Family Separation and Reunion

Families of Prisoners of War and Servicemen Missing in Action

For sale by the Superintendent of Documents, U.S. Government
Printing Office, Washington, D.C. 20401

Family Separation and Reunion

Families of Prisoners of War and Servicemen Missing in Action

EDITORS

HAMILTON I. MCCUBBIN

BARBARA B. DAHL

PHILIP J. METRES, JR.

EDNA J. HUNTER

JOHN A. PLAG

Dedication

This book is dedicated to "Military" families—men, women, and children who by their association with the military have intimately experienced the sadness of war.

Contents

Contents

Contributors

DOROTHY BENSON *received her B.S. degree in Educational Psychology from Montana State University, she is presently Executive Secretary of the Navy Relief Society, Naval Air Station, Miramar, San Diego, California and a part-time member of the Family Studies Branch of the Center for Prisoner of War Studies. Mrs. Benson is a social worker who has been responsible for conducting numerous interviews with RPW/MIA families.*

S. WILLIAM BERG *is a graduate of Wabash College and received both the M.S. degree in Psychopharmacology and the M.D. degree from Indiana University. Dr. Berg is presently a Lieutenant Commander in the U.S. Naval Reserve and is Head of the Medical Specialties Branch of the Center for Prisoner of War Studies. He was instrumental in the development of the Initial Medical Evaluation Forms (IMEF) and the publication "Medical Care for Repatriated Prisoners of War: A Manual for Physicians and Dentists," used during "Operation Homecoming".*

BARBARA B. DAHL *received her A.B. degree in Psychology from Vassar College and her M.A. degree in Psychology from Stanford University. From 1972 to 1973 Mrs. Dahl served as editorial assistant for the "Journal of Applied Psychology". She is presently a research psychologist and member of the Family Studies Branch of the Center for Prisoner of War Studies where she also serves as Publications Editor.*

Contributors

RICHARD C. W. HALL *received his B.A. from Johns Hopkins University and his M.D. Degree from the University of Florida College of Medicine. Dr. Hall was a Fellow in the Department of Psychiatry and Behavioral Services of The Johns Hopkins University from 1969 to 1972, and currently he is a Lieutenant Commander in the U.S. Naval Reserve serving at the Naval Hospital, Orlando, Florida and also holds the title of Assistant Professor of Psychiatry at the University of South Florida College of Medicine in Tampa, Florida.*

EDNA J. HUNTER *received an A. B. degree from the University of California, at Berkeley, the M.S. degree in Clinical Psychology from San Diego State University, and a Ph.D. in Human Behavior from United States International University. Dr. Hunter has been affiliated with the Navy Medical Neuropsychiatric Research Unit since 1967 as a member of the psychophysiology division prior to joining the Center in 1971. She is presently a clinical research psychologist at the Center for Prisoner of War Studies where she serves both as the Assistant Director for Administration of the Center and as a member of the Family Studies Branch.*

PATRICK T. MALONE *attended undergraduate school at Northwestern University and received his M.D. degree from the University of North Carolina at Chapel Hill. Following an internship at the Bethesda Naval Hospital, Bethesda, Maryland, he did his psychiatric residency at the Oakland Naval Hospital, Oakland, California. Since 1972 Dr. Malone has been Chief of the Neuropsychiatric Service, Naval Hospital, Orlando, Florida.*

HAMILTON I. McCUBBIN *received his B.S., M.S., and Ph.D. in Social Welfare and Sociology from the University of Wisconsin, Madison. As a Captain in the Medical Service Corps, U.S. Army, he served as Director of Research at the U.S. Army Correctional Training Facility in Fort Riley, Kansas, and Director of the Alcohol and Drug Rehabilitation program at Letterman Army Medical Center, San Francisco, California. In 1972 Dr. McCubbin assumed his present position as Head of the Family Studies Branch of the Center for Prisoner of War Studies and the U.S. Army Liaison to the Center.*

FLOYD G. MESHAD *received his B.A. degree in Psychology from Spring Hill College, Mobile, Alabama and an M.S.W. from Florida State University. From 1969 to 1971 he served as a Captain in the U.S. Army Medical Service Corps at Fort Leavenworth, Kansas and*

x

the 95th Medevac Hospital on the DMZ in South Vietnam. In 1971, Mr. Meshad Became Chief of the Vietnam Veteran Resocialization Unit at the Brentwood V.A. Hospital in Brentwood, California, where he is presently in charge of a community outreach program for the Vietnam Era Veteran.

PHILIP J. METRES, JR. *received his B. A. in Psychology from Holy Cross College and an M.A. in Social Psychology from United States International University. He served as a line officer in the U.S. Navy from 1964 to 1969, including a one-year tour of duty in Vietnam as a shipboard advisor to the Vietnamese Navy, and is presently a Lieutenant Commander in the U.S. Naval Reserve. Mr. Metres has worked as a research psychologist in the Family Studies Branch of the Center for Prisoner of War Studies since the Center's inception in 1971.*

WILLIAM N. MILLER *received his B.A. degree and his M.A. in Psychology from Colgate University. He has been working as a psychologist with the Defense Department and the military services since 1956. From 1964 to the present he has served as a consultant to military and civilian organizations with respect to their programs to train personnel to endure enemy detention. During the period from 1971 to 1973, Mr. Miller was in charge of the Environmental Stress Branch of the Center for Prisoner of War Studies.*

J. ROBERT NELSON *received both his B.A. degree and his legal training at the University of California, Los Angeles. He has served on active duty with the Judge Advocate General's Corps of the United States Navy as a Lieutenant since January 1972, and is currently on the Staff of the Center for Prisoner of War Studies where he is studying the legal problems of PW/MIA families.*

JAMES D. PHELAN *received his B.A. from the University of Arizona. He is presently a personnel research psychologist serving as Head of the Data Analysis Branch at the Center for Prisoner of War Studies where he has worked in this capacity since the Center's inception in 1971.*

JOHN A. PLAG *received his B.A. degree from Yale University his M.A. degree from Bradley University and his Ph.D. in psychology from Loyola University. Dr. Plag served as a civilian clinical psychologist at the Naval Training Center, Great Lakes from 1952 to 1960. For the next 11 years he was employed as a research psychologist at the Navy Medical Neuropsychiatric Research Unit where his research interests centered upon the establishment of procedures and criteria for the selection of Naval recruits. In 1971 he became Director of the Center for Prisoner of War Studies and is presently serving in this capacity.*

IRIS R. POWERS *is past Chairman of the Board of Directors of the National League of Families of American Prisoners and Missing in Southeast Asia. She has also served as the League's National Coordinator, Vice Chariman of the Board and Chairman of its Repatriation, Rehabilitation and Readjustment (Triple R) Committee. Mrs. Powers was a consultant to the Department of the Army, and is presently a consultant to the Center for Prisoner of War Studies regarding family matters.*

LUDWIG J. SPOLYAR *received his B.A. from San Jose State College and his M.A. and Ph.D. from Michigan State University. A Lieutenant Colonel in the U.S. Air Force Reserve and a graduate of the Air War College Associates Program, Dr. Spolyar has been involved in PW/MIA projects and programs since 1969 through the U.S. Air Force and the Repatriation, Rehabilitation, and Readjustment Committee of the National League of Families. He is presently the Director of the Campus Assistance Center and Assistant Professor of Educational Psychology at the University of Minnesota.*

CHARLES A. STENGER *served as a combat medic in World War II. He was captured during the Battle of the Bulge and remained a prisoner of war until the end of hostilities. He obtained his Ph.D. degree in clinical psychology at Case-Western Reserve University and was a Veterans Administration (V.A.) trainee. Since 1963 Dr. Stenger has been associated with the V.A. and is currently in the Mental Health and Behavioral Sciences Service. He has been Chairman, Vietnam Era Veterans Committee since 1970 and Vietnam Era POW/MIA Planning Coordinator for the Department of Medicine and Surgery since 1971.*

ROBERT E. STRANGE *is a CAPTAIN in the Medical Corps of the U.S. Navy. He is a graduate of the Indiana University School of Medicine and had internship and psychiatric residency training at the Naval Hospital, Oakland, California. Dr. Strange's assignments have included Staff Psychiatrist, Naval Hospital, Camp Pendleton, California; Head, Psychiatric Branch, USS REPOSE in Vietnam; Assistant Chief and*

Contributors

Director of Training, and Chief, Neuropsychiatry Service, Naval Hospital, Philadelphia, Pennsylvania. He is presently Head of the Psychiatry Branch of the Bureau of Medicine and Surgery.

LEONARD M. ZUNIN *received his B.A. degree from the University of Arizona and completed his medical and psychiatric training at the University of California, Los Angeles, Medical School. He served as a Lieutenant Commander in the Medical Corps of the U.S. Naval Reserve during the Vietnam War and, while assigned to Camp Pendleton, California, was instrumental in establishing a group therapeutic program for wives of servicemen killed in action. He is founder and presently the Director of Human Relations Consultants of West Los Angeles, and a psychiatrist in private practice. Dr. Zunin is currently psychiatric consultant to the Center for Prisoner of War Studies in San Diego, California.*

Acknowledgements

The editors are especially indebted to the Office of the Chief of Naval Operations, the Bureau of Medicine and Surgery, Department of the Navy, the Office of the Surgeon General, Department of the Army, and to the Commandant of the Marine Corps. We thank those individuals within these offices who generously gave of their time and interest in support of this endeavor: RADM D. Earl Brown, MC, USN; CAPT James H. Scott, USN; CAPT Jerald Zacharias, USN; CAPT Robert Strange, MC, USN; CDR Paul Nelson, MSC, USN; COL Glenn Williams, MSC, USA; LTC Donald Naylor, MSC, USA; COL Stewart Baker, MC, USA. We express our appreciation for the support provided by the Bureau of Personnel, Department of the Navy, the Office of the Adjutant General, Department of the Army, and, in particular, those officers and men of the casualty branches of the Armed Services who extended themselves to the PW/MIA and RPW families and provided invaluable support to our research effort. We particularly note the support of CAPT Gerald C. Canaan, USN; CAPT Thornwell F. Rush, USN; COL C. J. Bobinski, AG, USA; COL Archie W. Gratch, USAF; MAJ William Clark, USMC; CAPT James Johnson, USMC; and MAJ Robert Dietrich, USMC. Special acknowledgement is given to the Chaplain Corps of the Army and the Navy and, in particular, our appreciation is extended to Chaplain (Commander) John W. Berger, USN, for his continued efforts on behalf of PW/MIA families.

We recognize the support and contributions of the Defense Intelligence Agency and the Intelligence commands of both the Army and

Navy, with special recognition to Mr. Robert S. Boroughs, NIC, and LTC Wiley Watson, USA, ACSI. Additionally, we note the significant effort of Miss Elaine Mowery, Chief, Environmental Stress Branch of the Center, and those Naval Reservists who worked closely with her in the study of the captivity experience.

The editors also acknowledge the invaluable contributions of our colleagues whose job it was to contact and interview families throughout the world. Through their efforts we were able to establish rapport with these families and gain an understanding of the family situation. Their effort was without precedent. Specifically, we would like to thank Captain John Barry, MSC, USA; Captain Robert Sanderlin, MSC, USA; Captain Robert Jupe, MSC, USA; Specialist 5 Terry Weisbrick, USA; LTC David Jentsch, MSC, USA; LCDR Phillip Ballard, MC, USNR; Mrs. Dorothy Benson; and Mrs. Inez Dunning, A.C.S.W., former Head of the Family Studies Branch, CPWS. Additionally, many of the ideas in this volume emerged from the experience of the social work practitioners who are presently involved in the development and extension of services to MIA and RPW families. Appreciation and encouragement is extended to our colleagues with whom we have discussed or obtained ideas presented in this volume: Mrs. Lala Johnson, MSW, Naval Regional Medical Center, Bethesda; Mrs. Kate Powell, MSW, Naval Regional Medical Center, San Diego; Mr. Lester Hall, MSW, Naval Aerospace Medical Institute, Pensacola; Mr. David Huff, MSW, Naval Regional Medical Center, Lemoore; Mr. Benjamin Moss, MSW, Naval Regional Medical Center, Portsmouth; Mrs. Beulah Basham, MSW, Naval Regional Medical Center, Jacksonville; and LTC Paul Darnauer, MSC, USA, Social Work Consultant, Office of the Surgeon General, Department of the Army.

The editors gratefully acknowledge the continuing support and cooperation of the National League of Families of Prisoners and Missing in Southeast Asia whose officers encouraged the cooperation of family members in the Center's research efforts. Specifically, the editors are indebted to: Mrs. James B. Stockdale, Mrs. Iris R. Powers, Mrs. Mitchell O. Sadler, Jr., Mrs. Stephen P. Hanson, Mrs. Gordon M. Perisho, and Mrs. Herman L. Knapp.

We further acknowledge the generous cooperation, hospitality, and support extended to the editors by the High Flight Foundation. Participation in three of the religious retreats sponsored by High Flight permitted the authors to listen to and discuss the families' personal feelings and perceptions – observations upon which a number of chapters in this volume are based. Special thanks are extended to:

astronaut (Col.) James B. Irwin and his wife, Mrs. Mary Irwin, Dr. and Mrs. Bill Rittenhouse, and Mr. Charles Farr of the Foundation.

Finally, the editors owe much to their parent organization, the Naval Health Research Center (formerly the Navy Medical Neuropsychiatric Research Unit) and its subsidiary, the Center for Prisoner of War Studies (CPWS). Special thanks are due to CAPT David R. Ten Eyck, MC, USN, Commanding Officer, Naval Health Research Center; CAPT Ransom J. Arthur, MC, USN, and former Commanding Officer of the Navy Medical Neuropsychiatric Research Unit; Dr. Walter Wilkins, Scientific Director, Naval Health Research Center. We express our appreciation to our colleagues at CPWS who devoted themselves to seemingly endless requests for data analyses and preparation of manuscripts: Mr. Jim Phelan, Mr. Gary Lester, Mr. Lester Murphy, Miss Beverly Ross, Mr. John Deaton, Miss Nancy Shreve, Miss Carol Million, Mrs. Linda Mark, Miss Marie Hanson, Miss Susan Farish, Miss Nancy Cicalo, Mr. Steve Offut, Miss Jane Bryson, Mrs. Penny Brown, Miss Lynne Pugsley, Mrs. Lois West, and Miss Lucille Cheng. We are especially indebted to Miss Fran Jackson for her patience, persistence, and commitment to seeing this volume to its completion and for preparing the manuscripts of this book, many times over.

The conduct of this research and the preparation of this volume were supported by the Department of the Navy, Bureau of Medicine and Surgery, under work order request number WR-18-4-005, dated 29 June 1973 and by the Office of the Surgeon General, Department of the Army under military Inter-Departmental purchase request number 7401 dated 17 August 1973. This book is Naval Health Research Center Report No. 74-70.

The opinions and assertions contained herein are the private ones of the writers and are not to be construed as official or as reflecting the views of the Department of the Navy or the Department of the Army.

Preface

The Center for Prisoner of War Studies (CPWS) was formed in late 1971 and officially established in April 1972 as a special facility of the Navy Medical Neuropsychiatric Research Unit, San Diego, California. At that time the Navy's Bureau of Medicine and Surgery recognized the need for longitudinal medical studies of prisoners of war in order to document the effects of long-term deprivation and confinement upon physical and mental health in later life. It was also necessary to anticipate the physical and psychological needs of the repatriates so that the military planners could provide optimal medical care for them. Furthermore, the founders of the Center insisted that this country not again overlook the seldom-occasioned opportunity of acquiring new knowledge useful for increasing the nation's preparedness should future international events again subject our military forces to foreign incarceration.

For over a decade the Navy Medical Neuropsychiatric Research Unit,[1] had engaged in research dealing with the medical and psychological effects of unusual and highly stressful military environments. It was logical, therefore, that a facility for conducting studies in support of prisoners of war be established at this Command. In July of 1972, the United States Army became a working partner in the study efforts of the Center.

Since it was recognized that the American PW experience in Vietnam represented an unusually unique situation for gaining a

---

1. *In September, 1974 the Navy Medical Neuropsychiatric Research Unit became the Naval Health Research Center.*

better understanding of the long-term effects of stress upon both the incarcerated military member and the members of his family, policies and programs of the Center were aimed towards eliciting data of benefit to the research community as well as to the mobilization of needed health-care services. In broad terms, the Center was charged with the responsibility for developing and executing a study plan directed towards the establishment of an optimal and comprehensive health-care program for both repatriated prisoners of war (RPWs) and their families and the families of servicemen listed as "missing in action" (MIAs). Thus, in brief, the aims of the Center were to conduct scientific studies of the effects of captivity on subsequent adaptation of returned prisoners of war, and to explore the effects of long-term absence of the military member on the adjustment of the RPW and MIA families.

The first phase of this study plan began in 1972 when the staff of the Center, in conjunction with medical representatives of the Department of the Air Force, reviewed pertinent literature in depth and devised extensive medical examination forms and procedures. These procedures were subsequently adopted by the Department of Defense and utilized by the military departments for evaluating and recording the health of the PWs upon their return in early 1973. A manual for physicians and dentists, entitled "Medical Care for Repatriated Prisoners of War" was produced by the Center's Medical Specialties Branch for use during "Operation Homecoming". Also in 1972, and prior to the return of the prisoners, the Family Studies Branch of the Center personally interviewed over fifty percent of the Army, Navy, and Marine Corps PW/MIA wives in order to document the nature of their adjustment and to ascertain the need for clinical services by these families. A finding of treatable problems in a high percentage of the families led to the establishment of social service "outreach" programs by both the Army and the Navy.

With the return of the prisoners of war and the establishment of responsive health-care facilities and services by the military departments, the activities of the Center shifted towards the monitoring of the long-term health and adjustment of the returnees, their families, and the families of the MIAs, and towards the achievement of long-term research goals. Inherent in the thinking of those who planned the establishment of the Center for Prisoner of War Studies several years ago on behalf of the Surgeons General of the Army and Navy was the notion that valuable medical lessons could be learned through a careful but unobtrusive monitoring of the readjustment experiences of returnees and members of their families. Hence, research and services have been viewed as comprising a feedback loop of mutually enriching sources of data. This book, thanks to the untiring efforts of the editors, represents a major contribution towards the accomplishment of this objective.

The work of the contributors to this volume, as a result of numerous interactions with the PW/MIA families, has been a rewarding and enlightening experience. Cooperation of the involved family members with the staff of the Center has been outstanding. It has gradually become apparent that the effectiveness and proficiency of every military member is, in no small measure, related to the manner in which his family perceives the military establishment and understands the stresses to which he is subjected. Hence, it is hoped that many of the findings and procedures derived in the studies of PW/MIA families, as outlined in this book, will eventually have wider applicability to much-needed research with military families in general.

October 1974

John A. Plag, Ph.D.
Director
Center for Prisoner of War Studies
Naval Health Research Center

Introduction

Introduction

This book is an outgrowth of two major projects. The first is a research investigation, *the longitudinal study of families of servicemen missing in action and returned prisoners of war,* presently being conducted by the Center for Prisoner of War Studies; and the second, which had less to do with research and more to do with its implications, is the extension of services to families.

Through the research effort, which has provided the basic data for this volume, we became sensitive to the disruptive trends created by the families' adjustment to the stresses of father absence and reunion, trends which spurred our involvement in the development of an "outreach" and "follow-up" service to families of returned prisoners of war (RPWs) and those servicemen missing in action (MIA). The results of the initial stages of our prisoner of war and family research called attention to the immediate problems of family adjustment and pointed to the potential of future medical, psychological, social, and legal complications for the returning prisoner of war, his family and families of those servicemen who failed to return. Exposure to these families and their personal lives alerted us to the significance of our study; we became aware of their hurts and struggles and, at the same time, their resilience, adaptability, persistence and patience under trying circumstances. Had these families not been willing to share their experiences and thoughts and to reveal some of their innermost feelings, the publication of this book would not have been possible.

A symposium entitled "Family Adjustment and Reintegration" was conducted by the Center to train and provide some orientation for seven uniformed Army and six civilian Navy social workers who had been selected to act as regional coordinators of services to these families. The challenge to the social workers to extend and coordinate medical, counseling, legal and social services to the families was seen as consistent with the more progressive developments in the military program of family and medical services, the emphasis of which is upon prevention. The majority of the chapters selected for this volume were initially presented at this symposium held in San Diego, California in September, 1973.

This volume is concerned with the process of adaptation: the ways in which men responded to the stresses of war and captivity; the ways in which the family unit adapted itself to the prolonged and seemingly indeterminate absence of a father; how the returnee and his wife and children reintegrate their family unit after the long separation; and how a family copes with and prepares itself for a future without the father and husband.

Essentially the volume encompasses three major periods. First, the *waiting* period, from the early 1960's to February of 1973, during which time the families experienced the loss of their fathers, husbands, and sons and waited in anticipation and with hope for their return. Second, the *repatriation* period, from February of 1973 to April of 1973, during which time American prisoners of war in Southeast Asia returned to the United States and to their families. Third, the *readjustment and reintegration* period, from April of 1973 to the present, in which some families whose men returned have been working together toward a successful reintegration and stability while others have felt it necessary to choose independent and separate lives. During this period the majority of families whose men remained missing have continued to work toward some resolution of their circumstances and prepare themselves for a future without the serviceman. Within the framework of a longitudinal study, we organized the chapters and presented them in the context of these three major periods. The introductory chapters set the stage for the volume by providing an historical perspective of the PW and MIA situation as well as a demographic profile of the men and their families. In the second section, the casualty and waiting period, the complexity of family adjustment to father absence is emphasized. Beginning with a broad overview of family adjustment, based on interviews with 215 PW/MIA families, special emphasis is then given to the legal issues, the children's adjustment, and the wives' grieving process. The final chapter in this section examines the role of religion and religious beliefs in the family's adjustment to the PW/MIA situation. The third section of this volume is devoted to repatriation and the returned prisoner of war. The initial chapter describes the medical health of the returnees at the time of their repatriation. The remaining chapters explore hypotheses about the relationship between the returnees' experiences in captivity and their future adjustment to society.

The fourth section of the volume, which covers the readjustment and reintegration period, includes chapters devoted to descriptive accounts of some of the major dilemmas and factors involved in adjustment: the adjustment of families of returned prisoners of war and the adjustment of wives and parents of servicemen missing or killed in action. Since parents and wives may view the casualty and the future from different points of view, the final chapter in the section examines this issue. The final section of this volume, entitled services to families, examines the underlying assumptions, theories and concepts which characterize the military "outreach" and "follow-up" program for returned prisoners of war, their families, and families of servicemen missing in action. The chapter entitled "Consultants' Viewpoints" is intended to cast light upon the importance of follow-up services and the need for continuity of services to the returnees and their families. Special emphasis is given to the role of the Veterans Administration in the extension of these services. In the final presentation a counseling program for wives of servicemen killed in action is described.

Utilizing the concepts gained from past research, we tried to emphasize, when possible, the application of family system principles and concepts to describe and document our observations of family adjustment. We might have chosen to relate the book to concepts of individual psychological conditions such as a wife's depression or the returnees' possible feelings of "survivor guilt". However, it is our belief that the family must not only be seen as consisting of individual members but also as a transactional system—an interacting system of persons having its own unique rules, communication networks, alliances and pre-established modes of adjustment to stress.

We envisioned a volume which would not only communicate clinical observations and insights, but also would be useful to those professionals responsible for the provision of care and services to the returnees and their families and the families of those men who did not return from the Southeast Asian conflict. It is our belief that each of the contributors has succeeded in integrating the theoretical as well as the practical.

Each of the chapters of this volume has been written as a separate article, independent of the chapters contributed by other authors. As a result, historical data and the definition of terms are at times repetitive, particularly for the reader who reviews these chapters in consecutive order. However, it is for the reader who uses this volume to refer to a particular PW/MIA topic, he who wishes to find all relevant material in its entirety within a specific section of the book, that the material presented in this volume has been organized.

Our exposure to intimate family relationships has helped to broaden our understanding of the complex processes of family adjustment to father absence and to family reintegration following reunion. At the present time, however, and even with the completion of this volume, we are not able to elucidate what factors enable some families to cope with separation and reunion more successfully than others. The fact that we can at least explore these issues using scientific methodology is a significant step towards gaining a deeper understanding of not only PW/MIA and RPW family adjustment, but also the nature of the family and its adjustment in the military system generally. Only time will tell us whether research in support of this select group of families will constitute a significant turning point in the field of social and psychological research in the military. All the implications of the entire longitudinal study envisioned by the Center are far from realized. It is our hope, however, that this volume is at least a significant step in the direction of achieving that goal.

San Diego, California   Hamilton I. McCubbin
                                                          Barbara B. Dahl

History and Overview

1

The National League Of Families
And The Development Of Family Services

IRIS R. POWERS

In order to understand fully the development of counseling services for the families of Americans captured or reported missing during the long years of the Vietnam conflict, it will be necessary to start at the beginning and examine the role of an organization now known as the National League of Families of American Prisoners and Missing in Southeast Asia.

Because membership in the National League of Families consists of wives, parents, children and other close relatives of the prisoners and missing men, its involvement in government politics and military affairs from the beginning has been on a highly emotional and personal level. While these factors frequently acted as a handicap in some respects, they also afforded benefits. On the plus side they provided the most intimate knowledge possible of both the physical and emotional needs of the family members; needs that initially, in many instances, went seemingly unrecognized by the military establishment and were, therefore, felt to be unfulfilled.

In defense of the military establishment, it should be noted that in the beginning, however, while the needs may have been apparent to individual families, there was no collective experience on which to base recommended changes or corrective action.

To understand the evolution of the family services policies and programs, it is essential to present at least a brief historical summary of what transpired on the "family front" in the early years of the Vietnam War. Bear in mind that from 1964 until May of 1969 the general guidance to the families by the United States Government was to say as little as possible, publicly, about the prisoner-of-

1

war and missing-in-action issue. Our officials knew that not all Americans who had been captured by the other side had been identified as prisoners; that those whose capture had been acknowledged were not characterized as "prisoners of war" but as "war criminals," that most had been denied any communication with their families; and that none was receiving the humanitarian treatment prescribed by the Geneva Convention. Our nation's leaders believed that if these conditions were to be corrected, they could be achieved only through quiet diplomacy. But while these diplomatic overtures were taking place over a totally unanticipated period of more than five years, the fate of the prisoners and missing men and the plight of their families was almost totally obscured by the veil of secrecy which had developed around the issue.

Families were, of course, provided with information that their husbands or sons had been captured or were reported missing, and except for officially classified data, they were also advised as to the circumstances surrounding the men's capture or disappearance. At the same time, however, they were told this information was extremely confidential and not to be discussed with others.

The circumstances of being a PW or MIA next-of-kin was, therefore, complicated not only by the anxieties and fears for the captured or missing man, but by the concomitant frustration of having no normal outlet through which to voice these concerns. During this early period, it seemed to the families that there was limited personal contact with Government representatives, and little, if any, opportunity to raise questions about either personal family problems arising from the difficult situation, or questions about specific actions being taken by the Government to resolve the issue. On the other hand, some of the families made the assumption that everything possible was being done in their behalf.

However, as time went on there was a growing unrest among the families which eventually led to the creation of a family organization, to a decision by the Government to "go public" on the PW/MIA issue, and to the strengthening and formal activation of a "national" League of Families. Each of these events preceded and was an important factor in the eventual development of improved and essential family services.

One woman, the wife of a senior ranking officer who had been missing since the Fall of 1965, was responsible for founding the League of Families. Like so many other wives and parents during the early years of the Vietnam conflict, she had lived with terrible loneliness for long months after her husband first was reported missing in September

1965, and after he was subsequently identified as a prisoner of war. In a number of respects, she was more fortunate than many of those in similar circumstances, for eventually she began to receive sporadic mail from her husband. Quietly, in keeping with the Government policy of privacy, she began exploring the various Government avenues of communication. Then, because of another fortunate circumstance, the fact that she lived in a military community, she met another wife whose husband was also a prisoner.

Together, in late 1966, these two women tracked down other PW/MIA families in their area and before long had located 33 such families and had instituted informal group meetings. These meetings continued for almost two years as the number of families placed in the PW/MIA situation increased. While for a few families (about 100 all around the country) there continued to be a trickle of mail from PWs, but little else; for most families, the fate of their loved ones remained unknown. This trickle of mail, however, served as an important medium for discerning some information about at least a few of the men who had been allowed to write. In October of 1968 this information was disclosed to the press. The resultant news stories acted like the opening of a floodgate for families who had been in isolation all around the country. Finally they could express themselves and be heard. Equally important, they could now work actively and openly toward bringing their husbands and sons home.

It is necessary to keep in mind the fact that in many communities throughout the nation there were only one or two PW/MIA families and few of them had contact with anyone in similar straits. Even in cases where two men were shot down in the same plane, or captured from the same unit, neither family was notified that the same fate had befallen the other man. In most cases, families had no opportunity to share or exchange information. But with the release of the news stories in the public press, families from all around the country began to communicate. For the first time there was an interchange of information among families who previously had little, if any, recourse to resources outside their immediate family circle. While these events were transpiring, in several other areas around the country where there were large military populations, other families also began to "find" each other and to hold informal meetings.

In early 1969 a campaign was launched to have a group of the families flood the North Vietnamese delegation in Paris with cablegrams expressing concern about the prisoners and missing men. This was the first major organized activity in which a large number of families participated. For most, it meant the end of an era; the feeling of helplessness which had marked their prior existence slowly began to dissipate as they found more and more activities to occupy their minds and hands.

Meanwhile, the growing unrest among the families had not gone unnoticed in Washington. But the policy of diplomatic maneuvering and prodding, however well-meaning, had produced no results. The Department of Defense's list of prisoners and missing men was steadily increasing. In North Vietnam and the communist-controlled areas of South Vietnam, the captives were being constantly propagandized and continued to receive brutally inhumane treatment. Given such circumstances, chances were remote that the U.S. Government could continue its public silence on the prisoner issue indefinitely. It was also becoming equally clear that if the plight of the prisoners was to be relieved, if our missing men who had been captured were ever to be identified as captives, Washington would have to alter its strategy.

When the shift finally came, in May of 1969, with Secretary of Defense Laird announcing the Government's decision to lay the prisoner issue before the court of world opinion, the thrust of the action was on the "shocking conditions" in the prison camps and the refusal of the communists to identify all of those held captive. In other words, the U.S. Government's concern for the men was put forward as the underlying reason for the new policy. Yet, there can be little doubt that this concern, however genuine, was inextricably interwoven with the knowledge that the families were becoming increasingly dissatisfied and were slowly but surely taking the initiative in their own way, at their own pace, and without fear of political criticism. Swiftly, by the May 1969 decision to "go public" on the issue, the Government regained the confidence of those PW/MIA families who were beginning to doubt the wisdom of previous policy.

The families experienced new hope. Those who already had started to become active stepped up their activities. Those who had waivered in not knowing whether to follow the lead of others now began to emerge. The founder of the embryo League of Families was finding that it was increasingly difficult to cope with the correspondence, with suggested programs of action, and with the widening scope of activities in which families were beginning to take part. Also, as many family members began to turn to the Congress of the United States for succor, and to the State Department, Defense Department, and White House for information and help, it became clear that the League could best function with a national organization headquartered in Washington, D.C. The founder called for an ad hoc meeting in Washington in May 1970, and at that meeting, attended by wives and parents who were rapidly rising to leadership positions among the family groups, the formal structure and by-laws of the National League of Families of American Prisoners and Missing in Southeast Asia were hammered out.

On May 28, 1970 the League was incorporated, a temporary board of directors was named with the original founder as Chairman, and the Washington headquarters of the League opened its doors as a tax-free, non-profit, non-partisan, humanitarian organization under the direction of a newly appointed National Coordinator. The goals established by the League were four-fold. First, to obtain humanitarian treatment for the prisoners as spelled out in the Geneva Convention; second, to stimulate concern about the fate of the prisoners and missing men and the plight of their families; third, to improve communication and the dissemination of information among family members (as well as among government leaders and the news media); and foremost and finally, to obtain the earliest possible release of the prisoners and the fullest possible accounting of the missing.

What were the individual branches of the Armed Services doing about "family" services during this period? It is important to remember that the first American serviceman captured in the Vietnam War was taken prisoner on March 26, 1964. From that time until the date of the formal incorporation of the National League of Families, more than six years had elapsed, and some 1300 other Americans had been added to the captured and missing list. Those six years, in many respects, constituted a period of considerable trial and error as they related to official military policies concerning the families of the men.

Assistance programs were not designed to anticipate the special problems of PW/MIA families. The Survivors Assistance Program was basically designed to respond to the needs of those families of men killed or wounded in combat, or who died or were injured in other ways. However, this program was expanded to include PW/MIA families. Therefore, during the early years "survivor assistance officers" (SAO) were called upon to provide family support. This, however, was a sensitive situation for families of men who had been identified as prisoners of war, as well as for MIA families who still lived in the hope that their husbands or sons also had been taken prisoner. These families were not yet "survivors", and the use of the term served to add to their distress and anxiety. This situation serves to illustrate the extent to which the Armed Forces, in these early years, were unable to anticipate the special needs of a growing number of families who did not fit easily into ongoing programs.

The development of a program to address the needs of the PW/MIA family was without precedent. Therefore, its evolution was, to a large extent, based on trial and error. A typical, although somewhat fictionalized example of the kind of trial-and-error effort that existed is the story of a wife whose husband had been missing for three years. She discovered that the eight-year-old family automobile was about to chug its last chug and would have to be traded for another car. Very quickly thereafter she also discovered that the automobile was in her husband's name and that she had no power of attorney to sell or trade. Fortunately, she was wise enough to call the problem to the attention of her assistance officer who turned to his Service's legal office for help, and a solution ultimately was worked out. This type of situation, like many others to follow, clearly indicated the importance of inter-service communication and the need to adopt programs to help ease or eliminate similar family difficulties or to head them off before they developed.

Many of the personal family problems that arose were of a type that could possibly have utilized the services of a skilled social worker. Yet, it is significant to note that even though the Army, as an example, had many well-trained and qualified social workers in its hospitals and community service organizations, the professional abilities of these individuals were seldom, if ever, utilized by the PW/MIA families through those long and difficult years. For varying reasons, the families did not present themselves at medical centers. Also, the casualty sections, in an effort to protect the families' rights to privacy, rarely volunteered information about the families. Additionally, many non-career families were, for a long time, never fully aware of the full range of their benefits or entitlements. Some, and in particular the parents of draftees and other non-career enlisted personnel, knew so little about the military infrastructure that it didn't even occur to them to ask pertinent questions.

To clarify and underscore the plight of the PW/MIA families in the Fall of 1970, the mother of an Army man listed as missing in action together with the past National Coordinator of the League of Families, submitted a proposal to the Department of the Army outlining some of the major areas of concern that had come to the League's attention in those early months after the League became nationally organized. This proposal was single-service oriented, but it encompassed subject matter that in many respects was equally applicable to all Services.

The proposal, presented in a meeting at the Pentagon, on October 15, 1970, included an in-depth description of the desperate need of the wife or parent of a missing or captured man to "talk-out" their problems and frustrations to someone with whom they felt a sense of identity and trust. More specifically, the recommendation was made that a temporary consultant be appointed who could relate to those families and spend such time as might be necessary with each one to enable them to unburden themselves. The consultant could discuss issues which may be unique to an individual family's special circumstances, and could give them an opportunity to funnel back to the proper place any suggestions they may have that might be worthy of consideration, or any questions they may have which would merit an official reply. Most importantly, however, the consultant was to assist the SAO in gaining a better understanding of his all-important role from the point of view of a next-of-kin.

The result of this meeting, and the subsequent recommendations of a task force appointed to explore the subject further, was the assignment of a special consultant on PW/MIA family affairs whose duty was to report to the Army Chief of Staff "on ways the Army can best serve the families of soldiers captured and missing in Southeast Asia".

This consultant then set out to visit as many of the Army primary and secondary next-of-kin as possible both in the continental U.S. and in Europe. At the conclusion of the extensive four-month trip, another report with recommendations was submitted to the Army on July 20, 1971. As a result, a Family Services and Assistance Officer (FSAO) program was established. Other innovations were also initiated. The method of notifying the family of board-of-inquiry procedures was simplified and personalized; the method of transmitting the results of the report of this investigating board to the family also was overhauled, with the FSAO instructed to hand-deliver the information and remain with the family to answer questions (where answers were not immediately known, the FSAO was authorized to telephone the central Army Casualty Office, direct, and obtain an immediate answer).

Also, a comprehensive booklet was prepared for Survivor Assistance Officers and Family Service and Assistance Officers dichotomizing the functions of each; another comprehensive booklet was prepared for the next-of-kin, explaining the step-by-step procedures that ensue when a man is captured or reported missing. This booklet spelled out the kinds of services and entitlements available to both dependents and non-dependents. Additionally, it was recommended that families be given advance help to prepare them better for the eventuality of a "presumptive finding of death," and that the Army also begin to inform families about repatriation and rehabilitation plans, however incomplete.

The Army swiftly formed a task force to explore, expand and formalize programs further along these lines. It should be noted that this action took place almost two years before the first American prisoner was actually set free and returned to U.S. soil. The League, of course, was the springboard. There were numerous other inputs of a similar nature that were made by League members to the other Services over the same period of time.

By late 1971 the League was becoming increasingly encouraged by the prospect that the war might soon end and the long travail of the PW/MIAs and their families would be terminated; but the Board of Directors of the League at the same time was becoming increasingly alarmed that this happy event might transpire before the many family problems had been resolved, before they were fully prepared for the repatriation of their husbands and sons and their subsequent rehabilitation, and before these men and their families' own readjustment needs had been carefully delineated.

In December 1971 the Board of Directors created a new committee on Repatriation, Rehabilitation, and Readjustment. This committee, subsequently known as the Triple-R Committee, had a four-fold charter. It was charged with the responsibility of: (1) monitoring the plans and programs of all Service Casualty Sections, (2) making suggestions and recommendations in any area of policy where improvements appeared to be warranted, (3) acting as a link, in some instances, between family members and the casualty sections, and (4) assuring that all programs and policies developed by the Services for repatriation, rehabilitation, and readjustment would meet the needs (as envisioned by the League) of the men and their families.

At this point in time the Defense Department already was hard at work on a repatriation program. But plans for this operation had, up to this time, been formulated with little if any direct input from the families — the one group, except for the returnees, who would be most vitally affected by the planning.

Therefore, at the first meeting of the Triple-R Committee in March 1972, representatives of the Defense Department and of each of the Services were asked to meet with members of the Committee to discuss the plans. As it turned out, this was an expedient decision. For, while the plans in many respects were exemplary, it was also discovered that there were areas of family concern that the Defense Department and the Services simply had not thought about. But, more than that, the Committee session also brought to the surface many long, smoldering difficulties members of the League of Families were still experiencing with the Family Assistance Program — both errors of commission and errors of omission.

The National League of Families and the
Development of Family Services

One can easily understand how and why this happened. If the end of the war and the return of our men appeared imminent (as the intensified EGRESS RECAP planning anticipated), then some problems suddenly took on new meaning. Their resolution had been put off too long, and now there was a growing sense of urgency. The questions raised by the Committee members reflected widespread concern about many aspects of the ongoing assistance programs. As a result, 12 out of 28 recommendations, drafted in the Triple-R Committee's first report, dealt with proposed improvements in family assistance. For example, during the Committee sessions it became apparent that some families had told their respective Service that they preferred to have no contact with an assistance officer. The Committee, which felt that such an attitude on the part of the family may have been the result of many factors, ranging from unsatisfactory experiences to failure to establish rapport at the outset, urged the military to attempt to re-establish relations with these families.

There were, of course, other recommendations that highlighted family assistance problems, but the bulk of the recommendations growing out of the first series of Triple-R meetings dealt with repatriation and readjustment plans, many of which were approved and put into effect. A few of these recommendations will, perhaps, serve to demonstrate the scope of the committee's interest and concern:

1) The Department of Defense and the respective Services were urged to expedite the creation of special family counseling services.

2) Preparation of plans to send briefing teams around the country to talk with families were to be speedily concluded and set in motion.

3) Separate briefings were to be prepared for the children, with qualified psychiatrists, psychologists, or psychiatric social workers as participants.

4) Expert counseling was to be made available to MIA families whose husbands or sons might not return, with emphasis on long-range planning, and the need to make some advance preparations for such an eventuality.

5) Unity was urged with regard to the Center for Prisoner of War Studies; that is, all Services participating and assisting with funding.

From the June and October 1972 Triple-R Committee meetings, two additional sets of recommendations were transmitted to the Defense Department, months before the PW repatriation actually took place. Although these meetings and the recommendations will not be covered in detail, there are a few items of interest that should be mentioned. For example, one of the recommendations was that

9

establishment of counseling programs for both returnees and families should not be delayed until they had been perfected in every detail. It was felt that the need for knowledgeable, well-qualified counselors was of paramount importance and that if a mass release should come unexpectedly, it would be better to have an imperfect ongoing program than no formalized program at all.

Wives were beset with apprehensions. Many felt that they might be "weighed and found wanting". Had she saved enough of her husband's pay? Had she made the right decisions in raising and educating the children? Would her husband approve of her changed lifestyle, of her appearance, of the boys' long hair? Would he be angry or pleased that she had bought a new car, a new home? Few of the wives faced the eventual prisoner release with any equanimity.

At the same time, MIA wives encountered even greater fears in some respects. Some who had become resigned to the possibility that their man probably would not return, and who had begun to fashion new lives for themselves, were now faced with the prospect that the husband might, after all, come back. For those who had lived with the strong hope and expectation that their "missing" men would return, there were now new fears that perhaps he would not be among those repatriated, after all. For both categories, the realization of their worst fears would prove devastating.

The various pieces of each of these puzzles, of course, began to fall into place after repatriation. For some, the results have been shattering. Others have fared better than they expected. For a few, at least, the anticipated problems never materialized. But for many, including both families of returnees, some returnees, and for a large number of the families of the more than 1200 men who are still carried as "missing", there are a great many problems still to be resolved — pieces of a puzzle still to be fitted into place.

2

Army, Navy and Marine Corps Prisoners of War and Missing in Action: A Demographic Profile

EDNA J. HUNTER

JAMES D. PHELAN

Introduction

In April of 1972 the Center for Prisoner of War Studies (CPWS) was given the mission to plan and execute a longitudinal study of the health and adjustment of the Army, Navy and Marine Corps prisoners of war (PW) of the Southeast Asian conflict. The study of the Center was additionally concerned with the health and adjustment of the families of these servicemen, as well as the families of servicemen missing in action (MIA). Also included in the mission of the Center was the continuing compilation of data accumulated on returned prisoners of war (RPW) of previous conflicts; e.g., World War II, the Korean war, the Pueblo incident.

An essential part of the Center's longitudinal effort involves the establishment of a comprehensive data base regarding characteristics of these populations. The reader's knowledge of these characteristics would seem basic to understanding the total prisoner-of-war and missing-in-action situation and a prerequisite to further discussion. Therefore, the purpose of this chapter is to summarize briefly the Center's data base on the Army, Navy, and Marine Corps PW/MIA populations in order to provide background information for the chapters which follow.

The PW/MIA Population

Of the 899 Army, Navy and Marine personnel listed as prisoners of war or missing in action, 241 (27% of the total number of Army-Navy-Marine PW/MIAs) were returned to the United States in the early months of 1973.[1] Six hundred and fifty-eight men (73% of the Army-Navy-Marine PW/MIAs) did *not* return. For the purposes of this paper no attempt has been made to separate out those men who were reclassified as killed in action (KIA) or died of wounds (DOW) on the basis of information received from the returnees at the time of repatriation; for this paper this group of KIAs and DOWs is included in the statistics of the MIA group. It should also be noted that early releasees and escapees were not included in the figures for the returned prisoners of war group.

Sources of Information

Data used in the statistics presented in this paper were derived from multitudinous sources. A large proportion of the information for Navy personnel was drawn from the DD Form 1300, Report of Casualty, and from the Officer Data Card (1301/6). For Army personnel, information was likewise obtained from the DD Form 1300 and also from the Enlisted Qualification Record (DA Form 20), the Officer Qualification Record (DA Form 66) and the USA Personnel/ Financial Data Sheet. For Marine Corps personnel, the Marine Casualty Branch's POW and MIA Roster and the Marine Corps Service Record (NAVMC 118) were the primary sources of data. Other sources of data for all three services included the Record of Emergency Data (DD Form 93), Reports of Medical Examination and History (Standard Forms 88 and 89), correspondence files, and personal interviews with family members by CPWS staff members prior to the release of the men.[2]

The Returned Prisoner of War Population

Of the 241 Army, Navy and Marine returnees, 138 (57%) were Navy personnel, 77 (32%) were Army, and 26 (11%) were Marines. All Navy RPWs were officer personnel. The Marine returnees were 58 percent officer personnel and 42 percent enlisted personnel, while the majority of the Army returnees were enlisted personnel (64% enlisted to 36% officer), as shown in Figure 1.

---

1. *325 Air Force PWs and 23 U.S. civilian PWs were also released in February/March 1973.*

2. *In-depth semi-structured personal interviews with family members were conducted by professional psychiatrists, psychologists and social workers under the auspices of the Family Studies Branch of the Center for Prisoner of War Studies, Navy Medical Neuropsychiatric Research Unit, San Diego, California 92152.*

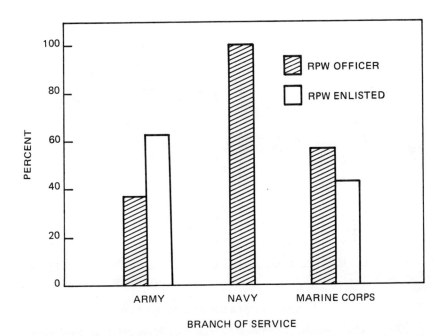

FIGURE 1: *A comparison of the percent of officer to enlisted returned prisoners of war (RPW) for the Army, Navy and Marine Corps.*

LENGTH OF TIME IN CAPTIVITY

The men held in captivity during the Southeast Asian war had been prisoners of war for longer periods than prisoners of war of any previous conflict (see Figure 2). The average time in captivity was in excess of five years for the Navy returnees (61.7 months) and only slightly less for Marine (51.1 months for officers; 60.0 for enlisted), and Army RPWs (44.3 months for officers; 52.1 for enlisted).

AGE

Figure 3 indicates the percent of Army, Navy and Marine returned prisoners of war who were in each of seven age groups at the time of casualty. Navy personnel were the oldest at casualty (mean age was 30.8 years), Marines were somewhat younger (30.1 years for officers; 20.5 for enlisted), and Army RPWs were the youngest (27.6 years for officers; 23.1 for enlisted). Many of the men were in their forties at the time of release and, as might be expected, enlisted personnel tended to be younger than officer personnel. The mean age for the total group of 181 officers at the time of release was 34.5 years; for the 60 enlisted RPWs, 26.3 years.

13

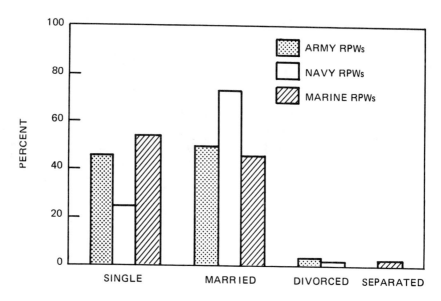

MARITAL STATUS AT TIME OF CASUALTY

FIGURE 2: *The number of months spent in captivity by the 241 Army, Navy and Marine returned prisoners of war (RPW).*

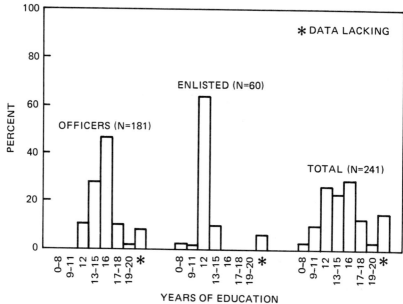

FIGURE 3: *The percent Army, Navy and Marine Corps returned prisoners of war (RPW) by age group at the time of capture.*

14

RACE, RELIGION AND EDUCATIONAL LEVEL

The majority of the returnees were Caucasian (See Figure 4), and their religious preference, as indicated by information supplied by the men themselves prior to casualty, was primarily Protestant; between 20 and 30 percent were Catholic.

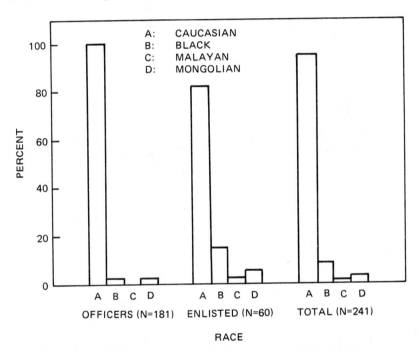

FIGURE 4: *Percentages of officers and enlisted Army, Navy and Marine returned prisoners of war (RPW) by race.*

Of the 60 enlisted returnees, over half completed high school. The majority of the officer RPWs had earned a college degree; a few had attained the masters or doctoral level. On the average, the officer returnees had completed fifteen years of formal schooling; the enlisted RPWs had completed twelve years of schooling (see Figure 5).

MARITAL STATUS

The majority (72.9%) of the officer RPWs were married at the time of casualty; the majority (61.8%) of the enlisted RPWs were single. There appeared to be inter-service differences with respect to the proportion of married to single personnel, as shown in Figure 6. However,

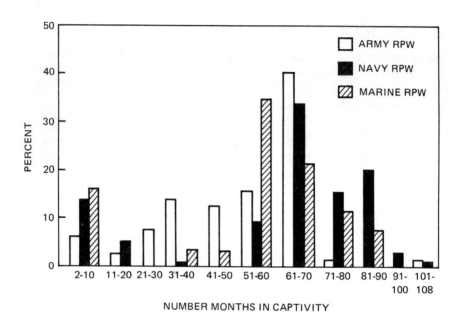

FIGURE 5: *Percentages of officers and enlisted Army, Navy and Marine returned prisoners of War (RPW) by educational level achieved prior to casualty.*

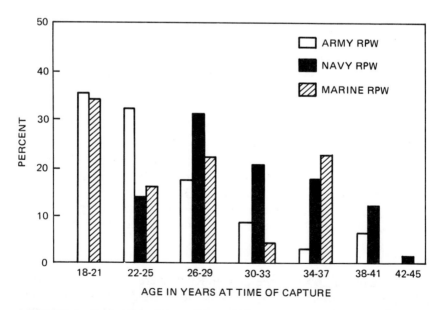

FIGURE 6: *Percentages of Army, Navy and Marine returned prisoners of war (RPW) by marital status at the time of casualty.*

these differences merely reflect the inter-service differences as to proportion of officers to enlisted RPWs that was previously mentioned.

Servicemen Missing Action: The Men Who Did Not Return

In a paper of this scope it also seems appropriate to examine the graphic profile of the men who did not return in 1973. Of the 658 MIAs, 367 (56%) were Army personnel, 177 (27%) were Navy personnel and 114 (17%) were Marines. Within the MIA population 55.3 percent were officer personnel; 44.7 percent were enlisted. Using paired comparisons there were significant inter-service differences with respect to the proportion of officer to enlisted MIAs (Navy: Army, $p < .001$, $\chi^2 = 184.4$, df = 1; Navy: Marines, $p < .001$, $\chi^2 = 119.6$, df = 1; and Army: Marines, $p < .001$, $\chi^2 = 31.7$, df = 1). Over ninety-five percent (95.5%) of the Navy MIAs were officers, 63.2 percent of the Marines, and only 33.3 percent of the Army MIAs were officer personnel.

The mean age of MIAs at the time of casualty was 26.4 years; 28.7 years for officers and 23.5 years for enlisted, with Navy MIAs being somewhat older than Army and Marine MIAs. As for race, over ninety-three percent (93.5%) were Caucasian. Average number of years of formal schooling was 14.9 years for MIA officer personnel and 11.8 years for enlisted. Twenty-five percent of MIAs were Catholic; sixty-eight percent were Protestant.

With respect to marital status, the majority (50.9%) of the MIA group were married at the time of casualty, 46.2 percent were single, and 2.7 percent were either divorced or separated. Of the 658 MIAs, 253 men had children, with a total of 576 children in those families where children were present.

Additional Information Derived from PW/MIA Family Interviews

Prior to February 1973 and the return of American prisoners of war, 215 Army, Navy and Marine PW/MIA families were interviewed by CPWS staff members (McCubbin, Hunter and Metres, 1973). Data from those interviews add to the graphic portrait of the PW/MIA family. At the time of the interviews, approximately one year prior to the men's release, the wives, on the average, had been married over ten years. Children ranged in age from less than one year (several were born shortly after the father's casualty) to 25 years. While most of the children were between 5 and 10 years of age at the time of their fathers' deployment, the majority were between 10 and 15 years at repatriation. The wives' ages averaged 34 years at the time of the release. The average educational level of the wives was slightly lower than that of their husbands. However, the wives' formal schooling was still, on the average, in excess of 12 years, and one-third of the group interviewed had earned college degrees. The husband's absence, in several instances, had apparently afforded the wives the specific opportunity needed to continue their education.

Comparison of the RPW and MIA Populations

Proportionately, there was a much higher percentage of MIAs compared with RPWs for the Army (77 RPWs to 367 MIAs) and Marine Corps (26 RPWs to 114 MIAs) groups than for the Navy. The number of MIAs to RPWs within the Navy sample was more evenly divided, with 138 RPWs to 177 MIAs. Comparisons as to the total number of service personnel involved, demographic characteristics for these men, and various family factors for both the MIA and the RPW populations are presented in Tables 1, 2, 3, and 4.

TABLE 1. *Distribution of Casualties by Service*

	RPW	*MIA*	*Total*
Army	77	367	444
Navy	138	177	315
Marine Corps	26	114	140
TOTAL	241	658	899

TABLE 2. *Comparison of Demographic Characteristics for Army-Navy-Marine RPW/MIA Populations (Age and Educational Level)*

	RPW	*MIA*
Mean age at casualty:		
Officers	30.2	28.7
Enlisted	22.6	23.5
Mean years of formal education:		
Officers	15.2	14.9
Enlisted	11.6	11.8

18

TABLE 3. *Comparison of Demographic Characteristics for Army-Navy-Marine Corps Populations (Race, Religion and Marital Status)*

	RPW %	MIA %
Race: Caucasian	94.2	93.5
Black	4.1	6.2
Other	1.7	0.3
Religion: Protestant	67.6	68.5
Catholic	25.4	26.1
Other	7.0	5.4
Marital Status:		
Officers: Single	25.4	30.8
Married	72.9	66.5
Divorced/Separated	1.7	2.7
Enlisted: Single	61.7	65.3
Married	36.7	31.6
Divorced/Separated	1.6	3.1

TABLE 4. *RPW/MIA Children*

	RPW N	MIA N	Total
Men with children	125	253	378
Total number of children	298	576	874

Based upon a comparison of officers only, in order to rule out the officer versus enlisted differences, it was found that the RPW and MIA officer populations were similar for race, religion, education and marital status. However, there was a statistically significant difference ($p < .01$, $t = 3.1$, $df = 543$) between the RPW and MIA officer populations for age at time of casualty. Mean age for the RPW officer group was 30.2 years; for the MIA officer group 28.7 years. There was also a significant between-group difference ($p < .05$, $t = 2.5$, $df = 539$) for average number of children per officer, with the MIA group having fewer children. However, this latter difference may merely be a reflection of the younger age of the MIA group and the larger percentage of RPWs who were married (73% of the RPW officers compared with 66% of the MIA officers).

Summary and Conclusions

A demographic profile of the 899 Army, Navy and Marine Corps prisoners of war and missing in action populations has been presented to provide a basis for understanding descriptive and statistical information to be presented in subsequent chapters. The 241 prisoners of war who were repatriated in the Spring of 1973 had been absent, on the average, for five years, during which time their families sought to cope with an undefined and indeterminate situation. A second group of 658 men did not return, and their families continue to wait or prepare to adapt to a restructured family unit without the missing serviceman.

Within the MIA and RPW groups are 874 children who experienced or are still experiencing prolonged periods of father absence. Additionally, there are 489 wives who experienced the trauma of having a spouse that was either missing or a prisoner of war. Three hundred and four of these women continued in their "limbo" status beyond the mass release of prisoners in 1973; for many of them, resolution remains to be attained.

Of course, it should be kept in mind that the characteristics of the RPW and the MIA populations do not necessarily reflect the characteristics of the total population of men in the armed services. Furthermore, what bearing the basic characteristics presented above, in particular the family characteristics, may have upon the adjustment of the returnee, his family, and the family of the serviceman still unaccounted for remains to be examined.

The Casuality and the Waiting Period

3

Adaptation Of The Family To The PW/MIA Experience: An Overview

HAMILTON I. MCCUBBIN

EDNA J. HUNTER

PHILIP J. METRES, JR.

Introduction

Over the years behavioral scientists have continued to extrapolate and document lessons learned from prisoner of war experiences. The classic studies of the trauma of concentration camps (Bettelheim, 1953; Eitinger, 1964; Frankl, 1968), prisoner of war experiences (Biderman, 1967), stresses of captivity (Schein, 1957; Schein, Schneir and Barker, 1961), and coping behavior in captivity (Ballard, 1973) indicated the significance of these unique experiences and their possible influence upon the longitudinal adjustment of repatriated prisoners (Schein, Cooley and Singer, 1960; Segal, 1973). In contrast, there is a paucity of research attempting to answer questions surrounding the adjustment of families of servicemen missing in action (MIA) or prisoners of war (PW), family adjustment during the internment period, and the role families play in the long-term rehabilitation of repatriated prisoners.

Existing research on the general problems of family adjustment to father absence in the military, however, indicates the importance of this line of inquiry. Baker et al. (1967, 1968) documented the serious nature of father absence and its potentially deleterious effect upon the family, and in particular its effect upon the children. Montalvo's (1968) study of the adjustment of 55 families whose fathers were stationed overseas spotlighted family assistance programs (medical, social and psychological) and the social value of the military community as major contributors to family adjustment. His conclusion that family adjustment to father absence could be enhanced by maintaining the family in the military community throughout the serviceman's tour was examined and reaffirmed later by Allen (1972) in his survey of Schilling Manor, a military community in Salina, Kansas, which was designed and operated to serve military families of servicemen performing a tour in Southeast Asia. Collateral findings were also evident in an assessment of the impact of father absence in the Navy (Dickerson & Arthur, 1965) and the Navy's study of family adjustment to the prolonged absence of fathers serving on board submarines (Pearlman, 1970). Exploratory studies (MacIntosh, 1968; Spellman, 1965) and descriptive papers (Hartog, 1966; McKain, 1965) on family adjustment have continued to emerge and add to our growing knowledge of patterns of family adjustment under a wide range of stressful situations in the military setting.

The adaptation of the PW/MIA family to an indeterminate and unprecedented length of father absence, has only been alluded to in past research. Hill (1949) cited one family in his total sample who experienced the ramifications of a husband missing in action. Even though PW/MIA families were present at Schilling Manor, Allen (1972) did not take this factor into consideration. Recent papers by Spolyar (1973), Hall and Simmons (1973) and Brown (1972) attempted to describe the grieving process, adjustment problems and coping behaviors of PW/MIA wives and children; however, none of them were based on any systematic assessment of such families.

It is paradoxical that while professionals are expected to continue the extension of comprehensive medical, legal, psychological, psychiatric and social work services to repatriated prisoners and their families, we as yet lack clarity regarding the nature and extent of the problems the families faced in the past and the resulting family dynamics, adjustments, and concomitant problem-solving behaviors which evolved during the serviceman's absence. Knowledge of the history of family adjustment is essential to the analyses of any future family or individual problems, the establishment of counseling and treatment relationships, and the development of family services.

The study reported here, in part, represents an effort to determine the nature and extent of adjustment problems experienced by families of servicemen missing in action or prisoners of war in Southeast Asia. These families were studied solely because they were in a unique situation of adapting to prolonged and indeterminate husband absence and not because they had been referred for help with emotional, financial, or medical problems. The underlying hypothesis was that when a family is called upon to adapt to the absence of a husband/father listed as missing or a prisoner in a war zone, the occurrence of adjustment problems (in the broadest sense) must be anticipated as

part of the natural history of the situation. A corollary to this hypothesis is the assumption that these families must uniformly be offered
assistance with their adjustment if the goal of comprehensive medical,
social, psychological and legal services and care is to be realized.
    The purposes of this study were threefold:
  (a) To determine the nature and incidence of social, emotional,
       medical and legal problems encountered by this group of
       families;
  (b) To discover and classify the processes of adaptation to a here-
       tofore unstudied family crisis; and
  (c) To determine the relative value of existing services and need for
       future services.
    The importance of the data collected to the professionals and service
delivery personnel stimulated the timely presentation of findings as
soon as phases of analysis were completed. The findings presented in
this text will be limited in scope to a broad overview of the families
and their basic problems.

Sample

    The study reported here was conducted over the period April 1972
to February 1973 by the staff of the Center for Prisoner of War Studies
(CPWS), San Diego, California. Families included in the sample[1] were
drawn from the total population of PW/MIA families of the Army,
Navy and Marine Corps. The sample, for this part of the total study,
was limited to families of procreation (those in which the PW/MIA
serviceman has a status of spouse), because of their "dependent"
status and the responsibility of each of the armed services to provide
them comprehensive care during the serviceman's absence.
    The sample consisted of 215 families; approximately 50 percent of
the total number of wives of PW/MIA servicemen of each service,
Navy, Army and Marine Corps. The majority (55.3%) of the sample
was represented by Navy families, followed by the Army (32.6%) and
in turn the Marine Corps (12.1%). Of the sample, 100 families (46.5%)
were of servicemen classified as captured in Southeast Asia and the
remaining 115 families (53.5%) were of servicemen listed in the
casualty status of missing or missing in action. The sample included
405 children. Three-fourths (76.3%) of the sample were families of
officer personnel, an additional 2.8 percent of warrant officers, and
20.8 percent were families of enlisted personnel.

    1. *The research design included interviewing all PW/MIA families; however, interviewing
was only possible up to the time of repatriation in February 1973. To maximize the achievement of a representative sample while working towards interviewing the total population,
emphasis was placed upon conducting interviews in regions of the United States with high
concentrations of Navy and Marine families.*

Hamilton I. McCubbin, Edna J. Hunter, Philip J. Metres, Jr.

Method

Family interviews were conducted using a structured interview format. Single in-depth interviews, ranging in length from two to eight hours, were conducted with PW/MIA wives located throughout the Continental United States, Hawaii, Puerto Rico, and Europe. The 215 interviews were conducted by professional staff of the CPWS Family Assistance Branch[2] consisting of a Navy psychiatrist, civilian clinical psychologists, military and civilian social workers, and assisted by clinical social workers of the U.S. Army.[3] The Army social workers were selected on the basis of their extensive experience with military families and were given additional training in PW/MIA problems and the application of the structured interview schedule.

The interview schedule was used to insure the systematic collection of data. The questions elicited specific demographic information and data related to family history as well as psychological, social, and medical factors conceivably related to family and individual adjustment. The schedule was modified on two occasions subsequent to the initiation of the study; thus, the number of wives responding to each question sometimes varied. The wives usually gave the information and described their experiences in a candid and forthright manner with an apparent eagerness to share their feelings and concerns which had fomented over the preceding years. For many wives this situation represented their first meaningful opportunity during the long period of adjustment to express fully and freely the many conflicting, complex personal feelings surrounding their "in limbo" status. The clinical skills of the interviewers and the need of the wives to "tell their story" resulted in interviews which often proved supportive and therapeutic as well as informative. Those families indicating active social, psychological, medical, legal or financial adjustment problems were referred to the appropriate civilian or military resources for continued assistance.

Findings

Population Characteristics.[4] The sample of families consisted of wives between the ages of 20 and 49 with an average of 33.2 years of age at the time of the interview. The educational level of the majority of wives was in excess of twelve years; one-third had received college

2. *Mrs. Inez Dunning, A.C.S.W., Chief, Family Assistance Branch; LCDR Philip Ballard, M.D.; Mr. Philip Metres, Jr., M.A.; and Mrs. Dorothy Benson.*

3. *LTC David Jentsch, D.S.W.; Captain Robert Jupe, A.C.S.W.; Specialist Terry Weisbrick, B.S.*

4. *Data analysis was conducted by Jerry Goffman, Ph.D., Chief, Data Analysis Branch, Center for Prisoner of War Studies.*

24

degrees. While the families averaged two children, one-fifth (20.5%) had no children. The 405 children ranged in age from less than one year to 25 years of age, with the majority (53.8%) between the ages of eight and fifteen. The majority of wives (55.2%) had a marital history in excess of 10 years. Prior marriages were infrequent for both husbands (9.8%) and wives (8.4%). At the time of the interview extended families (both or either parent) existed for most of the PW/MIA husbands (91.6%) and wives (92.1%). Religious affiliations were similar for both husbands and wives and were predominantly Protestant (64.6%).

The Situation. The situation common to these families was that each family had been confronted with a report of casualty listing their husbands/fathers as missing in action or prisoners of war. The length of absence of these men extended from less than one year to over eight years. One hundred thirty-nine (64.6%) of these absences were extended over a period of three to six years.

General Adjustment. Families appeared to seek some degree of stability as well as change following notification of casualty. The majority of families (71.6%) made at least one change of residence; one-fourth (25.1%) made three or more moves.

During this period of prolonged husband absence, the wives involved themselves in a wide range of activities which, for the most part, were both enhancing to their self-esteem and productive. Recreation and leisure-time activities were satisfying and provided an outlet for the wives. While television and movies, social group activities, and hobbies ranked high, the military service clubs received the least emphasis of those activities mentioned.

TABLE 1. *Satisfying Recreational and Leisure-Time Activities*

Activities	Number of Responses*	Percent
Hobbies	193	89.8
Television	170	79.1
Social group	170	79.1
Movies	164	76.3
Sports	160	74.4
House remodeling/redecorating	115	59.6
Educational classes	104	49.3
Volunteer work (non-military)	87	40.6
Church	80	41.4
Military service clubs	32	15.6

*N varied due to revisions in the questionnaire.

Hamilton I. McCubbin, Edna J. Hunter, Philip J. Metres, Jr.

Adaptation of the family to its inherent social responsibilities requires that family members, the wife in this particular situation, have the authority to negotiate all legal transactions. This area of responsibility proved to be one of unexpected difficulty. Although less than one-third of the families emphasized legal problems as a major area of difficulty encountered during the period of husband/father absence, when these problems did occur, they affected the family's financial stability and credibility. The absence of or the expiration of a power of attorney, which deprived the family of the authority to act on behalf of its members in all negotiations, was the most frequently mentioned legal issue confronting the wives. Transactions involving the purchase or sale of real or personal property were also areas of difficulty precisely because of the power of attorney problems already mentioned. Of lesser import were problems related to financial credit, preparation of wills, court, tax, and insurance matters, as well as law suits, probate matters, and business ventures. Additionally, it is important to note that 21 families (10.9%) sought answers to questions surrounding termination of marriage.

TABLE 2. *Legal Issues Confronted by PW/MIA Families*

Legal Problems	Number of Responses*	Percent
Power of attorney	66	30.8
Purchase/sale of real property	46	21.5
Purchase/sale of personal property	46	21.5
Obtaining credit	27	13.8
Wills	25	13.0
Termination of marriage	21	10.9
Court appearance	20	9.3
Tax problems	15	7.8
Insurance problems	14	7.3
Probate	10	4.7
Law suits	5	2.3
Business ventures	5	2.6

Number of respondents varied.

Role Adjustments. An analysis of intra-family adjustments indicated that families often adapted to new responsibilities and modification in family roles with accompanying anxieties, frustrations, and feelings of insecurity engendered by the situation. One hundred and twenty wives (72.3%) reported the lack of husband's companionship as the most difficult area with which they had to cope. Concomitantly, difficulties with feelings of loneliness, lack of suitable social outlets, concern for personal health, and guilt feelings were emphasized by the wives. Both traditional and inherited responsibilities were intensified for the wife tasked with the dual mother-father role. Seventy-one wives (33.0%) were employed either on a full or part time basis. Almost two-thirds of the group (62.3%), however, were unemployed. Decision-making, disciplining of the children, handling of family finances, and the health of the children were cited as additional perplexing family problems.

TABLE 3. *Intra-Family Adjustments*

Adjustment Problems	Number of Responses*	Percent
Lack of husband's companionship	120	72.3
Feelings of extreme loneliness	78	47.0
Making decisions alone	66	39.8
Lack of social outlets	45	27.1
Disciplining children	31	18.7
Time for dual mother-father role	30	18.1
Feelings of guilt	23	13.9
Handling family finances	22	13.3
Health of wife	18	10.8
Health of children	7	4.2

Number of respondents varied.

Wife's Perception of the Marriage. It seems reasonable to hypothesize that the indeterminate separation would have some discernable and differential effect on the wives' perception of their marriages because of the large within group variance in lengths of marriage before casualty and the length of husband's absence. In contrast with the wives' retrospective assessments of their marriages prior to casualty in which the majority (79.9%) rated their marriages as being either satisfactory or very satisfactory, less than half the group (44.2%) felt the same degree of satisfaction with their marriages at the time of the interview. There was a 35.7 percent decrease in perceived satisfaction. This change in feelings about the marriage was evident in other areas. There was an increase in the number of wives who planned to obtain a divorce or separation (1.2% to 9.2%). Initially only 10 (6.1%) wives expressed ambivalence about their marriages; 53 wives (32.5%) reported uncertainty of their marital situations at the time of the interview.

27

TABLE 4. *Wife's Perception of Her Marriage**

	Pre-Casualty		At Time of Interview	
Wives' Assessments	*Number*	*Percent*	*Number*	*Percent*
Requested divorce/ separation	3	1.8	1	0.6
Planned divorce/ separation	2	1.2	15	9.2
Chronic conflict	8	4.9	2	1.2
Uncertainty of situation	10	6.1	53	32.5
Family difficulty not insurmountable	10	6.1	20	12.3
Satisfactory	31	18.9	14	8.6
Very satisfactory/very close	100	61.0	58	35.6

*Number of respondents varied.

Physical Adjustment of the PW/MIA Wife. The physical status of the mother is a critical factor in the maintenance and stability of the PW/MIA family. Although personal health problems were not considered one of the most difficult areas for the PW/MIA wives, they did report a variety of physical illnesses which required medical attention during the interim period.

TABLE 5. *Wives' Physical Illnesses Requiring Medical Treatment*

Illnesses	*Number of Respondents*	*Percent*
General: flu, allergens	101	47.0
Respiratory	62	28.8
Gastro-intestinal	28	13.0
Hepatic	10	4.7
Biliary & Pancreatic	6	2.8
Genito-Urinary	4	1.9
Cardiovascular	1	0.5

The most common ailments were influenza and allergens, mentioned by 101 (47.0%) of the wives. Respiratory ailments (28.8%) and gastro-intestinal disturbances (13.0%) were also frequently mentioned. In general, the wives maintained surveillance over their health and, on the average, had received a thorough physical examination within the preceding fifteen-month period. Data from the interviews showed that a noticeably larger percentage of the wives (13.2%) rated their general health as a handicap during the period of husband absence than had been the case prior to their husbands' casualties (7.3%).

When in need of medical attention for physical ailments the families tended to seek care from civilian resources (40.2%). The importance of civilian programs to PW/MIA families gains significance when we consider that an additional forty percent (41.1%) of the families utilized both military and civilian medical services. The remaining families (18.7%) obtained care solely from military medical programs.

Emotional Adjustment of PW/MIA Wives. Emotional and psychological adjustments seemed more prevalent than the physical health problems of PW/MIA wives. Out of twelve emotional symptoms covered by the interviewer, nearly three-fourths (73.5%) of the sample reported having experienced five or more symptoms during the period of husband absence. The most frequently reported symptom was that of feeling depressed or "down in the dumps", mentioned by almost the entire sample (89.8%). Disturbed sleep patterns were cited by more than seventy percent of the sample. Additionally, over three-fourths (78.6%) of the sample cited feelings of jumpiness or being "uptight" during the same period.

TABLE 6. *PW/MIA Wife's Emotional Symptoms*

Symptoms	Number of Respondents	Percent
Depressed, "Down in dumps"	193	89.8
Jumpiness, "Uptight"	169	78.6
Fitful sleep	149	73.8
Difficulty falling asleep	144	67.0
Waking, not rested	130	64.4
Bored	109	54.5
Rapid mood fluctuations	115	54.5
Headaches	108	50.2
Feeling life is meaningless	85	40.5
Poor digestion	85	39.5
Shortness of breath	56	26.0
Accident-prone	36	17.9

Additional indices of emotional adjustment noted were that over half the group (58.2%) were taking or had taken tranquilizers during their husbands' absences, and 53.2 percent had experienced body weight fluctuations of 15 pounds or more in either direction during that period. Although almost half of the group (48.2%) were non-smokers, 32.9 percent reported they now smoked more heavily than they had prior to their husbands' casualties. Slightly over ten percent were nondrinkers, while 23.8 percent found they imbibed in alcoholic beverages more heavily than previously. For 6.7 percent of the group, alcoholism was reported to be a potential, if not already existent, problem. Over forty percent (40.5%) of the group reported frequent feelings that life was meaningless, and 37.2 percent reported entertaining suicidal thoughts at some time during their husbands' absences, although only 16.4 percent felt they had ever really seriously considered suicide.

Coping with Emotional Stress. The sample of 215 families reported a wide range of symptoms related to emotional and social adjustment that they found to be moderately or severely difficult to manage. It appears that the occurrence of emotional problems and correlated symptomatology in the unique PW/MIA situation is predictable and therefore should be anticipated. In many instances the families did seek professional help to cope with the situation. One-third of the wives depended upon the family physician (34.2%) and an almost equal percentage turned to the minister or priest (27.4%) for assistance. Mental health professionals, including psychiatrists, psychologists and social workers, were consulted by over one-third (35.2%) of the wives.

TABLE 7. *Family Use of Professionals for Emotional Adjustment*

Professionals Used	Number of Responses*	Percent
Physician	53	34.2
Minister or priest	42	27.4
Psychiatrist	40	26.3
Psychologist	9	5.6
Social Worker	5	3.3
Teacher	4	2.6
Family Counselor	1	0.6
Other	17	10.8

Number of respondents varied.

Because of the military's commitment to provide services to families and to maintain continuity in the care provided, the source of family support takes on greater import. Families who did use mental health services reported a slightly greater use of family services offered by the military over civilian services through CHAMPUS (Civilian Health and Medical Programs of the Uniformed Services).

Adaptation of the Family to the PW/MIA
Experience: An Overview

TABLE 8. *Family Use of Mental Health Services*

Type and Frequency	Number	Percent
Military Family Services		
No contact	177	82.3
One contact	5	2.3
2-3 contacts	12	5.6
Contacts over several months	18	8.4
No response	3	1.4
Champus Family Services		
No contact	182	84.6
One contact	1	0.4
2-3 contacts	8	3.7
Contacts over several months	18	8.4
No response	6	2.8

The efficacy of treatment received in either program is beyond the scope of this report. However, of the wives who used either or both CHAMPUS and military mental health programs, the majority (76.4%) endorsed the programs as being of some or considerable help to them.

Personal religious beliefs were also mentioned as a source of support and consolation for the PW/MIA wives. One hundred and seven wives (49.8%) reported that their religious beliefs had been very helpful to them in coping with their husbands' absences. A minority (20.5%) did not find religion a source of support. The degree to which religion proved helpful to the family varied with time since the husband's casualty. Some wives (11.2%) found religion to be important initially, but not at a later time. On the other hand, a few (4.2%) found the opposite to be true.

Wives in Treatment. Interview data showed that 31.3 percent of the wives were either receiving therapy at the time of the interview or had been in treatment at some time during the husband's absence. An additional 51.4 percent of the wives appeared to be in need of psychological assistance at the time of the interview but were not then in treatment. If those who might benefit from therapy are added to the number actually in treatment, it would appear that 57.5 percent of this group of PW/MIA wives would profit from psychological or psychiatric assistance (see Table 9). The interviewers also noted that it was probable that approximately 80 percent of the families would benefit from marriage or family counseling during the repatriation period.

31

TABLE 9. *Psychological/Psychiatric Treatment Received by or
Recommended for PW/MIA Wives
(N = 214)*

Status at time of Interview	Number	Percent
Wives receiving treatment	13	6.1
Wives who received treatment in past, but		
not now in treatment	54	25.2
Wives who never received treatment	147	68.7
Wives for whom treatment was		
recommended who were not in treatment	110	51.4
Families who may need counseling at time		
of repatriation	170	79.4

Adjustment of Children of PW/MIA Families. The physical and emotional adjustments of children of servicemen missing in action or prisoners of war are important indices of both individual and family adjustment. Children's problems represent another source of stress for both the mother and the family unit. Seven of the wives (4.2%) reported that the physical health of children presented major problems during their husbands' absences. The most frequently reported physical health problems among this group of 405 children were the common childhood diseases, accidental injuries and surgery. Other physical problems are shown in Table 10.

TABLE 10. *Children's Health Problems During Father Absence*

Health Problems	Number of Responses	Percent*
Common childhood diseases	166	41.0
Accidental injuries	73	18.0
Surgeries	48	11.8
Enuresis (past age 3)	31	7.6
Acute illnesses	27	6.7
Chronic illnesses	25	6.2
Special handicaps	17	4.2
Other physical problems	17	4.2

Based upon total number of children in the sample: N = 405

In contrast with the children's physical status, their emotional adjustment appeared slightly more problematic. Seventy of the PW/MIA children were judged by their mothers to have had significant emotional problems during the period of father absence. For the families with children, the average number of emotional or behavioral problems was 4.3 per family. The most frequently reported symptoms which might reflect adjustment difficulties were unwarranted and frequent crying (14.1%), nightmares (13.1%), rebelliousness (12.1%), shyness (10.4%), nail biting (10.4%), and fear of the dark (10.4%). Other symptoms reported by the mothers are listed in Table 11.

TABLE 11. *Children's Emotional and Behavioral Adjustment*

Children's Symptoms	Number of Responses	Percent*
Cries easily	57	14.1
Nightmares	53	13.1
Rebelliousness	49	12.1
Overly shy	42	10.4
Nail biting	42	10.4
Fear of the dark	42	10.4
Frequent temper tantrums	32	7.9
Enuresis (beyond 3 yrs. of age)	31	7.6
Overly aggressive	20	4.9
Sulky	20	4.9
Sleep walking	19	4.7
Difficulty adjusting to new situations	18	4.4
Destructiveness	16	4.0
Lethargic	14	3.4
Stealing	14	3.4
Speech problems	13	3.2
Drugs	10	2.5
Encounters with law enforcement	6	1.5

Based upon the total number of children in the sample: N = 405

The social and interpersonal adjustments of the children were also areas of concern to the mothers. Thirty-nine (9.6%) children were reported to have displayed behavior problems in the school setting. Almost the same percentage (9.1%) had difficulty with peer relationships (Table 12).

TABLE 12. *Children's Interpersonal and Behavior Problems*

Child Problems	Number of Responses	Percent*
School behavior problems	39	9.6
Difficult peer relationships	37	9.1
Behavior problems at home	35	8.6
Poor relationship with mother	29	7.2
Poor relationship with other adults	22	5.4

Based on the total number of children in the sample: N = 405

Use of Children's Services. The families were involved in the full range of medical services available to them in providing care for the children. Of those families where physical health problems for the children did arise, over half (56.7%) utilized both military and civilian medical resources. One-quarter (29.3%) obtained all medical services from civilian sources. A minority (14.0%) utilized military medical assistance only.

Some of the mothers did seek the assistance of mental health professionals when they felt their children had emotional problems. However, of the 69 children judged by their mothers to have significant emotional problems, only 37 children had received professional counseling. The remaining 32 children who needed help (46.4%) received no professional assistance. The future significance of child adjustment gains added importance when we consider that over one-quarter (27.9%) of the PW/MIA wives with children expressed concern that their returning husbands would experience difficulty in coping with the array and severity of the emotional and behavioral problems presented by the children.

The interviewers made a clinical judgment of the children's needs for psychological or psychiatric assistance on the basis of mothers' comments and reports of their children's behaviors and symptomatology during father absence. Wherever possible, personal interviews were conducted with the children. Results showed that 102 children (25.2%) of the 405 children were evaluated to be in need of psychological/psychiatric counseling at the time of the interview (See Table 13).

TABLE 13. *Psychological/Psychiatric Treatment Received by or Recommended for PW/MIA Children*

Status at time of Interviews	Number	Percent*
Children receiving treatment	12	3.0
Children who received treatment in past but not now in treatment	25	6.2
Children who were never in treatment	368	90.8
TOTALS	405	100.0
Children for whom treatment was recommended who were not already in treatment	102	25.2

*Based upon the total number of children in the sample: N = 405

To provide continuous service to and liaison with families of servicemen missing in action or prisoners of war, the armed services established a casualty assistance program: Casualty Assistance and Calls

Adaptation of the Family to the PW/MIA Experience: An Overview

Officers (CACO) were assigned to Navy and Marine families; a Family Service Assistance Officer (FSAO) was assigned to each Army family. These selected individuals were responsible for providing and coordinating services to PW/MIA families. As one part of the interview, the Casualty Assistance Program was evaluated by the wives. Almost half the PW/MIA wives interviewed reported they had been very satisfied with the Family Assistance Program. Add those wives who were moderately or to some extent satisfied with the assistance program (25.0%), and it appears the wives favorably endorsed the assistance program (Table 14).

TABLE 14. *Wives' Assessments of CACO/FSAO Program*

Satisfaction Rating	Responses	Percent
Very satisfied	106	49.4
Moderately satisfied	46	21.4
To some extent satisfied	10	4.6
Not at all satisfied	2	0.9
Question not posed*	51	23.7
TOTAL	215	100.0

*Revised questionnaire

The interpretation of this general endorsement, however, must be tempered by consideration of additional findings. Over one-fourth (26.1%) of the wives emphasized the need for more effective or more highly trained family assistance officers, and almost forty percent (39.8%) expressed the need for receiving more information about services available to them. The frequent transfers of casualty assistance officers coupled with the prolonged period of husband absence resulted in extreme variance in the number of family assistance officers assigned to a particular family over time. Over forty percent (40.1%) of the wives had been assigned five or more family assistance officers; three wives had as many as fifteen family assistance officers assigned to them during the period of husband absence.

In recognition of the important role of family assistance officers and the need for careful selection of such personnel, the interviewers solicited the wives' impressions of desirable qualities and traits for any family assistance officer. Heading the list of desired attributes was maturity (mentioned by 96.3%), followed by the ability to make referrals for services (95.7%), empathy (91.5%), and the ability to establish a professional relationship (84.8%). Other qualifications deemed essential by the wives are cited in Table 15.

Hamilton I. McCubbin, Edna J. Hunter, Philip J. Metres, Jr.

TABLE 15. *Desired Characteristics of Family Assistance Officers*

Characteristic	Number of Responses*	Percent
Maturity	158	96.3
Referral Ability	156	95.7
Empathy	150	91.5
Ability to establish a professional relationship	139	84.8
Volunteer for the job	104	63.4
Married	85	51.8
Career officer	69	42.1
Married with own children	60	36.6
Behavior science background	59	35.9
Similar age as husband	52	31.7
Similar rank as husband	36	22.0
Not in flying status	19	11.6

N = 164 due to revised questionnaire.

The wives' concerns about repatriation were additional indices of the difficulty in the adjustment of PW/MIA families. For the returnee repatriation would be the time when he would be confronted with the family's behavior during his absence; for the wives, it represented a critical time of accounting for their stewardships during the husbands' absences. For other wives, repatriation meant facing the fact that their husbands were not coming back. The husbands' reactions to their wives' increased independence was a primary concern mentioned by 41 percent of the group. Dating (22.9%) and handling the finances (23.5%) were also emphasized as potential areas for disapproval by the husbands. A few of the wives (12.0%) expressed concern over the husbands' judgments of the manner in which the children were raised. Over-indulging in alcohol was reported by nine (5.4%) wives as a potential subject of disapproval (Table 16).

TABLE 16. *Wives' Concerns About Repatriation*

Concern	Number*	Percent
Becoming too independent	68	41.0
Not saving more money	39	23.5
Dating	38	22.9
Manner in which children raised	20	12.0
Drinking too much	9	5.4

N = 166 due to revised questionnaire.

Repatriation also meant the wives must come to terms with their fantasies about the physical and emotional status of their husbands. The majority (61.2%) of the wife group emphasized concern over their husbands' abilities to adjust to the rapid social change which had occurred during their absences. Half of the wives indicated concern about their husbands' health and over one-third exhibited anxiety about the husbands' abilities to assume the husband and father roles and continue a career in the military. Of lesser import were the wives' concerns over the husbands' premature aging, sexual inadequacy, violent behavior, in-law problems and driving ability.

TABLE 17. *Wives' Concerns for their Husbands at Repatriation*

Concern	Number of Responses	Percent
Adjustment to social changes	131	61.2
Husband's health	108	50.2
Resumption of husband role	85	39.5
Resumption of father role	83	38.6
Ability to resume career	78	35.8
Premature aging	59	27.0
Ability to cope with children's problems	53	31.0**
Sexual inadequacy of husband	43	20.0
Violent behavior	37	19.5*
In-law problems	35	18.4*
Driving ability	30	15.8*

*N = 190 due to revised questionnaire.

**N = 171 based on number of families with children.

The wives emphasized the need for family and individual services at the time of repatriation for both the family and the returning prisoner of war. Heading the list of desired services was psychological counseling for the returning men (59.0%). Of nearly equal importance were educational counseling (52.4%) and occupational counseling (50.5%) for the returnee. Over 40 percent of the wives expressed the need for marriage and family counseling, legal counseling and job retraining at the time of repatriation. Other service needs at the time of repatriation are cited in Table 18.

TABLE 18. *Services Required at Time of Repatriation*

Service	Number of Responses*	Percent
Psychological help	125	59.0
Educational counseling	111	52.4
Occupational counseling	107	50.5
Marriage/family counseling	103	48.6
Job retraining	101	47.6
Legal counseling	92	43.4
Physical therapy	75	35.4
Financial counseling	65	30.7
Spiritual counseling	64	30.2

*$N = 212$

Discussion

The emotional and social adjustment of the military family to the absence of a husband/father who is missing in action or a prisoner of war is the primary focus of this study. How the families adjust to the absence of a PW/MIA husband/father and the families' expectations regarding his return are seen as important areas for research since there has been little documentation of family adjustment in the literature. The data revealed the value of this line of inquiry and the variance in patterns of adjustment to this unprecedented situation of indeterminate and protracted father absence.

The population of PW/MIA families is not, demographically, a homogeneous group. The wives presented a full spectrum of ages, socioeconomic levels, and levels of education. The sample varied with respect to the number of families with children, number of children per family, and the age range of children. However, within this diversity are demographic characteristics which may suggest a greater or lesser potential for the family's adaptation to the situation. MacIntosh (1968) in his study of family adjustment to separation in the military found a positive relationship between wives' past experiences with husband absence and educational level of the wife with the subsequent successful adjustment to separation. For the most part, the wives in this study had relatively high levels of education and college degrees. Concomitantly, the wives for the most part had marriages of generally long standing. Pending further data analysis, the correlation of this data with overall adjustment remains a hypothesis.

Adaptation of the Family to the PW/MIA Experience: An Overview

The family members responded to the separation by involving themselves in social, individual and family activities. The wives focused upon activities which appeared to build their self-esteem and occupy them both emotionally and mentally. Participation in social functions indicated that the wives attempted to involve themselves in numerous activities outside the home. Efforts to engage in the military community and its social activities, however, appeared minimal. This may be due in part to their inherent discomfort in performing the social roles without a husband and their anxieties about exploitation. Striking out to establish the independent role as a wage earner of the family was not evident for most. This was, in part, due to the allotments received from their husbands' salaries which lessened any desire to supplement income. It may also be that the wives recognized the added importance of their dual role as mother and father, and their presence in the home assumed added importance.

The unprecedented length of absence brings into focus the complexity of the situation. The wives were immediately confronted with basic questions which had to be answered to their personal satisfaction. Should they plan for his eventual return or a confirmation of his death? In most cases families had to plan for both. Under normal conditions an immediate notification of death quickly sets into motion several emotional reactions and social behaviors leading to a new future. However, in the PW/MIA situation the normal emotional and social adjustment processes were thwarted. Complex adjustments in the family's life-style were required for some. Personal, financial, legal, and medical needs evolved and were extended over an unknown and unpredictable period of time.

Adaptation of the family to the normal demands of living and planning for its future is dependent upon the determination of its legal status, its rights, and its responsibilities. One area of unexpected difficulty was the wives' legal status to negotiate all transactions on behalf of the family. Wives were, in some cases, unable to perform normal tasks such as the purchase or sale of a home due to a lack of or an expired power of attorney or an inability to obtain credit. Although the wide range of persistent legal issues confronted by the families can be simply stated, the issues were, in fact, complex: to invest money in property, purchase an automobile, purchase a home or to terminate a marriage. These issues became more difficult because of the variance in legal interpretations within the military and the lack of uniformity in State laws governing all PW/MIA legal transactions. The legal difficulties experienced by the wives put into perspective both the need for established guidelines for servicemen which anticipate the wide range of potential problems inherent in a combat tour and the value of adequate preparation of military families for every eventuality.

Adjustment of roles within the family was evident. The PW/MIA situation precipitated a reallocation of tasks and responsibilities among family members: among other tasks, mothers assumed greater responsibility for making decisions, disciplining the children and handling family finances. The children inherited father-related responsibilities including a heightened awareness of and responsiveness to the mothers' demands and needs. Those family members assuming such responsibilities were called upon to lengthen their commitment in recognition of the fact that their father might not return. Many wives reported in the interviews that their relationship with the children was perhaps a closer one than it would have been had the father been present in the home. The statistic indicating "time for dual mother-father role" as being a lesser problem, is deceptive; while it may be true that the *time* required to perform the roles may be of little consequence, the responsibilities were perplexing as well as difficult to cope with. Even under normal conditions it is difficult for the average mother to raise a family single-handedly. The PW/MIA wife had total responsibility for the family and planning for its future. She often experienced feelings of frustration and guilt, realizing that she was to be held accountable by her husband for whatever the outcome of her efforts upon his release. For the MIA wife, the paradox of starting a new life for the family, as well as for herself, while maintaining a role for the husband who might not return, fostered feelings of insecurity, guilt, and a continuous struggle with problems of self-esteem (Brown, 1972). The shifting of family roles, responsibilities, and the intensification of relationships among family members suggests the evolution of a family unit without the father. The closing of ranks within the family was described by Hall and Simmons (1973) as part of their clinical portrait of PW/MIA families. Hill (1949) also noted this pattern of adjustment to be a common phenomenon among families experiencing father separations during World War II. While these may be indices of normal adjustment, Hill (1949) reported that the type of reorganization which made for successful separation adjustment appeared to lead to poor adjustment at time of reunion.

In spite of the wives' efforts to perform their roles well, they received little satisfactory feedback and had to deal with the realization that there were few, if any, socially acceptable outlets to enhance their self-esteem. The guilt associated with performing their dual roles and establishing new lives without husbands was a significant factor in the wives' adjustment. With each accomplishment and increment of improved self-esteem, the wives' experienced a growing sense of independence which added to already existing feelings of guilt. Brown's (1972) conclusion seems appropriate: "Even the most stable and mature wives experience emotional problems ... (p. 12)."

The impact of the PW/MIA situation and the families' attempts to develop without a husband was most evident in the wives' devaluation of the marital relationship. Part of the change may be accounted for by the indeterminate nature of the situation and the natural inclination to avoid building unrealistic hopes and expectations. They relied on a "wait and see" attitude, as exemplified by the large number who changed their assessments of their marriages to being "unsure of the situation". The wives' increased independence which evolved during the separation appeared to influence their feelings about their marriages. Marriages were now seen by some wives as renegotiable with demands that consideration and recognition be given to their independence, acquired abilities, and new skills. What the marriage in the future holds for the independent wife must be reassessed upon final determination of the husband's status. For some wives the marriage contract will be terminated. Reunion for the wives who sought to develop and were proud of their independent role will be difficult. Hill (1949) in his study of military families under the stress of father separation found that wives who managed well during the separation period and who enjoyed their newfound freedom did not, in general, have good reunions.

In general, health problems requiring medical attention in the family were not a major area of concern. However, the data indicated frequent family contact with the physician for emotional support, especially for the wives. Similarly, the presentation of emotional problems through manifested physical symptomatology as a mode of coping with stress was a common finding by Hall and Simmons (1973) in their case study of two groups of PW/MIA wives.

The frequent use of tranquilizers to cope with the PW/MIA situation points out the importance of a careful assessment of our medical services to families. The high percentage who used tranquilizers was not matched by the percentage who contacted mental health professionals; in particular, psychiatrists. There appears to be a reluctance on the part of the physicians to make referrals to psychiatrists, even if indicated. Hall and Simmons (1973) stated that wives "shop around" in search of medical care from those physicians who will provide them with the medication needed to overcome the immediate stress; the underlying problems remain untreated.

The emotional adjustment of PW/MIA wives to the contradictory demands placed upon their lives was a major area of difficulty for the families. The range and frequency of emotional symptoms reported by the wives reflect the basic universal psychological reaction to extreme stress, such as "depression, disturbed sleep and traumatic dreams, anxiety and apprehension, headache, difficulty in concentrating, impairment of memory for names and recent events, and tension and irritability" (Hocking, 1970). The reactive depression may, in part, be accounted for by the indefiniteness and unpredictability of the situation. The future remained uncertain and any attempt to resolve the situation was fraught with feelings of ambivalence and guilt. This ambivalence may be partially accounted for by two general factors: first, the absence of complete information regarding the status of the men captured or lost in enemy territory; secondly, the military policy of retaining the men in the missing-in-action or prisoner-of-war status rather than risk a premature judgment of killed in action. Spolyar (1973) described the grief reaction of MIA wives and emphasized that this type of situation creates a certain amount of anxiety and unknown fear; the wives and children are suspended or "in limbo" until more definite facts are known.

Other classic adjustment behaviors related to depression and anxiety under stress were also evident in the PW/MIA wife population. Extensive weight fluctuations and increases in smoking and alcohol consumption for some of the wives reflected their efforts to deal with the situation. Both the unpredictable future, and the covert as well as overt pressure from the military to discourage a wife from verbalizing feelings and displaying family problems which might possibly lower the morale of her husband or distort his image as a professional soldier play a part in the wives' frustrations, depression, and lowered self-esteem. This reactive depression is well documented as an inherent part of the adjustment behavior of wives who have experienced chronic separations from their military husbands (Isay, 1968; Pearlman, 1970). Isay (1968) postulates that the depression may be related to a guilt response to their unacceptable rage at having been left alone or deserted and to their frustrated longing to be cared for adequately.

The difficulties experienced by the children of PW/MIA families were reported by wives to be relatively few in number. From the analyses completed to date it is impossible to know if a small number of children exhibited the majority of the symptoms and problems reported. If this were the case, it would further reduce the significance of child adjustment problems as a major issue. To state this as a conclusion, however, may be premature. When we consider the relatively small number of children seen in treatment and the additional 25 percent recommended for treatment by the interviewers, the issue takes on greater importance. The discrepancy may be accounted for by a host of factors. There was perhaps a reluctance on the part of the wives to report child behavior problems; the wives may vary considerably in their judgments as to what constitutes a problem child, and the wives may have been reluctant to seek help. The issue of child adjustment problems should not be ruled out. The French (M. Marcoin, personal communication, 1972) in their assessment of PW families of the Indo-China War found both behavior and academic difficulties among the children long after the repatriation of their fathers. The possible deleterious effects of father separation upon child adjustment were underscored by Gabower (1960) in her controlled study of behavior problems of children in Navy families. The influence of separation upon child behavior cannot, however, be dissociated from the other variables, such as the manner in which the mother and children interact and play out their respective roles. Hall and Simmons (1973) pointed out the subtle but effective ways in which some PW/MIA wives were able to undermine the children's social and emotional developments; for example, mothers sometimes used psychophysiologic symptoms to prevent their sons from dating seriously.

The wives' assessment of the military's Family Assistance Program pointed out the program's strengths and its weaknesses. In general, the program was judged to be very satisfactory in that it accomplished what it was basically designed to do; that is, to provide close liaison between the military and the family and administratively assist families with matters pertaining to allotments, medical benefits, transportation, etc. and to keep the families informed as to the serviceman's casualty status. The needs of the families and the demands placed upon the family assistance officers, however, exceeded the expectations envisioned by the military. These family assistance officers seldom had formal training in the assessment of emotional adjustment of adults and children and were not professional counselors. They were often unaware of the problems even where they existed; covertly presented symptoms were left undetected. Feelings of anger which may have been directed towards the assistance officer were often misinterpreted by the assistance officers as direct attacks upon their performances rather than as manifestations of the wives' frustrations in coping with the situation. When problems were apparent, some family assistance officers were often unaware of the appropriate services to which the family might be referred. While it should be noted that there were family assistance officers who performed all functions most ably, training programs, in addition to careful selection, appear needed to prepare these officers for the full range of responsibilities unique to the Family Assistance Program.

Hamilton I. McCubbin, Edna J. Hunter, Philip J. Metres, Jr.

The limitations of family assistance officers cannot alone account for the gap between the PW/MIA families in need of services and the comprehensive services available to them. Families have tended to avoid seeking help for reasons ranging from denial to abortive and unsatisfactory experiences with health professionals. Additionally, the total system of providing services to military families must also be called into question. Hunter and Plag (1973), on the basis of a study of a select group of Navy PW/MIA families, suggested the need for an aggressive program and proposed the development of a more flexible, coordinated, and professionally-based Family Assistance Program for PW/MIA families. While the value of an aggressive service delivery approach to PW/MIA families remains to be evaluated, the concept has face validity in light of the results of this study.

The discrepancy between the number of wives and children who received treatment and those recommended for treatment by the interviewers deserves further explanation. The responsibility to "carry on" despite all that has happened was a shared feeling among the wives. To admit that personal emotional problems existed would be an admission of defeat; such an admission is not a generally accepted response for military families. Denial, therefore, was a common defense mechanism employed by the wives. Those wives who recognized their difficulties tended to postpone and/or rationalize away the need to seek help. It was not uncommon to hear the wives relate how the problems and feelings they experienced would be resolved upon the husbands' return, or that their relationships with other men would be justified should he not return. These rationalizations were enough to sustain most wives throughout the long period even though at the sacrifice of their self-esteem and emotional health.

The wives' apprehensions about the future were focused upon the time of repatriation and family reunion. For some this period would be a time of dampened hopes and dreams; their husbands would not return. For others it would be the start of a new life or the continuation of a life already forged. For most wives it would be the initial test of the stability and future potential of their marriages. Reunion also represented a challenge. The wives were reluctant to give up control over the family, finances, and the children. A realistic appraisal of the wives' concerns about repatriation also suggested that reunion posed a threat to one or more of the gratifications that the separations provided: the opportunity to assume greater freedom, an independent income with the latitude to determine its use, and the avoidance of any confrontation with the manner in which the wives conducted themselves during their husbands' absences. These findings are consistent with those established by Isay (1968) in his study of the submariners' wives. The French social workers (M. Marcoin, personal communication, 1972) cited also these very problems as major areas of difficulty and contributing factors to family discord following the repatriation of the French PWs.

Women's independence may be viewed as part of the wives' broader concern for the husbands' adjustment to rapid social change which had taken place in the United States during the men's absence. Changes in social values, liberal attitudes towards sex, and rejection of authority are all part of the "now" society. The difficulty in coping with social change and its potential impact upon the returning PW has been well documented in public news media (Toffler, 1973), popular books (Toffler, 1969) as well as the research literature (Segal, 1973). The wives' desires for psychological counseling for their husbands at the time of repatriation were not only based upon the anticipated need for the returning husbands to cope with the residuals of their captivity experiences and their adjustments to family problems, but also to the adjustment to social change. Rapid change was also a factor in the wives' recommendations for personalized care for their husbands; job retraining, employment counseling, educational counseling, and career counseling were seen as necessary steps toward dealing with obsolescence brought about by changes in technology and advances in the military.

The variance in the social and psychological hardships experienced by the families would indicate that the PW/MIA situation does not produce a crisis in every case. Some families suffered only the obvious hardships of the absence of the husband/father from the home, while other families experienced a wide range of difficulties, not all directly related to the husband's departure. These difficulties, however, may have been intensified or complicated by his absence. Consider, for example, the situation of a wife who even prior to casualty was independent and managed the family affairs in an orderly and systematic manner. Frequent prior tours by the husband requiring his absence provided this wife the experience needed to cope with the present situation. Adjustment may have been eased by a sort of rehearsal or graduated immunization. Family life continued for this family with only a minimal break in the usual routines. In contrast, the totally dependent wife, inexperienced with the responsibilities brought about by the casualty, was confronted with a crisis, and to further complicate matters, she perhaps responded to the situation by withdrawing, thereby neglecting a host of other family responsibilities.

45

Hamilton I. McCubbin, Edna J. Hunter, Philip J. Metres, Jr.

The meaning of the PW/MIA situation varied from family to family. On one hand was the family where the husband, wife and children were in constant conflict, where the husband's drinking and physical abuse of his wife were added complications. For that family the father's absence was a relief in spite of guilt feelings about his loss. On the other hand, we witnessed a family which prior to casualty worked and functioned as a unit, sharing responsibilities as well as recreation. For that family the casualty came as a traumatic shock, and recovery was and continues to be extremely difficult.

Conclusions

The existing literature on prisoners of war has been criticized for its tendency to limit attention to the prisoner alone, to his experiences in captivity and to his subsequent adjustment. A consideration of the importance of the PW/MIA families' adaptation to the servicemen's absence has been slighted. For the most part, scientists seeking explanations for the adjustment behavior of returned prisoners have focused solely upon morbidity statistics and upon psychological, and physiological data on the returnee, and have ignored the history and influence on the family. The data presented here suggest the significance of family adjustment as a separate line of inquiry.

This paper examines data related to the adjustment of families of servicemen missing in action or prisoners of war. Several major findings appear to emerge from the interview data. Because research on family adjustment and the analysis completed to date can hardly be seen as beyond an exploratory phase, it would seem reasonable to conclude with a statement of these findings in a propositional form.

I. Basic patterns of adjusting to the absence of husband/father are compounded by the unprecedented length and indeterminate nature of the PW/MIA situation.

II. The probability of major adjustments in family roles and interaction is high for families in the PW/MIA situation.

III. PW/MIA wives are likely to pursue a wide range of individual and social activities which will enhance their self-esteem and contribute to the stabilization of the family.

IV. Over time, PW/MIA families are most likely to be confronted with complex legal issues surrounding their rights and privileges.

V. The probability of modification in the wives' assessments of their marriages is high for the PW/MIA families.

VI.   The emotional difficulties experienced by the wives and children strongly reflect the complexity and difficulty of coping with the PW/MIA situation.

VII. The discrepancy between the families' need for services and their limited contacts with such services is suggestive of the need for a more effective approach to extending services to PW/MIA families.

VIII. The family's adjustment over the years and their apprehensions about repatriation must be considered important factors in the formula for the successful reunion and readjustment of each returned prisoner of war.

Collectively the eight propositions, along with the corollary implications suggested in the body of the analysis, provide the beginning of an empirical portrait of PW/MIA families under stress.

There is a need for more information about other aspects of PW/MIA family adjustment and the coping processes. There is also a need for comparative analyses which will provide answers to many of the following questions. Are there discernable family patterns of adjustment unique to each of the Armed Services: Army, Navy, and Marines? What constitutes successful adjustment among PW/MIA families? What are the differences between PW and MIA families in how they adapted to the situation? Does receiving letters from a PW have any bearing upon family adjustment? Does the proximity of the family to a military installation make a difference in the services the family received? The intracacies of PW/MIA family adjustment have been slighted in the field of behavioral research. However, as these and other related questions are answered more completely, a general theory of family adjustment to stressful situations will be advanced.

4

The Legal Plight of the PW/MIA Family[1]

J. ROBERT NELSON

Introduction

"The cauldron of war has left an aftermath of problems which can only be solved by the application of practical common sense."[2]

Implicit in the foregoing quotation, penned by a Pennsylvania judge ruling on the taxability of accumulated military pay of a deceased serviceman after World War II, is a recognition of the peculiar legal issues that can arise in a wartime context. In response to certain of those legal problems encountered by the fighting man, the federal government has enacted legislation which shields the soldier against inability to defend adequately a suit because of his military commitments,[3] provides for status determinations of those missing or within enemy control,[4] and designates the procedure for payment of accumulated military earnings upon determination of a

1. *This article embodies the substance of remarks delivered on September 28, 1973 to a group of social workers responsible for assisting the families of former Vietnam prisoners of war and missing in action. The intent of that address and of this article is to identify those stress-creating legal problems that either have been encountered or can reasonably be anticipated which could impede satisfactory family adjustment. Hence, the following remarks should not be viewed as a thorough exposition or analysis of the applicable law but merely as a touchstone for effective family assistance. Further, the opinions expressed are the author's alone and not an official statement of the Judge Advocate General of the Navy.*

2. *Stones Estate, 58 Pa. D. & C. 154, 157 (1946)*

3. *Soldiers and Sailors Civil Relief Act, 50 App. U.S.C. Sections 510-590 (1970)*

4. *Federal Missing Persons Act, 37 U.S.C. Sections 551-557 (Supp. 1973)*

serviceman's death.[5]   Although these enactments were intended to alleviate stresses which potentially could detract from the fighting man's efficiency,[6] they have, directly or indirectly, been the source of a substantial number of problems.[7] These difficulties have been accentuated during the recent Vietnam conflict for approximately 2000 military personnel designated prisoners of war (PW) or missing in action (MIA) and their respective families.[8]   The so-called "common sense approach" has often been sacrificed to rigid application of statutory controls, thereby imposing additional stresses on families overwrought with other emotional concerns.   The following article will cursorily examine certain legal problems commonly encountered by families of prisoners of war/missing in action and thereafter will focus on legal difficulties attributable to the aforementioned federal statutory schemes.

Commonly Encountered Legal Problems

It is only reasonable that the prolonged absence of the head of a household will give rise to emotional and psychological displacements. Accompanying such manifestations are the legal problems engendered when a wife is called upon to coordinate the daily family business in her spouse's absence.   Potential legal problems arise on a frequent and recurring basis in even the most mundane daily routines, as the wife undertakes actions affecting the family welfare.   A series of interviews, conducted by the staff of the Center for Prisoner of War Studies in the fall of 1972, revealed a significant number of stress-creating legal problems that had been encountered or were anticipated by the families.   The problems that were voiced covered the entire legal spectrum.   For example, correspondence from 42 wives of

5. ·*10 U.S.C. Section 2771 (1970)*

6. *See Wissner v. Wissner, 338 U.S. 655, 660 (1950)*

7. *This anomalous result is best illustrated by reference to the legislative history of 10 U.S.C. Section 2771 which reflects: "Also, under existing law, the 'father desertion' and 'foster parent' cases present tremendous problems. As to the first class, objection often is raised to payment . . . to a father who deserted his wife and family while the children were small. As to the second class, a natural parent usually receives the balance due the decedent to the exclusion of a foster parent who may have reared the serviceman from infancy to manhood." H. R. Rep. No. 833, 84th Cong., 1st Sess. (1955)*

The amended enactment which resulted from these Congressional deliberations, attempted to correct the aforementioned inequities. In so doing, however, the new statute created other equally grievous injustices. See accompanying notes 46-51 infra.

8. *Excluding 566 returned Vietnam PWs, the Defense Department listed 1363 servicemen as still missing in action at the termination of hostilities.*

missing military personnel received at the Service Casualty branch of one of the military departments, provides a general summary of the broad types of legal problems encountered by wives during their husbands' absences. Table 1 reflects the nature of the problem and the frequency of its mention.

TABLE 1. *Legal Problems Encountered by Wives During Husband Absence*
(N = 42)

General Area of Legal Concern	Specific Problem	Frequency of Response
Purchase, Sale & Disposition of Property	Questions regarding power of attorney	13
	Difficulty purchasing or refinancing home	3
	Difficulty selling automobile	1
	Establishing conservatorship	4
Domestic Problems	Divorce procedures in husband's absence	6
	Propriety of remarriage without divorce	2
	Impact of Soldiers and Sailors Civil Relief Act on divorce action	5
	Impact of divorce on military allotment	2
	Legal status or remarriage should serviceman return	1
	Adoption attempts in husband's absence	1
Status Determinations and Declarations of Death	Military procedures for declarations of death	14
	State court procedures for declarations of death	1
	Impact of state determinations on military declarations of death	4

General Area of Legal Concern	Specific Problem	Frequency of Response
Availability of Federal Benefits	Disposition of serviceman's pay	3
	Impact of state declaration of death on availability of military dependent's benefits	1
	Impact of divorce on allotment	2
	Increasing or decreasing allotment	42
	Military movement of household goods	42
	Procurement of military identification cards	42
	Availability of VA benefits	3
Estate Administration	Intestate procedures	1
	Impact of divorce on inheritance	4
	Disposition of husband's accumulated earnings	3
	Federal and state inheritance tax abatement	2

A few examples will illustrate the scope and nature of the most frequently encountered difficulties.[9] The sale of homes, automobiles, stocks and other belongings in the absence of PWs and MIAs was often complicated by the fact that the property was jointly owned. To facilitate such transactions, many servicemen executed powers of attorney prior to their departure for the combat zone. Unfortunately, the prolonged period of absence generally meant that the once valid

9. *In the context of this article, the term "legal problems" is broadly defined to encompass those difficulties perceived by the families as posing legal issues. Admittedly, such a definition would circumscribe questions which are more administrative than legal (identification card procurement, movement of household goods); nevertheless, such perceived problems would be included within the definition.*

power had expired before it could be used to affect the disposition of property.

Even in those cases in which the power of attorney, by its terms, was still effective, transactions which it supposedly accommodated might nonetheless be invalid. Unless a power is "coupled with an interest" (e.g. power in regard to jointly owned property), it automatically terminates on the death of the grantor. Where death is established by irrefutable evidence, it is not difficult to determine when a power becomes ineffective under this rule. In numerous instances during the Vietnam conflict, however, there has been no such positive evidence of death. Rather, many servicemen are merely listed as missing in action while their true status remains unresolved. Thus, the mere possibility of a serviceman's death has also placed a damper on even those sales transactions facilitated by an apparently valid power of attorney, simply because the power might have been invalidated by a prior death.[10]

Many wives found that numerous problems were created by the uncertainty of their spouse's true status. Had they been assured of the husband's demise, they could have begun the painful task of starting anew. With status in doubt, however, such a new beginning was impossible. Naturally, without a declaration of death, a wife could not receive life insurance proceeds or accumulated but unpaid military earnings so necessary to afford her some degree of financial stability. She would likewise be unable to probate her husband's estate or to take sole ownership of jointly held property and thus facilitate sales or other dispositions thereof. Finally, any remarriage without a declaration of death or a divorce would be at the possible risk of a bigamy conviction.[11] Of course, the social stigma of divorce from a PW coupled with the potential loss of military

---

10. *To avoid wholesale emasculation of otherwise valid powers of attorney of those listed as missing in action, California has adopted legislation which affirms acts performed under a power if done in good faith and without actual knowledge of death. CAL. CIV CODE Sec. 2356 (West Supp. 1973). In 1972 the legislature provided that the grantee of an apparently valid power of attorney would not be deemed to have actual knowledge of death until receipt of a finding of death from the Service Secretary. Id at Sec. 2356 (b).*

11. *"Like such a mistake it will not excuse if not based upon reasonable grounds, but a bona-fide and well-grounded belief that the other spouse is dead should entitle the defendant to an acquittal in a bigamy case unless the language of the statute precludes this defense."* R. M. Perkins, *CRIMINAL LAW 837 (1957) and cases cited therein.*

privileges and the possible forfeiture of benefits under a husband's estate[12] made this a highly undesirable alternative.

To resolve this quandary, some wives attempted to pressure the Service Secretaries to issue presumptive findings of death under the Missing Persons Act, or alternatively, contemplated actions in state courts which could ultimately result in a judicial declaration of death.[13] Neither of these alternatives proved totally satisfactory. First, such actions exposed deep-rooted differences between family members, often turning one against the other. Thus, while wives, on the one hand, might have actively sought a death determination, parents strongly resisted this alternative, viewing such a course as abandonment of their son.

Beyond the emotional divisions, however, a wife faced monumental logistical difficulties in securing either a judicial or an administrative declaration of death. A judicial determination was normally based on the presumption of death that arose only after the absence of the husband for seven years. While an action could be brought prior to the expiration of seven years, its success could only be predicated on a strong showing of evidence by the wife pointing to death at an

12. *Divorce prior to a serviceman's death would foreclose the wife from inheriting as an intestate successor. See, e.g., CAL. PROB. CODE Sec. 221 (West 1956). Further a divorce in most jurisdictions would likewise nullify an existing will. See Rogers v. Rogers, 152 So. 2d 183 (Fla. App. 1963); CAL. PROB. CODE Sec. 70 (West 1956). But a divorce which antedates a military as opposed to civil determination of death would not necessarily preclude the wife's inheritance under state laws. Since a presumptive finding of death issued by the Service Secretary establishes the fact of death for service-related purposes alone and "does not mean that death occurred on that or any other certain day," 32 C.F.R. Sec. 718 (1954), a state court could consider the evidence and reach an independent determination regarding the date of death. See Haynes v. Metropolitan Life Ins. Co., 262 Md. 255, 277 A. 2d 251 (1971); In re Thornburg's Estate, 186 Ore. 570, 208 P.2d 349 (1949); Lukens v. Camden Trust Co., 62 A. 2d 886 (N.J. 1948). Thus, if the state court establishes the date of death at some time antecedent to the divorce, the wife would retain her normal rights of inheritance.*

13. *Evidence of determinations of death by a Service Secretary constitute prima facie evidence of the fact of death in the following states: Alabama, California, Colorado, Connecticut, Delaware, Florida, Georgia, Hawaii, Indiana, Iowa, Maine, Maryland, Michigan, Minnesota, Mississippi, Nevada, New Hampshire, New Jersey, New York, North Carolina, North Dakota, Oklahoma, Oregon, Pennsylvania, Rhode Island, South Carolina, Tennessee, Vermont, Washington, West Virginia, and Wyoming. Unless overborne by other evidence, this document will sustain a state court determination of death. See Stone's Estate, supra, note 2 at 157; Lukens v. Camden Trust Co., supra, note 13; In re Jacobson's Estate, 143 N.Y.S. 2d 432 (1955). On the other hand there is no evidence that a state court determination of death will necessarily compel or even affect a military finding of death.*

earlier time.[14] In most instances such compelling information was unavailable since the truth was shrouded in uncertainty. A wife's hesitancy in pursuing such recourse is understandable in view of the costs involved, the evidentiary burden imposed, and the emotional impact of forcing a wife to prove her husband's death affirmatively. Further, while such an approach could facilitate remarriage, distribution of the husband's estate and insurance settlement, it would have no impact whatsoever on the military's obligation to release the serviceman's accrued pay and allowances to the designated beneficiary.[15] This fund, which often represented the single most important asset in a serviceman's estate, was excluded from state testamentary control by a federal statute[16] permitting disposition of the sum only after the Service Secretary concerned had entered either a determination of death or a presumptive finding of death. State court declarations of death in no way compelled a like Secretarial finding. Thus, many wives were forced to await a Secretarial determination to realize the full benefits of their husband's estate.

Even a Secretarial determination did not insure all wives the full benefit of their husbands' accumulated pay. That fund was distributed to a beneficiary designated by the serviceman. In a number of cases the beneficiary was someone other than the wife.

14. The burden of establishing death at some time prior to the lapse of seven years falls on the petitioning party and can be satisfied by a showing of "specific peril" encountered by the absent individual, Davie v. Briggs, 97 U.S. 628, 634 (1878); Herold v. Washington Nat. Ins. Co., 128 Pa. Super. 563, 566 (1937); In re Wylie's Estate 134 Misc. 715, 236 N.Y.S. 370 (1929), or through other circumstantial evidence. In re Woods Estate, 62 A.2d 883 (1949); Cox v. Ellsworth, 18 Neb. 664, 26 N.W. 460 (1886). The concept was explained in GREENLEAF, EVIDENCE, Vol. 1, pt. 1, Chap. IV, Sec. 41, at 46-48 (Redfieldt's Ed.):

Thus, where the issue is upon the life or death of a person, once shown to have been living, the burden of proof lies upon the party who asserts the death. But after the lapse of seven years, without intelligence concerning the person, the presumption of life ceases, and the burden of proof is devolved on the other party . . . upon an issue of life or death of a party, as we have seen in the like case of the presumed payment of a debt, the jury may find the fact of death from the lapse of a shorter period than seven years, if other circumstances concur . . . But the presumption of the common law, independent of the finding of the jury, does not attach to the mere lapse of time short of seven years . . .

See generally Continental Life Ins. Co. v. Searing, 240 F. 653 (3d Cir. 1917); Connor v. N.Y. Life Ins. Co., 179 App. Div. 596, 166 N.Y.S. 985 (1917). Death can be established prior to the expiration of the seven-year period on a "fair preponderance of clear and convincing evidence, direct and circumstantial" Herold v. Washington Nat. Ins. Co., supra at 566.

15. See note 14 supra.

16. See note 30 infra and accompanying text.

Whether this result was intended by the serviceman or was merely an oversight in failing to change the beneficiary at the time of marriage, the result was unacceptable for the wife who had actively supported her husband only to find that she was deprived of the most valuable asset in his estate. This inequity was compounded when wives either continued to permit deposits of earnings in a federal savings program or failed to petition the Secretary's designee for release of funds under the erroneous assumption that they would be the ultimate beneficiary of the account.[17] Instead, a parent or friend reaped a windfall, while the wife, often burdened with raising a deceased serviceman's children, was left nothing.

While the foregoing examples represent but a sampling of the legal issues confronting the families of prisoners of war and missing in action, they are a fairly accurate indicator of the nature and scope of problems that were encountered by PW/MIA families during the husband's absence or upon Secretarial determination of his death.

Federal Statutory Solutions

The problems experienced by the families of Vietnam PW/MIAs were by no means novel; similar legal issues were encountered during World War II and the Korean conflict.[18] However, the unprecedented duration of absence resulting from the protracted Vietnam conflict undoubtedly accentuated the difficulties. In response to similar problems in earlier wars, the federal government enacted a panoply of legislation to protect the fighting man. These statutes include the Soldiers and Sailors Civil Relief Act,[19] the Federal Missing Person's Act,[20] and a provision governing the payment of a serviceman's accumulated earnings and allowances upon his death.[21]

The Soldiers and Sailors Civil Relief Act was enacted to foster the spirit of the fighting man by providing a shield against civil liabilities during a serviceman's period of active service. Before entering a default judgment, the Act requires a court to secure from the plaintiff an affidavit reflecting that the defendant is not in the

17. *See note 48 infra.*

18. *See TIME, Sept. 14, 1953, at 26.*

19. *See note 3 supra.*

20. *See note 4 supra.*

21. *See note 5 supra.*

military service.[22]   Where such an affidavit is not filed, the judge is also given discretionary authority[23] to stay any action unless it appears that the serviceman's defense will not be materially prejudiced by his absence.[24]   Such a default judgment can be reopened by the serviceman on his release from active duty if it appears that he has a "meritorious or legal defense" to the action.[25] When a default judgment is entered, the court can require the plaintiff to post a bond to indemnify the defendant should the judgment later be set aside.[26]

Recognizing that a sizeable number of servicemen are captured, confined, or disappear in enemy territory during an armed conflict, the federal government enacted the Missing Persons Act which defines missing status and permits the government to continue pay and allowances to the serviceman while he continues to be listed as missing.[27]   The statute likewise contains provisions mandating periodic reevaluation of status and upon which, where warranted, presumptive findings of death are based.   Since the avowed purpose of this presumptive finding is merely to set a point at which the serviceman's military record will be closed and his account settled,[28] the official date of death will rarely, if ever, conform to the actual date of death.

When pay records have been closed as a result of a military finding of death, the accumulated earnings must be disbursed to an appropriate party.   In 1956, a new statute was enacted which for the first time permitted a serviceman to designate personally the primary beneficiary of accumulated but unpaid earnings.   This procedure, intended by Congress to permit a testamentary disposition of

22. *50 App. U.S.C. Sec. 520 (1) (1970)*

23. *Id.*

24. *50 App. U.S.C. Sec. 521 (1970)*

25. *50 App. U.S.C. Sec. 520 (1970)*

26. *Id.*

27. *Missing Persons Act, 37 U.S.C. Sections 552-53 (1970)*

28. *See, e.g., In re Thornburg's Estate, supra note 13, at 352.*

property,[29] replaced an earlier provision which required the government to pay the accumulated earnings first to a qualified representative of the deceased's estate for distribution under a will or under state laws of intestacy.[30]

The Shortcomings of Federal Enactments

Subjected to the rigorous test of lengthy periods of confinement during the recent Vietnam struggle, these federal provisions, intended to protect the civil affairs of the fighting man during his absence and to facilitate a more normal life for his dependents in his absence, have revealed several potentially serious flaws which need to be relieved.

Soldiers and Sailors Civil Relief Act. Designated primarily to alleviate the burden of defending a law suit where the ability to defend is materially affected by one's military status, the Soldiers and Sailors Civil Relief Act has created or poses problems of consequence for the wives and families of Vietnam PWs and MIAs. In an attempt to protect the status quo, the enactment has served to shackle the wife's discretion to make certain highly personal domestic decisions as well as to enter into transactions deemed necessary to maintain some degree of normalcy and to enhance financial stability. Thus, both marital dissolution and property disposition have been, or potentially could be, affected by provisions permitting judicial proceedings to be stayed or subsequently challenged under the Act.

Several wives have dissolved their matrimonial bonds during their husband's prolonged absences. During World War II the Act was advanced as a bar to divorces in several cases in which the husband's ability to defend himself was materially affected by his absence.[31] While the decision to stay a divorce action for this reason rests in the judge's discretion, certain factors would seemingly favor the grant of a stay in the case of prisoners of war or missing in action. Not only is it clear that the ability of these individuals to defend a suit is materially affected by their status, but the plight of the

29. *H.R. Rep. No. 833, 84th Cong., 1st Sess. (1955)*:

The proposed legislation will permit the soldier himself to designate a beneficiary for his final pay. The measure in substance, by permitting a designated beneficiary, provides for a testamentary disposition by the serviceman of that part of his estate representing his final pay. See Goldberg, Is Armed Services Retired Pay Really Community Property? 48 CAL BAR J. 12, 16-17 (1973)

30. *60 Stat. 30 (1946), as amended 10 U.S.C., Sec. 2771 (1956)*

31. *See Roark v. Roark, 201 S.W. 2d 862 (1947)*

misfortunate PW/MIAs is bound to elicit a sympathetic ear from the judge.

Strict application of the Act in this context reflects a Congressional judgment that a serviceman's rights should override the wishes of his spouse. As such, it disregards a determination by the wife that the relationship is irrevocably shattered and denies her the opportunity to begin life anew. That such an approach concentrates on the serviceman's rights rather than on the wife's desires or on the continued viability of the marriage is evident from the fact that ex parte divorces are recognized by virtually all jurisdictions despite the non-appearance of one spouse.[32] This latter rule manifestly emphasizes the viability of the marriage over requirements of personal appearance. Hence, it is clear that Congress has carved out an exception to the general rule permitting ex parte divorces in those cases where non-appearance stems from military service and materially impedes one's defense of an action. In the cases of wives of long-absent PW/MIAs, such an outcome reflects a blatant disregard for the feelings of the wife and for the prerequisites of a successful matrimonial relationship.

Next, the Act poses several problems in the area of alienability of property which severely restrict the wife's legal capacity to freely dispose of personal and real property, armed even with a power of attorney or after appointment as conservator of a missing serviceman's estate. To illustrate this shortcoming, the case of *Bristow v. Pagano*,[33] recognized the absent husband's right to challenge subsequently the sale of property received by his wife in a divorce proceeding in noncompliance with the statute but nonetheless found that the buyer received marketable title. Simplified to its basics, this holding means that in all cases in which a wife's claim or authority to sell property arises from a judicial action in which the missing serviceman is a party or is directly affected, the transaction can potentially be challenged upon the serviceman's return.[34] This rule would extend to quiet title actions, property settlements accompanying divorce, and even, arguably, to sales by court appointed conservators. Such a result is seemingly at odds with federal and state legislation designed to facilitate such transactions. Congress, in the past year, enacted legislation which extended

---

32. *See Williams v. North Carolina*, 317 U.S. 287 (1942); *Williams v. North Carolina*, 325 U.S. 226 (1944); *Crouch v. Crouch*, 28 Cal. 2d 243, 169 P2d 897 (1946)

33. 238 Iowa 1171, 15 N.W. 2d 423 (1947)

34. *See* note 26 *supra.*

expired powers of attorney until the serviceman's return[35] and several states have passed statutes which greatly facilitated procedures for appointments of conservators of a PW/MIA's estate.[36] The potential impact of the Act could, for the most practical purposes, render this legislation nugatory and thereby seriously impede the wife's attempts to dispose of property.

Missing Persons Act. With the significant amount of national attention that was focused on military accounting for servicemen still missing behind enemy lines in the aftermath of the Korean War,[37] a similar concern for status resolutions among a small but vocal segment of the civilian sector during the Vietnam hostilities was not altogether surprising. In the emotion-charged atmosphere surrounding status determinations, where dwindling hopes fanned by persistent though generally unfounded rumors, the Service Secretaries were, on occasion, criticized for their handling of the accounting operation.[38] These criticisms eventually culminated in a constitutional attack against the Federal Missing Persons Act,[39] the statutory authority for Secretarial determinations of status.

Basically, the argument of the petitioners in *McDonald v. McLucas* reduced itself to two related contentions, each directed at the alleged unconstitutionality of the statute. First, the petitioners argued that the statute as drafted provided inadequate guidelines for functionaries applying the enactment regarding procedures to be followed, evidence to be considered, and standards of proof to be applied under the statute.[40] The gravamen of this argument,

---

35. *Public L. No. 92-540 (Oct. 24, 1972)*

36. *CAL. PROB. CODE Sec. 1751 et. seq. (West 1973 Supp.); Sec. 747.02 Fla. Statutes.*

37. *The concern for American servicemen allegedly held captive in Mongolia after the termination of the Korean hostilities eventually resulted in a federal district court action filed by 33 relatives of missing servicemen declared KIA who sought $33,000,000 from the government. The case was dismissed for lack of jurisdiction. See THE NEW YORK TIMES, Aug. 4, 1956, at 12.*

38. *Address by Brigadier General Robert Kingston, USA, in Washington, D.C., July 27, 1973.*

39. *McDonald v. McLucas, 73 Civ. 3190 (S.D.N.Y. July 20, 1973)*

40. *37 U.S.C., Section 555 (1970) reads as follows:*

(a) When a member of a uniformed service entitled to pay and allowances under section 552 of this title has been in a missing status, and the official report of his death or of the circumstances of his absence has not been received by the Secretary concerned, he shall, before the end of a 12-month period in that status, have the case fully reviewed. After that review and the end of the 12-month period in a missing status, or after review which shall be made when warranted by information received or other circumstances, the Secretary concerned, or his designee, may —

(1) if the member can reasonably be presumed to be living, direct a continuance of his missing status; or

(2) make a finding of death.

which suggested that the statute was void-for-vagueness, was that such broadly drafted language could permit an arbitrary exercise of discretion by the Secretary concerned. Next, the petitioners suggested that the foregoing potential for abuse was increased by the guarded nature of the proceedings which, in the past, had denied the families directly affected an opportunity to challenge the information considered, examine witnesses, or participate in a hearing. This, it was contended, constituted a denial of constitutionally mandated rights of due process. The federal court affirmed this latter argument and, in its decree, ordered the Service Secretaries to thereafter insure certain minimal hearing requirements.[41] In response to the decision in this case, the services developed and implemented detailed administrative guidelines which provided for the offer of rights stipulated in the final decree, including that of a hearing as a prerequisite to any status change.[42]

While the debate regarding the alleged constitutional shortcomings of the Missing Persons Act awaits final resolution in some higher tribunal, certain inequities arising from its application, in conjunction with testamentary dispositions, can presently be ascertained.

To illustrate, the date of death, as determined by a Service Secretary, controls the availability of certain federally administered benefits. This date of death for military purposes is established either by a determination of death, in which case the date is fixed by actual demise, or by a presumptive finding, which merely establishes a presumptive date of death for administrative convenience and probably does not comport with the actual circumstances which are unknown.[43] The availability of non-retroactive federal benefits dates from the time of enactment. Thus, if one casualty results in a determination of death and another, at some later date, eventuates only in a presumptive finding of death due to a dearth of evidence regarding the circumstances of disappearance, it is entirely conceivable that the individuals who may have actually died on the same day might not share the same benefits. Thus, the benefits available under

---

41. McDonald v. McLucas, 73 Civ. 3190 (S.D.N.Y. Feb. 14, 1974)

42. The Navy directive implementing McDonald v. McLucas, 73 Civ. 3190 (S.D.N.Y. Feb. 14, 1974), SECNAVINST 230922, dated 26 March 1974, provides for the first time, significant administrative clarification of specific procedures for status determinations under the Federal Missing Persons Act.

43. ?Y U.S.C., Section 555 (1970); see C.F.R., Sec. 718(a) (1954):
"A finding of presumptive death concerning an officer or enlisted man of the Navy means simply that as of the date thereof he is for the purposes of Naval administration no longer alive. It does not mean that death occurred on that or any other certain date."

Uniformed Services Group Life Insurance policies were recently increased from $10,000 to $15,000.[44] The applicable limits were initially controlled by the date of death determined by the Services. The inequity outlined above finally resulted in extension of the additional coverage to all individuals irrespective of the mode of death determination.[45] Ideally, the availability of benefits established specifically for prisoners of war and missing in action should not turn on the distinction between a determination of death and a presumptive finding of death.[46]

Distribution of Unpaid Pay and Allowances: U.S.C. Sec. 2771. The enactment of 10 U.S.C., Sec. 2771 in 1956 marked the first time that a serviceman could personally designate the beneficiary of his unpaid pay and allowances. In passing a statute specifically intended by Congress to permit testamentary disposition and thereby to preempt inconsistent state probate or intestacy laws, legislators sought to enhance military morale by assuring servicemen that their military earnings would be passed on to the object of their beneficence. In several circumstances during the Vietnam conflict, however, the strict application of this statute has operated to deprive a wife of a substantial fund and, at the same time, has conferred a windfall on another individual.

Several cases will suffice to illustrate the potential inequities that have arisen through application of 10 U.S.C., Sec. 2771. In one instance, a serviceman married shortly prior to deployment for Vietnam. At that time, his mother was designated as beneficiary. In the increased pace of operations attendant to the forthcoming deployment, the man failed to change the beneficiary. Consequently, when a presumptive finding of death was issued by the Service Secretary, the mother rather than the wife reaped the benefits of the serviceman's military service. While it is most difficult to fathom the true intent of the deceased, it is at least arguable that such a

44. *38 U.S.C. Section 767(a) (1973) Supp.*

45. *28 C.F.R. 9.5(d) (Nov. 22, 1972)*

46. *A further problem emanating from the Missing Persons Act involves the impact of the presumptive finding of death on rights of succession. Thus, In re Thornburg's Estate, supra note 13, under a will challenged the inheritance rights of a serviceman found by the Service Secretary to have died subsequent to the death of the individual whose will was in probate. The legatees successfully established that although the presumptive date of death would permit the serviceman to inherit, his actual date of death, established in the court action, caused the gift to lapse. The reverse of this situation can likewise pose problems as devices and legatees under a serviceman's will must determine the testator's date of death for purposes of determining possible lapse of bequests.*

result would not comport with his wishes. Similarly, in certain cases, a friend or relative was designated beneficiary, probably as an expression of gratitude and affection and under the misapprehension that the sum of unpaid pay and allowances would represent but a minor token. In most cases, however, it constituted the major portion of one's estate.

These inequities were moderated by provisions which permitted the wives to petition the Service Secretary for release of accumulated pay and earnings deposited in a Uniformed Services Savings Deposit Plan account drawing 10 percent interest.[47] This resolution disregards the fact that such a distribution was discretionary and was cautiously approached to conserve the serviceman's assets. Further, in withdrawing the funds, a wife would necessarily forego the highly lucrative interest accruing on the deposited funds.

There is something morally offensive about a procedure which permits a husband to shirk his legal obligation of spousal support[48] even where that result is intended. Where that outcome is merely from inadvertent oversight, however, it is even more unacceptable. Various state statutes have been enacted to assure the wife a fund for her support and to prevent even intentional exclusion from a deceased husband's bounty.[49] Under one such provision, the wife would seemingly have an absolute claim to one-half of the accumulated earnings as her share of community property regardless of the husband's designation of beneficiary. However, since the Supreme Court has ruled that contrary state law of community property is preempted in the area of Servicemen's Group Life Insurance beneficiaries,[50] it is highly probable that the same result would apply to preclude claims in the realm of accumulated earnings as well.

Conclusion

Like most products, the propriety and effectiveness of laws, statutes and regulations can only be properly tested in the crucible of application and practice. Flaws and uncertainties which might originally be concealed from even the most perceptive eye are often revealed in times of substantial stress. The recent Vietnam conflict

---

47. *Interview with Capt. Frank Rush, Head, Office of Prisoner of War Affairs, Bureau of Naval Personnel, on October 15, 1973.*

48. *Schlaefer v. Schlaefer, 71 App. D.C. 350, 112 F. 2d 117 (1940); In re Guardianship of Bagnall, 238 Ia. 905, 29 N.W. 2d 597 (1947)*

49. *See, e.g.,CAL CIV. CODE Sec. 5110 (West 1970)*

50. *Wissner v. Wissner, 338 U.S. 655 (1950)*

has produced just such a milieu in which to observe various federal enactments designed to prevent or solve legal difficulties commonly encountered by American servicemen in time of war. The duration of the most recent struggle, coupled with the prolonged absence of servicemen held by enemy nations, exposed serious flaws in the Soldiers and Sailors Civil Relief Act, and a provision governing payment of a serviceman's accumulated but unpaid military earnings. From the foregoing discussion, it is apparent that these statutory schemes should undergo careful analysis, reevaluation, and regulatory clarification or amendment that has already occurred in the context of the Federal Missing Persons Act as a result of recently successful constitutional challenge of that enactment.[51] Only if these lessons of the Vietnam struggle are carefully studied and the problems resolved, can the same stress-creating difficulties be avoided in a future conflict.

51. *See note 41 supra.*

5

Children in Limbo

HAMILTON I. MCCUBBIN
EDNA J. HUNTER
PHILIP J. METRES, JR

Introduction

The absence of father caused by his assignment to military combat in a foreign country, presents some difficult problems for any child. When a father is missing in action (MIA) or a prisoner of war (PW) there are the additional burdens for the child, and mothers must not only cope with their own problems and feelings but also with those of their children during the prolonged and indeterminable period of the father's absence.

There is a paucity of research attempting to answer questions surrounding a child's adjustment to and his perceptions of a father missing in action or a prisoner of war. Although the adjustment of children of PW/MIA families was emphasized and described by McCubbin, Hunter, and Metres (1973) in their report of a world-wide study of PW/MIA families of the Vietnam Conflict, their data were based primarily on the mother's perceptions of the children's problems, needs and feelings. The number of children interviewed personally for that study was small however, and precluded meaningful conclusions. In a recent report by Hall and Simmons (1973) an attempt was made to describe aspects of the child's role in the emotional adjustment of PW/MIA mothers. Here again no direct assessment of the children was made nor was there any attempt to explore fully the nature of the children's behavior. It should be noted that lack of knowledge about the children's reactions to father absence may be attributable in part to the mother's desire to protect her children from the trauma of dealing with father's absence and also to the disquieting nature of the subject which brings with it an awareness of the children's vulnerability. Additionally, the child's emotional reaction to father's absence, the realization that a child desires to maintain high hopes for father's return, as well as the realistic limitations of therapeutic intervention in such situations often inhibit the involvement of mental health professionals. The importance of understanding children in this unique situation, however, cannot be ignored.

Problem

For the purpose of this presentation, the child is seen as involved in a cumulative family crisis. The child plays his part in the family's effort to resolve the crisis and to maintain family stability. The child, in turn, is affected by the community's attitudes towards the war and the family. His behavior is also influenced by a number of other factors — by his own personality, by his relationship with peers and their expectations, by mother's attitude and behavior, by the roles he plays in the family, as well as by the family's solidarity and self-sufficiency. Ordinarily, while in a crisis situation such as a death in the family, members may draw on cultural definitions of appropriate behavior which can lead to a personal resolution of the crisis. However, this is not so for the family having a father as a prisoner of war or missing in action.

The military's view of how the family should behave has been made clear — it is in the best interest of the father that the family do all that is necessary to maintain stability, unity and solidarity. But, for the family which has to face not only the day to day crises, but also make necessary legal, personal, emotional and social adjustments without a father, what should be done to preserve the family's future is less clear. Information to assist families has been primarily administrative in nature and of minimal value as specific guidelines for coping with total family adjustment. Thus, the PW/MIA family and, in particular, its children, is faced with an unstructured situation and must discover the techniques for handling this position through the process of trial and error.

The basic question as to how children should react to a situation in which father's fate is unknown is, at best, controversial. Grieving is the most common concept used when describing children's reactions to father separation. However, the published reports by McCubbin et al. (1973) and Hall and Simmons (1973) allude to child adjustment but do not reference the grief reaction. The literature is neither clear nor uniformly consistent on the subject. Bowlby (1960) mentioned the existence of the psychological processes of mourning even in young children experiencing separation. On the other hand, Freud (1943) and Deutsch (1937) in their studies of children separated from fathers during World War II emphasized that children for their own protection are not likely to grieve as adults do. A search for the usual symptomatology of grief, such as anger, somatic distress and guilt, is not likely to produce meaningful information. The most viable proposition which seems applicable to PW/MIA children is offered by Hilgard, Newman and Fisk (1960) who pointed out that children who lost their father before nine years of age displayed extreme sensitivity to their mother's reaction to the loss, rather than displaying a personal grief.

Purpose

The present paper is based on a study initiated by a concern with children's reactions to the absence and in some cases, the return of a father missing in action or a prisoner of war. The study was conducted by the staff of the Family Studies Branch of the Center for Prisoner of War Studies in an attempt to understand these reactions and to determine whether mental health intervention might be beneficial in such situations.

Procedure

Data were obtained from group discussions with children of servicemen who were listed as missing in action, or prisoners of war, or of recently returned prisoners (RPW) of the Southeast Asian conflict. The sample included children of families in attendance at three of the five week-long religious retreats sponsored by a nonprofit organization.[1] Of a possible 75 families[2] with children who were in attendance, 65 mothers were willing to have their children participate. A total of 124 children were involved in the group discussions; eight of those children were from families where the father had returned (RPW).

For each retreat the children were separated into four age groups: 3-6 years, 7-9 years, 10-13 years, and over 14. The groups engaged in discussion periods of up to one hour with the exception of the 14 and over group, which was scheduled for 3 hours of discussion.

1. *High Flight Foundation sponsored an all-expense paid religious retreat program for families of returned prisoners of war, missing in action, and listed prisoners of war. The retreats were held in Estes Park and Granby, Colorado during the period of 16 June through 27 July 1973. The Foundation is under the leadership of astronaut Jim Irwin and Dr. Bill Rittenhouse.*

2. *All branches of the Armed Services were represented: 10 percent were Marine Corps families, 20 percent were Army families; 30 percent were Navy Families, and 40 percent were Air Force families.*

Hamilton I. McCubbin, Edna J. Hunter, Philip J. Metres, Jr.

This paper will primarily emphasize the findings derived from the discussion group for the 14 year olds and over since their reactions and comments were representative of the other groups, but seemed to present a greater depth of feelings.

The children's discussion groups were scheduled as integral parts of the retreat program; the children were invited to attend and were informed that the topic of father absence would be discussed. The groups were led by a team of behavioral scientists[3] skilled in group counseling, with ministers and youth counselors as support personnel. The discussions were semi-structured and primarily focused upon three major themes: (a) the children's perceptions of father's absence, (b) their feelings about father's absence, and (c) their perceptions of their mother's adjustment.

Findings

Coping with the Unknown. All of the children involved in the group discussions expressed initial reservations about discussing father and his absence. However, the conditions surrounding father's casualty were familiar to each and served as a legitimate point of departure for reflecting on father's loss. The ring of the doorbell, men in uniform, mother's crying, sadness in the home and the news of father's casualty were vividly described by the more articulate children, while others nodded tearfully in agreement with the close similarity to their own personal experiences. Like a casualty report, the children read the personal "facts" to each other.

Father's absence from the home was unquestionably real. As the children shared experiences and notes, however, little else remained clear. Is he alive? Was he killed immediately? How much hope can we continue to keep? What else can we do? Do we have all the information about him? The children expressed frustration with the lack of more definitive information as to the fate of their fathers. As if to present their mother's position, some children were able to relate what seemed to them to be gaps in the information they did receive. One child, after describing how his father had been on a patrol which received heavy enemy fire, and how the report of casualty revealed little other than the fact that a return sweep of the area was unable to produce a trace of his father, still was able to say, "I feel he is alive."

3. *The team consisted of a psychiatrist, three psychologists, two social workers, and three ministers with the support of three youth counselors on the staff of the High Flight Foundation.*

For the MIA children, father's future became more questionable and their perceptions, hopes and fantasies less clear as the children discussed the recent return of American prisoners of war. Operation Homecoming[4] symbolically represented two seemingly conflicting points of view. On one side of the coin, it meant that all the children, RPW and MIA alike, had reason to be extremely happy and proud. After all, they, along with their mothers had hoped and prayed for this event, and most families took an active part both locally and nationally in the effort to bring the men home. On the other side, however, Homecoming presented a threat to the hopes and fantasies of the MIA child about father's return. Did the return of American PWs mean that the remaining fathers would definitely not return? How should they feel and how should they now act? Wasn't it time for them to prepare for their own future without father, or work harder and make a greater commitment to account for father's loss? The questions were posed and seemingly acknowledged by all the children, but the answers were left for each to resolve at his own pace.

With this brief but meaningful introduction to the questionable nature of father's return, the children seemed to recognize the acceptance and understanding within the group. The group became an acceptable setting in which the children could discuss more personal feelings and seek opinions and impressions. It should be noted, however, that the group experience itself played a minor role in creating this impression of "being a safe place". The atmosphere of the total retreat and the opportunity to share similar experiences with other children who "really understood" because they had been through the same struggle set the stage for the discussion. The children provided each other with mutual support, without any attempt to attenuate the free expression of pain, hurt and frustration which had accumulated over the months, and in most cases, the years of waiting and uncertainty. As the discussions continued, the children began to express personal beliefs. For some, there was no question in their minds that their father would not return, that he had died in Southeast Asia.

Given the facts surrounding the casualty, the negotiations and cease-fire, and finally, the return of the American PWs, the children felt that the prospect of their father's return was realistically questionable. This position was not presented to the group without associated expressions of guilt, self-doubt, and the need for accept-

4. *Operation Homecoming was the name given to the total plan for processing of returned American prisoners of war in February and March of 1973.*

ance by the other group members. The twenty-one-year-old daughter of an Air Force pilot, missing in action, after documenting why she believed her father died, also expressed how uncomfortable it was for her to feel this way: "Somehow I feel I am letting my father down by not doing everything possible for him. I feel guilty for not keeping the hope alive. I still hope that he will come back, but I have to get on with my life." The group members responded to this expression of honesty and discomfort with personal acknowledgement of similar feelings. "My father would not want me to think about him this way. He would want me to get on with my life and not wait for him. He loves me and would have encouraged me to become someone. He would not want to hold me back."

Any discussions of the possibility that some fathers would not return was interpreted by some children as an outright challenge and a threat to their personally held belief that their father was still being detained as a prisoner. Hope for them had to be maintained in spite of any facts to the contrary. As long as there was any discrepancy or gap in information these children seemed to believe that hope should be maintained. They responded with comments such as: "We can never really be absolutely sure about whether they returned all of the prisoners." "Some might still be in the South, but they may not have heard of the cease fire." "The Joint Casualty Resolution Center will determine whether my father is alive. I believe he is alive somewhere."

Father's New Image. Following the casualty, during the years of waiting, the children's perceptions of their father and feelings toward him had undergone some evaluation and change. In a few instances, the emotional reactions to father's absence were linked to disquieting memories of father, real or imagined. Some of the children had difficult experiences with their fathers before casualty, and the discussion touched off feelings of guilt, fear, shame or disgust. Sudden outbursts of emotions, of anger and frustration as to "why did he go, he had already been two times before," or "why my father," were intermittently present. For most of the children, the description of their father that they presented to the group was obviously not the father the children once knew, but the glorified parent who is perpetuated in the fantasies of these young adults. It is not uncommon to hear the children speak of their fathers totally in terms of the ideally good, understanding and compassionate father. Their own feelings toward father had become ideally loving and understanding.

70

Dreams. Children's dreams about father's absence were seldom mentioned. In those few instances in which they were referred to, the children symbolically described the paradoxical nature of the PW/MIA situation. A twelve-year-old son of an MIA father described a frightening dream of years ago which he had never forgotten. "I dreamed my father returned but he was in two parts; one half was alive and the other half was dead." The dismemberment may have represented the child's ambivalence about the possibility of father's return. Or, perhaps the amount of distortion was related to prior information about the atrocities in Vietnam and was further influenced by the subtle messages that hope must be kept alive, even though father is very likely to be dead. The information from the children's discussions suggested that fantasies of father's return are either more clearly conscious or more readily expressed in adolescence than at younger ages. It seems likely that the children's fantasies of father's return may be a more closely guarded secret in younger children. Wolfenstein (1966) believes that a readiness to admit such fantasies, thus risking confrontation with the facts and reality, may represent one of the many important steps towards accepting the permanence of father's loss or giving up the lost parent.

Self-consciousness. The children appeared deeply self-conscious about having a father missing in the Southeast Asian conflict. Perhaps because the father is felt to be part of each child and an inalienable possession without which the family is incomplete, the children emphasized their need to conceal the fact that their fathers were PWs or missing in action. Although the children were aware that publicity and special recognition accompanied their special status, they also felt a painful inferiority to children with intact families. These feelings were apparently fostered by the public's questionable attitude towards the war. The children made numerous references to verbal insults they received in school. One fourteen-year-old daughter of an MIA father presented an interesting question to the group: "What should I say to a very close friend of mine who was angry at me and told me my father deserved it?"

Emotional Trauma. The experience of having a father missing in action was difficult for all children of MIAs, and exceedingly traumatic for a few. A twenty-year-old girl who sat noticeably quiet throughout the early stages of the discussion, presented her unique experiences. A few months after the report of her father's casualty she found herself experiencing a strong identification with her absent father. Seemingly in an attempt to keep her father's image in the family, this young lady, who was 15 at the time of casualty, began to wear father-like clothing. Military fatigues and jacket with appropriate patches became her usual daily attire. The loss of her father had meant that she was forced to carry on with her psychological development in the absence of an essential figure, she felt she had to compensate for this loss. As she put it: "I behaved as I thought he would have wanted me to." This led to distortions in development and complications in the resolution of the otherwise normal and typical conflicts of adolescence. Gradually increased depression in this case led to an attempted suicide and subsequent treatment as an in-patient in a military medical center. Her presence in the group and her willingness to share the experience with the group were sincerely appreciated and respected by all and served as testimony of not only the difficulties she experienced, but also of the personal effort she had made to overcome this difficult situation successfully.

Suppressed Emotions. The group experience was charged with emotionality. From the outset, crying, and in some cases sobbing, became a legitimate and accepted way of expressing the pain, frustration and anguish built up over the long period of waiting and hoping. As the children discussed the meaning of the sudden and contagious flood of emotions, it became apparent to the group leaders that suppressed emotions played a unique part in the adjustment of the PW/MIA family. Although the open display of emotions was acceptable in the group, the children expressed the feeling that it was not a generally accepted mode of behavior at home. Crying was not ordinarily tolerated because "I didn't want to upset my mother, she is easily upset." "I was afraid that I would not be able to stop once I started." "I was supposed to be strong and crying meant that I was weak." Suppression of emotions seemed to be one prerequisite for keeping the family on an even keel.

A related topic that was brought out during the discussions of suppressed emotions, was the commonly shared "understanding" within these families that it was dangerous to upset mother. For if upset, mother may break down and cry, may become depressed, or possibly angry at them, and they, the children, may be adversely affected by this. The thing to do, therefore, was to be good to mother and not do anything to upset her, even though it meant sacrifices on their part. Szasz (1959) pointed out the potentially deleterious effect of this very situation and emphasized the child's vulnerability in the family dynamics: "The child, even more than the adult is prone to think that if mother is upset, he must have caused it. He is ready to assume responsibility and blame for others' distress" (p. 293). The child, in the absence of father, is even more dependent on the mother's integrated behavior for his own survival and comfort. Hence, he has a pragmatic motive for keeping mother happy. The seriousness of this type of relationship between mother and child was also referred to by Hall and Simmons (1973) in their study of PW/MIA wives. Playing on the children's fears, the mothers were reported to use psychophysiological symptoms and emotional outbursts to control their children. Szasz (1959) indicated that this type of parental behavior was stimulus *par excellence* in developing the child's dread of parental anguish.

RPW Children's Reactions. The eight children of returned prisoners of war who were present in the group struggled with their feelings of discomfort which resulted from being among children whose fathers failed to return. They felt uncomfortable with themselves because of their own good fortune. One young lady was not aware of the basis for her crying and discomfort until well into the meeting. Then, after listening to others, she was able to express what was actually troubling her and what had motivated her to attend. Because of her compassion for the other children, she wanted to share with the others the happiness she felt over her father's return. She prefaced this disclosure by absent-mindedly citing how she too missed her father. The conflict between her past identification with the other members of the group, her desire to continue being part of and accepted by the group, and her altered status due to father's return contributed to her guilt feelings and discomfort. Some support from the other children through their understanding of her dilemma and, at the same time, recognition of her good fortune, appeared to put her feelings of self-worth together once again; although such feelings, it was judged, may resurface from time to time.

Mother's Adjustment. The children who experienced the loss of a father still have one parent. But is the surviving mother an adequate supporter of the children and is she a person to whom the children can transfer the feelings they had for the father? The information gained through the group discussions indicates that the children tend to perceive their relationship with their mother with some ambivalence. Mother represents authority, nurturance, support and foundation for their future. As one child described her mother: "she is not a mother and a father, rather she is a big momma." The children expressed some difficulty in dealing with a single surviving parent, a parent who is grief-stricken and hypersensitive. From the child's point of view, mother seemed to take little comfort from his presence or his efforts to comfort her. On the other hand, there appeared to be an intensification of positive feelings for the absent father. The absent father was idealized; the surviving mother was placed on trial. The children emphasized the necessity of "keeping hopes alive for father's return". Mothers were expected to conduct themselves in a manner which reflected this hope and commitment to father's return. Any deviation from the norm was suspect and called into question by some of the children. A few children voiced the opinion that it was inconceivable for mother to even entertain the thought of starting a new life for herself and the family — without father. The children's fantasies included the belief that if hope and continued search for father's whereabouts were to be given up, they, as well as their mother, could be blamed for his death.

These feelings, although present, were not uniformly experienced by all the children. Some children, in response to the question of "how is mother doing", were pleased to acknowledge that their mother had begun dating and was starting a new life for herself. They justified mother's actions in terms of her "vanishing youth" and the fact that they, the children, would soon be moving out of the home and starting a life of their own. "Mother should look out for herself." It would appear they felt their future separation from the family was in some way inextricably bound to mother's security and independence. If mother believed father was dead and began dating, it would then be legitimate for the teenage daughter to start her life.

A fifteen-year-old girl took exception to this seemingly mature and understanding approach to mother's dating. Mother's dating was a "cop out" which she (the child) could not understand, but she could tolerate. For this young lady, however, the crusade would continue; she believed that someone in the family must continue to pursue the truth about father's missing status. This was to be her mission in life. Interestingly enough, the group responded to this expression with questions about "her" future and "her" individuality. The other children made the point that her father would have wanted her to develop herself, not design a life around his loss. This presentation of another perspective by her peers was warmly received and acknowledged, although not pursued any further within the context of the group.

Staff Reaction. The staff of ministers, psychologists, social workers, youth counselors and a psychiatrist became totally involved in these brief but intense group experiences. Because the staff themselves had experienced a wide range of personal emotions, they were able to relate with empathy and, during subsequent staff meetings, were able to reflect more openly upon their reactions to the children.

Despite the exhaustion and emotional drain felt by most staff members after each group experience with the children, there was a feeling of having accomplished something and of having extended oneself fully to others. Yet, there were also the disquieting feelings of having observed and empathized with severe loss and grief. In almost every staff member, the group experience aroused repressed memories of past personal loss, anxieties, and thoughts of the possibility of future loss of family members. Staff meetings, informal discussions, and independent reflections helped to reconcile the arduous events of each experience.

Summary and Conclusions

In applying Bowlby's (1961) concepts of grieving to these children of fathers missing in action, one may consider the childrens' free expression of their demands for his return to be essential in attaining the conviction that father's loss may in fact be irretrievable. Bowlby has emphasized the therapeutic value of these overt expressions of what he calls "protests" in reaction to father's absence, an awareness which appears to be a prerequisite step towards reality testing and eventual tolerance for accepting the permanence of father-loss.

The denial of the existence of any facts which may suggest the possibility of father's death co-exists with a correct conscious acknowledgement of what may be reality. The children had little difficulty verbalizing that father may not return and even referred to the precarious circumstances surrounding their fathers' casualties. Yet, this superficial deference to facts remained isolated from the persistence on a more emotional level of hopeful expectation of father's return. Both Wolfenstein (1966) and Furman (1964) referred to this process as splitting of the ego in the defense process. Freud (1957) not only acknowledged this defense against accepting an unbearable piece of reality, but also emphasized the commonality of these occurrences in childhood.

The staff was impressed with the similarities in basic feelings and reactions of the children with those presented by their mothers who were interviewed earlier. However, the underlying motivations and feelings appeared to differ. The children's reactions did not appear to be attributable to the grieving process, but rather to the emergence of various struggles with identity formation, interpersonal relationships, and peer relationships which may be unique to children at different ages. Nagera (1970) emphasized the limited value of making comparisons between the mourning of adults and the mourning of children. He pointed out that, "Many factors contribute to the specific form of 'mourning reactions' observed in children following the loss of important objects. They (the children) vary . . . according to the different levels of development reached in a number of areas of the personality at different ages" (pp. 366-367). His conclusions seem to fit the PW/MIA situation; while adult-child comparisons may show similarities, they should not be misconstrued as identical, nor should it be assumed that identical metapsychological processes underlie the superficial similarities.

Unfortunately, because of the small size of the study sample and the potential of bias in the sample at the religious retreats, it is impossible to make any comparisons based on differences in religious affiliation, education or age. It seemed, however, that the absence of father was an equally difficult experience whether the loss was recent or one of long standing, whether it was sudden or unconsciously expected, or whether mother felt this loss to be permanent or merely temporary.

Although it is necessary to have more complete and clinically quantifiable data gathered on the children to determine whether the reported reactions are predominantly normal or pathological, it appeared that in those situations where child adjustment had been a major difficulty, mothers had taken the appropriate action and sought professional help. The area of more appropriate concern was the mother's ability to cope with her children's responses and needs. In discussions held with all the parents following the children's groups, the mothers indicated this was indeed one of their primary concerns. They worried about how they could help their children adjust to father's absence and, more importantly, how they could help them accept the possibility that father may not return. In the final analysis, this may be the most difficult task of all.

6

The Grieving Process In MIA Wives

LUDWIG SPOLYAR

Introduction

The Southeast Asian military conflict spotlighted a unique situation in which over 1200 American servicemen were listed as Missing in Action (MIA). Their families underwent or are presently undergoing a process of grieving which for some has extended over a period of up to nine years. This situation was created by two highly unusual aspects of this war: the fact that its strategies and policies were complicated by an unconventional type of jungle warfare and the fact that a full accounting of the status of the men who had been captured or lost was denied by the enemy. Thus, because of very limited information, many of these men, who under other circumstances might have been declared dead or presumed dead after a period of time, were still carried as MIA by the U.S. Government. Some of these men have turned up as prisoners, some were verified as deceased after the PWs' return, and some may never be verified as deceased due to a lack of evidence or inaccessibility of crash-site locations, (e.g. an aircraft lost at sea). For the latter a presumption of death may eventually be made.

What is the emotional process being faced by the wives of these men? Is he dead or alive? How do the wives plan for his possible return or a confirmation of his death? In most cases, they had to plan for both. Whether he returned or not, the process of grieving (grief cycle) was started and it is an important factor in the future life and adjustment of the wife, no matter what the results.

The purpose of this paper is to explain the process these wives underwent and to suggest ways their grief cycle may be completed in some satisfactory manner.

Background

Prior to going overseas, the expectation of death was a possibility. Most wives considered the separation, the safe return, the possibility of injury, and even the possibility of death. It may not have been openly discussed, but the silent considerations were there.

When the military authorities notified her that her husband was "missing in action", there was the initial shock followed by hope for rescue or the known status of being a prisoner. When this hope was not immediately realized there were many problems to be faced. An immediate notification of death quickly sets into play several dynamic self-operations of grief, but in the MIA situation, the grieving process is expanded or drawn out over a period of time. The concerns of family living, financial, legal, medical, and personal needs are extended over an unknown and indefinite period of time. It is a unique situation; one that is too infrequently considered.

The Process of Grieving (Grief Cycle)

Grief has been defined by Jackson as, *essentially the emotional and related reactions that occur at the time of and following the loss of an important person in the emotional life of an individual who has reached the state of development where he or she has the capacity for object love. Grief is the emotion that is involved in the work of mourning, whereby a person seeks to disengage herself from the demanding relationship that has existed and to reinvest her emotional capital in new and productive directions for the health and welfare of her future life in society.*

The MIA wife is faced with the possible loss of a person who is very important in her emotional life. Not knowing the actual status (prisoner or dead) of the MIA, the wife has difficulty in trying to disengage herself from the previous relationship because she does not know for sure if death has occurred. Nevertheless, she can still attempt to reinvest her emotional capital in new and productive directions until and/or after a final status is determined.

After the notification of possible death or tragedy, there is a deep-set craving for details of the situation. Any information about the circumstances is anxiously desired, received, and considered. Unfortunately, in the case of the MIAs, the complete details of the circumstances were not usually available and this situation created a certain amount of anxiety and fear of the unknown. So, the MIA wife found herself emotionally suspended until more definite facts were known about the status of her MIA husband. However, the process of grieving slowly began.

As mentioned above, shock is usually the first phase of the grief cycle. There is commonly a slight sense of unreality, a feeling of increased emotional distance from other people, and an intense pre-occupation with the image of the missing person. This will usually be followed by an emotional release which is a normal channel for the relaxation of tension. A sudden "breaking down" or weeping spell does not represent "failure", especially if such concessions to one's human frailty are reserved for one's private moments or intimate friends. Eliot (1946) points out that this element of grief displayed at intervals should not be interpreted as failure or weakness, nor should it be encouraged or stimulated as proof of acceptable "devotion" or to secure attention and sympathy. An emotional release is normal and necessary. It should not be suppressed permanently and in some cases, not released all at once, but in installments.

There are two other emotional states which have some relationship to grief: anxiety and depression. Both of these states may be involved to some degree in the process of grieving, but can be minimized if the individual has a better understanding of the grieving process and directs his energies towards the future in a healthy and normal fashion.

Anxiety is a threat to some value which the individual holds essential to her existence as a personality. Depression is a feeling of inadequacy and hopelessness, and involves a loss of self-esteem with possible aggressive feelings toward others or herself. Normal grief involves no loss of self-esteem; there may be a normal amount of self-accusation and feelings of guilt, but only on a temporary basis.

In the grief cycle, there may also be physical symptoms of distress. These may include a tightness in the throat, a shortness of breath, a lack of strength, frequent periods of exhaustion, dietary problems, and certain psychosomatic conditions such as ulcerative colitis, rheumatoid arthritis, and asthma.

Guilt. Guilt is almost universally present in grief. The nature of human relationships breeds the possibility for guilt responses among normal people. It is testimony to the ambivalent nature of the love relationship. This love relationship produces a certain amount of inner conflict. Wherever love exists there is also a certain amount of reaction against it, for love demands limitation of freedom and extended responsibility. This negative reaction can build up over a period of time and when it is released, it normally results in lovers' spats or marriage conflicts. In a normal ongoing marriage, when husband and wife are together, the conflict is usually resolved through some type of dialogue or communication. However, for the wife whose husband is not present to help resolve the conflict, the reaction may increase in intensity. On top of this, further guilt feelings may result in the wife when she realizes that her husband is not present to represent his side of the conflict.

The wife may search the times prior to or during the missing period for evidence of failure to do right by her husband. She may accuse herself of negligence and exaggerate minor situations which can increase the guilt feelings. The absence of the man precludes an immediate resolution of most guilt feelings, but the talking out of guilt feelings can often be accomplished with close friends, clergy, professional counselors, or medical personnel.

Identification. A bereaved person may sometimes seek to overcome the pain of grief by becoming one with the lost love-object. A certain amount of identification is essential and desirable, but too much identification or incorporation of the lost one over a long period of time can be undesirable. In order to achieve a greater degree of self-fulfillment, a person should live in terms of the future rather than in terms of the past. Because our society makes women identify with and depend on their husbands for many essentials of life, socially and economically, women have a greater tendency to identify with their lost husbands. Faced by the loss of a husband, the wife may try to protect this loss of self-esteem and security by identifying with her husband through becoming the breadwinner, running her husband's business, or continuing to maintain the home as if she were fulfilling a dual role. An MIA wife is almost forced into the identification role because her security and self-esteem is continued as a military wife whose husband is away. If and when this status is terminated, there should be a phasing away from too much identification or incorporation which could destroy the personality.

Substitution. Another response to grief may be an active effort to externalize, project, and substitute an image or an object for that which has been lost or missing. Where identification tends to be personal and internal, substitution tends to be external and more impersonal. Substitution may take two directions. One may involve the act of changing the meaning to something that is more readily acceptable by substituting a completely different but related meaning for that which is too painful to accept. For example, going to church across town on Sunday rather than going to the neighborhood church where the wife and husband were married may be less painful. A second method is to relate the emotional meaning to an external object, person, or idea as a substitute for the internal feeling one would escape. Sometimes this may be desirable or it may be disruptive to the emotional life of a person. Some substitution is probably involved in every normal grief situation because the bereaved person should try to separate herself from the binding ties to the lost person. An example of substitution would be the establishment of scholarships in the name of the lost or missing person.

Hostility. During the grief cycle, there is often a disconcerting loss of warmth in relationships with other people, a tendency to respond with irritability and anger, and a wish not to be bothered by others at a time when friends and relatives make a special effort to keep up friendly relationships. These feelings of hostility, brought on by anxiety, depression, and frustration, are to be expected, but they are usually specific and often directed towards certain persons. In some cases, this hostility is directed inwardly toward the person herself. If the hostility continues for a long period of time or is intensified, this may appear to the individual as a sign of approaching mental instability and create greater guilt feelings. In the process of fighting against these feelings of hostility, she may develop a formalized, stiff manner of social interaction.

The working out of hostile feelings can take several directions. The most detrimental direction would be towards herself which can also intensify her guilt feelings. Hostile feelings may often be directed towards the lost person too. Hostile feelings directed toward family and friends can lessen the needed social interaction and support. Sometimes, hostility may be directed towards institutions like the military services and governments. Occasionally, various techniques are used to vent hostility in a non-destructive way. (One woman would bake bread and the strenuous pounding and kneading of the dough would help her release the tension.) Verbalizing the hostility to professional counselors or empathetic friends can be of positive value. Most important, however, is the awareness and understanding that hostile reactions are an expected phase of the grief cycle and, hopefully, are temporary in nature.

Anticipatory Grief

Of particular significance in the MIA situation is the problem of anticipatory grief. Anticipatory grief usually develops, not as a result of definite death, but with those who have experienced a separation which is under the threat of death. The person is so concerned with her adjustment after the potential death of her husband she goes through all the phases of grief–anxiety, depression, heightened preoccupation with the departed, a review of all forms of death which might befall him, and anticipation of the modes of readjustment which might be necessitated by it. She may have completed her grief work so effectively and emancipated herself so well from dependency on her husband prior to any finalization of death that it may serve as a safeguard against the impact of a permanent separation.

There are several problems related to anticipatory grief. First, if the wife has previously worked out her grief process prior to the actualization of death, there may be an absence of feeling for the death at the time it is made certain. As a result there may be a sense of guilt or a feeling of shame brought about by the cultural directive to mourn. Second, in cases where the man returns and the wife has emancipated herself through the process of anticipatory grief, the readjustment must now be directed towards new interactions. In other words, a new relationship will have to be developed, since it will be most difficult to reverse or disregard the emotionality experienced during the grief cycle.

Conditioning for the Grief Cycle

The dynamics of grief reaction may be influenced in at least four ways. First, the personality structure of the wife is important. An emotionally mature person with adequate self-acceptance will be better able to handle a grief situation. Second, there are social factors involved. In the military community, the loss of a loved one is not uncommon and the attitude toward it is conditioned by a tradition and a sense of duty. Third is the importance of the husband in the life cycle of the wife. Fourth is the value structure of the wife as it relates to a loss of her husband. A value structure which perceives the loss of a husband not as an appalling tragedy, but rather an incident set in a long chain of other incidents, will have the effect of moderating the grief reaction of those who are bereaved.

Readjustment to Reality

One important concept to remember is that the husband would not wish his wife to act in futile, destructive, or regressive ways. She should act so that the husband would be proud of her. She should continue to preserve the values represented by the husband which seem most worth carrying on into life. The bereaved wife may never again be fully "the same", but who else (bereaved or unbereaved) stays the "same"?

The grief cycle is a necessary but difficult human task. No words, written or spoken, can truly express the process of grieving. However, the explanation of the grief cycle may aid in the understanding and awareness of this human experience to those who undergo it.

Finally, one may ask how recovery or signs of the completion of the grief cycle are recognized. Eliot (1946) supplies the same norms that one applies in appraising social normality anywhere:

There is reasonable physical health.

There is interest in self, life, the future, and others.

There is productivity, and some out-giving activity in leisure.

There is intellectual acceptance of the loss and emotional assimilation of the experience, without too great a break in the continuity of personality.

There is relaxation of tensions in relation to the deceased, and renewed emotional control and stability.

When memories come, they are without pain, neither sought nor avoided, but spontaneous and welcome.

Sympathies are broadened and mellowed.

New love-objects gradually supervene without sense of competition or fear of jealousy.

Conclusion

The wives of military personnel missing in action will find themselves emotionally involved in a unique situation which includes the process of grieving, an emotional suffering. They are in a double bind, for they do not know for sure whether their loved one is dead or alive. Unfortunately, this emotional state continues for an indefinite and unknown period, creating greater anxiety.

Accompanying the separation, potential loss, or actual loss of a husband, the process of grieving is a normal, human and necessary experience. Further, it is essential that the grieved wife successfully complete the grief cycle and begin a different and realistic life.

By understanding the psychological elements of the grief cycle, a wife can better cope with the experience and hopefully return to a new and productive life. The psychological elements include shock, emotional release, anxiety, depression, physical symptoms, guilt, identification, substitution, and hostility.

Of particular significance to the MIA situation is that of anticipatory grief, which develops, not as a result of definite death, but with those who have experienced a separation which is under the threat of death. Here, even though there is no finalization of death, a wife may still go through the grief cycle.

There is no common or universal grief experience because each person, due to individual circumstances and personality characteristics, will undergo the grief cycle differently. The final phase should result in a readjustment to reality and a future life of social normality.

Several other related issues have become apparent and influential in the unique grief process of the MIA wife. Although these issues may not be classified as "psychological" elements of grief, they could be very important in resolving or completing the grief cycle. First, if children are involved, they can either aid or cause additional difficulty in the grieving process. There are many variables to this aspect such as the ages of the children, how the wife has explained their father's absence, the children's perception of death or potential death, and of course, the usual one-parent family problems. There are many situations where the children have been exceptional in providing supportive strength to their mother. Second, many wives have found religion to be helpful and have found strength and guidance in spiritual activities. Third, conflicts or cooperation with in-laws, especially the parents of the husband, have an influence on the wife's grieving process. Parents often perceive the emotional loss of a son far differently from a wife who loses a husband, and this may produce conflict and difficulty for the wife. Finally, there is always the possibility that the MIA wife may have experienced intimate relationships with other men during the long absence of her husband. Such experiences can create guilt, anxiety, or other psychological problems which further affect the grieving process.

Professionals working with MIA wives and assisting them in undergoing the grieving process, must bear in mind that there are many factors to be considered. No two situations will be exactly alike, but common elements will be found in many cases.

7

Religion And The PW/MIA Family

EDNA J. HUNTER
HAMILTON I. MCCUBBIN
PHILIP J. METRES, JR.

*"God was there with me and he helped
me make the best of a bad existence".*
Gaither, 1973

Introduction

The church service held at Clarke Air Force Base by the released prisoners of war immediately prior to their return to the United States, their statements before the television cameras upon return, and the books written by returnees now beginning to appear in print: *Seven Years in Hanoi* (Chesley, 1973), *With God in P.O.W. Camp,* (Gaither, 1973), and *In the Presence of Mine Enemies* (Rutledge & Rutledge, 1973), present convincing evidence that religion was, indeed, effectual in aiding these men to cope with the extreme stresses of their captivity experiences.

But what about the prisoner of war (PW) and missing in action (MIA) families? Were their personal religious beliefs helpful in coping with the prolonged and indeterminate period of husband/father absence, as the men's beliefs appeared to have been in dealing with their long captivity experience?

In a manual specifically written for Navy chaplains who minister to the families of prisoners of war and missing in action, the observation was made that although each man's experience differed, the "terrible experiences of the PWs were nonetheless more uniform than the variety of problems encountered by their waiting families" (Westling, 1973). Hunter and Plag (1973), in their survey of one particular group of PW/MIA families several months prior to the release of the prisoners from Southeast Asia, also found a great deal of variance among the families as to their social and psychological hardships associated with the PW/MIA situation. They found that while some families suffered only the usual hardships related to any period of husband/father absence, other families experienced a wide range of difficulties.

Edna J. Hunter, Hamilton I. McCubbin, Philip J. Metres, Jr.

During the ten-month period prior to the return of the prisoners of war in early 1973, professional staff members of the Center for Prisoner of War studies in San Diego interviewed 215 Army, Navy, and Marine PW/MIA wives (McCubbin, Hunter and Metres, 1973). Interview data from that study showed that although almost fifty percent of the wives reported that their religious convictions had been very helpful to them in coping with the extended absence of their husbands, another twenty percent of the group had not found their personal religious beliefs a source of support in any way. During the period of husband absence, approximately thirty percent of the wives reported having consulted a minister or priest for assistance with emotional as well as other adjustment problems, and a similar percent indicated that they believed spiritual counseling services should be available to their families at the time of repatriation. Additionally, over forty percent of the women in this study group reported church activities to be a satisfying form of spending leisure time since the occurrence of their husbands' casualties. On the other hand, smaller groups of wives from this study reported that religion was either helpful at first but not later (11.2%), or not helpful immediately but became a source of support over time (4.2%).

Purpose

The purpose of the present study was to determine whether those wives who reported that religion had been very helpful in coping with the PW/MIA situation in the McCubbin et al. study presented a pattern of coping behaviors or demographic characteristics which differed from those of the wives who indicated religion was of no value to them.

Procedure

A comparison was made between the group of 107 PW/MIA wives who had indicated religion as a source of help during husband absence (designated as the R Group) and a second group of 44 wives who had reported receiving no help whatsoever from religion (designated as the NR Group) in adjusting to their PW/MIA situation. Analyses were carried out to compare the between-group variance on a number of demographic factors as well as on physical, psychosocial, and role adjustment factors for both the wife and the children during the prolonged absence of the husband/father. A 2 x 2 chi-square test was used to determine the statistical significance of between-group differences.[1]

1. *Data analysis was conducted under the supervision of Dr. Jerry Goffman, former Head, Data Analysis Branch of the Center for Prisoner of War Studies.*

86

One hundred fifty-one PW/MIA wives, including 51 Army wives, 21 Marine wives, and 79 Navy wives served as subjects. Sixty-seven of these women were wives of men classified as prisoners of war (PW), and 84 were wives of husbands classified as missing in action (MIA). The sample was predominantly Protestant (64.2%) or Catholic (25.8%), well-educated (almost seventy percent had continued their schooling beyond the high school level), and the average age was 32 years. Within the 151 families there were 289 children, ranging in age from less than one year to 25 years. Although twenty-nine of the wives were childless, the majority had either one or two children.

Results and Discussion

Demographic factors. Comparing the number of wives in each group who were 32 years of age or older, there were more older wives in the religious-oriented group (44.8% of the R group were 32 years or older; only 22.7% of the NR group were in that age bracket). It would seem that religion was a greater source of support or consolation for the older wife ($\chi^2 = 6.5$, df = 1, p < .05). There was no statistically significant difference between the MIA wives and the PW wives with respect to their feelings about religion as a source of support. In addition, no significant differences were found among Army, Navy, and Marine wives as to whether religion was seen as helpful during husband absence. There was evidence, however, that geographical factors may be related to the wives' feelings about religion. In comparing the wives residing in the northern half of California (N = 30) with those residing in southern California (N = 66), it was found that significantly more wives ($\chi^2 = 4.4$, df = 1, p < .05) from the group who found religion helpful resided in the southern part of the state. It should be noted that because a relationship exists, such a relationship does not necessarily imply that geographical location affects one's perception of religion. It may be that the wives who viewed religion as a source of assistance were also the ones who tended to move to certain areas to wait out their husbands' absences, or to move away from certain areas (e.g., from the military base) following their husbands' casualties. However, it is also possible that this finding may very well be attributable to the type of community in which they resided. This phenomenon cannot be fully explained on the basis of the existing data.

The finding that the two groups did not differ on average number of years of formal schooling (13.7 years for the R Group and 13.9 years for the NR Group) is perhaps in and of itself significant as it refutes the contention sometimes held that the less-educated turn to religion in times of crisis. While there was a small difference observed

87

between the religious background of the wife and whether or not she viewed religion as supportive (82.1% of the Catholic wives indicated they received consolation from their faith; 71.1% of the Protestant wives said that religion was helpful), this difference did not reach statistical significance ($\chi^2 = 1.7$, df = 1, p < .20).

Satisfying leisure-time activities. The two groups were compared on a wide range of activities in which they had participated and found satisfying during their husbands' absences (see Table 1).

Both groups indicated high participation in hobbies, social group activities, and television viewing, but differed only slightly ($\chi^2 = 3.3$, df = 1, p < .10) on home participation projects (remodeling and redecorating), and significantly on church-related activities ($\chi^2 = 8.9$, df = 1, p < .01). Despite the fact that wives frequently expressed the distinction that it was their own personally held religious beliefs which provided the source of help, and not the institutional church, it appeared that those who found religion very helpful were also the ones who found church activities more satisfying, and participated more frequently in them.

Satisfaction with the marriage. What were the wives' present feelings about their marriages after the long separations? A significantly greater number of those who reported religion as helpful still viewed their

TABLE 1. *Leisure Activities Found Most Satisfying During Husband Absence*

| | R Group | | NR Group | | |
Activity	Frequency++	Percent	Frequency++	Percent	χ^2
Hobbies	65	60.8	25	56.8	NS
Social Groups	42	39.2	19	43.2	NS
TV	41	38.2	18	36.4	NS
Sports	30	28.0	16	36.4	NS
Educational Classes	27	25.2	12	27.3	NS
Church Activities	30	29.7	2	4.9	8.9**
Remodeling/Redecorating	18	17.8	13	31.7	3.3+
Volunteer Work	18	16.8	10	22.7	NS
Movies	14	13.1	8	18.2	NS
Military Service Groups	5	4.7	1	2.3	NS

NOTE: *The R Group contains those PW/MIA wives who reported that religion was very helpful in coping with their husbands' absences; the NR Group contains those who reported that religion was not a source of support for them.*

++Number of respondents varied due to revised questionnaire.

**p < .01

+Approached significance (p < .10)

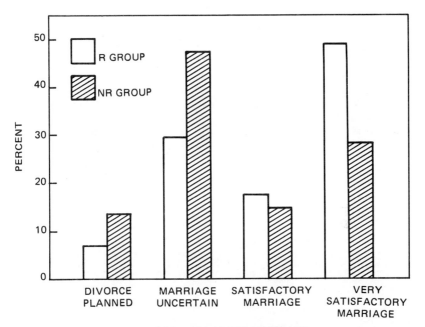

FEELINGS ABOUT MARRIAGE

marriages as satisfactory (χ^2 = 12.9, df = 1, p < .01). At the time of the interviews, over twelve percent of the NR group indicated that they were considering divorce, while only seven percent of the religious-oriented wives indicated that intention (see Figure 1). This relationship between high marriage satisfaction and support reportedly received from religion is congruent with the high value placed upon marriage by the institutional church, particularly the Catholic church.

Difficult areas of coping. During the interviews the wives were asked about the most difficult areas of coping experienced during the period since their husbands' casualties. Both groups mentioned the lack of the husband's companionship and their feelings of extreme loneliness, making all decisions alone, and the discipline of the children as difficult areas. However, none of the between-group differences was statistically significant.

When asked if there were any regretted decisions, small differences were found between the groups for their expressed regrets associated with "marking time" (23.1% of the NR wives had regrets; only 13.8% of the Rs) and dating (10.3% of the NRs; 5.8% of the Rs); however, the between-group differences were not statistically significant. On the other hand, significantly more wives in the non-religious group had

TABLE 2. *Difficult Areas of Coping During Husband Absence*

Activity	R Group Frequency++	Percent	NR Group Frequency++	Percent	χ^2
Lack of husband's companionship	64	72.7	27	69.2	NS
Feelings of extreme loneliness	38	43.2	22	56.4	1.9+
Discipline of the children	17	36.4	7	35.9	NS
Making all decisions alone	37	42.1	12	30.8	NS
Lack of social life	26	29.6	9	23.1	NS
Guilt feelings	6	6.8	5	12.8	NS

NOTE: *The R Group contains those PW/MIA wives who reported that religion was very helpful in coping with their husbands' absences; the NR Group contains those who reported that religion was not a source of support for them.*

++Number of respondents varied due to revised questionnaire.

+Approached significance (p <.20)

dated during the husband's absence. Stated conversely, 54.6% of the wives who reported religion very helpful had never dated while only 31.6% of the other group had never dated (χ^2 = 5.6, df = 1, p < .05). This finding is consistent with the wives' present feelings of satisfaction with their marriages; if marriage is valued less, then one would expect the wife to be more apt to date and to have more guilt feelings about dating. This situation presented a problem for the PW/MIA wife, for if she was religiously-oriented it appeared that she found it difficult to close the door on her past life and begin dating. During one particular interview a wife stated, "I had to give up my church because it was inconsistent with dating another man."

Anxiety-Depression symptoms. During the period subsequent to the husband's casualty, most wives reported experiencing a number of problems associated with anxiety-depression symptomatology, for example, sleep disturbances, feeling "down in the dumps," mood fluctuations, etc. The two groups were compared as to specific complaints and number of emotional problems reported. Depression was the most frequently mentioned symptom for both groups. None of the between-group differences for any of the symptoms covered was statistically significant; however, the largest differences were with respect to mood fluctuations, boredom, depression, and feeling that life was meaningless.

TABLE 3. *Symptoms Experienced by R and NR Groups During Husband Absence*

Activity	R Group Frequency++	Percent	NR Group Frequency++	Percent	χ^2
Depressed, "down in the dumps"	38	35.5	18	40.9	NS
Rapid mood changes	25	23.4	16	36.4	2.7+
Jumpiness	38	35.5	16	36.4	NS
Sleep problems					
Fitful sleep	35	32.7	14	31.8	NS
Difficulty falling asleep	31	29.0	11	25.0	NS
Waking early, not rested	25	23.4	13	29.5	NS
Feeling bored	19	17.8	11	25.0	NS
Headaches	24	22.4	8	18.2	NS
Poor digestion	17	15.9	7	15.9	NS
Feeling life is meaningless	9	8.4	6	13.6	NS
Shortness of breath	10	9.3	2	4.5	NS

NOTE: *The R Group consists of those PW/MIA wives who reported that religion was very helpful in coping with their husbands' absences; the NR group consists of those who reported that religion was not a source of support for them.*

++Number of respondents varied due to revised questionnaire.

+Approached significance (p <.20)

Suicide. There is often a close relationship between depression and suicide, and the wives were questioned as to whether they had ever contemplated suicide subsequent to their husbands' casualties. Their responses indicated that a significantly greater number of the nonreligious wives ($\chi^2 = 6.4$, df = 1, p < .05) had entertained suicidal thoughts than had those wives who found religion supportive. Again, this finding appears to be congruent with the larger percentage of Catholics in the religious-oriented group and the traditional Catholic view on suicide.

Religion and the need for psychiatric treatment. Religion did not seem to be related to the need for psychiatric help on the part of either the wives or their children. This was indicated not only on the basis of those who had received treatment in the past, but also on the basis of those recommended by the interviewer as needing treatment.[2] The children within the two groups were also compared as to the frequency of a wide variety of physical, behavioral, and personal adjustment problems, without finding any significant between-groups differences. There was no indication from these results that wives who had

2. *Based upon one-time, in-depth personal interviews lasting from two to eight hours, an evaluation was made by the interviewer as to the present need for psychological counseling for the wife and children.*

Edna J. Hunter, Hamilton I. McCubbin, Philip J. Metres, Jr.

TABLE 4. *Children's Feelings Toward Returning Father*

Feeling	R Group Frequency	R Group Percent	NR Group Frequency	NR Group Percent	χ^2
Will not remember him	53	24.8	28	37.3	4.3*
Will blame him for deserting them	10	4.7	6	8.0	NS
Will treat him as an interloper	16	7.5	17	22.7	12.7***
Will resent him	33	15.4	31	41.3	21.6***

NOTE: *The R Group consists of those PW/MIA wives who reported that religion was very helpful in coping with their husbands' absences; the NR Group consists of those who reported that religion was not a source of support for them.*

* *p<.05*

****p<.001*

not received any religious support sought support either for themselves or their children from mental health sources.

As part of the interview, the mothers were asked how they believed their children would feel towards their father upon his return, and several highly significant differences emerged between the two groups (see Table 4). Those mothers who had not found religion helpful in coping with their husbands' absences reported that they believed the children would not remember their father, would be more apt to resent him, and would treat him as an interloper. Although it may be possible that these children would not remember their father simply because they were too young at the time he left to recall his presence (40.0% of the children from the NR group were eight years of age or under; 34.1% of the children from the R Group were in that age group), such an explanation cannot fully account for the difference. Perhaps the mothers simply had not taken positive steps to keep their children aware of father during his absence. These findings may also reflect the reorganization within the family structure with a closing out of the father's role. The present authors have noted that the "shifting of family roles, responsibilities, and the intensification of relationships among family members suggest the evolution of a family unit without the father" (McCubbin, Hunter and Metres, 1973). The mother's devaluation of the marriage and her decision to begin dating point to a reorganization in process. Mothers may be overtly or covertly passing on to the children the message that father would not return. Although some mothers reported their children would view father as an interloper upon his return, this finding may not, in reality,

92

reflect the children's feelings, as it could be projection on the part of the mothers who were moving out and attempting to attenuate conflicting inner feelings during the period of family reorganization.

Conclusions

From the findings of this study, the wife who indicated she found religion a source of support throughout her husband's absence had certain personal attributes which differentiated her from the wife who did not turn to religion for help in coping. She took an active part in church-related affairs to fill her leisure time. She was somewhat older than the wife who did not find religion helpful in coping with her limbo state. She was less apt to date, and she had fewer guilt feelings than her counterpart who found religion was not a source of emotional or personal comfort.

It is possible that the manner in which the PW/MIA wife perceived religion as a source of help was influenced by her early family background; it may also be a measure of the degree to which the family had moved on into a phase of family reorganization. Perhaps, even redecorating or remodeling the home symbolized for the wife a reorganization; that is, a sign of closing the door on the old life and starting a new one. Religion and "moving on" to a new life may be mutually exclusive; in this case, if the wife holds on to religion, she may feel too much guilt associated with beginning a new life for herself. Perhaps those wives who reported that religion was of no help were also those who had moved on towards a reorganization of the family and a closing out of the husband's role, but not without feelings of guilt and emotional ups and downs which, at times, included contemplation of suicide. Understanding the coping process and being sensitive to where the families are in their own adjustment is crucial, not only for the clinician, but for the pastoral counselor as well.

Repatriation

8

Medical Aspects of Captivity and Repatriation

S. WILLIAM BERG

Introduction

In January 1973 four years of planning reached fruition as Operation Homecoming was put into effect by the release of 591 Americans held prisoner in Vietnam. Although the plan was wide-ranging in scope and massive in detail, emphasis was on the medical evaluation and treatment of the prisoners of war (PWs). Toward that end a minimum 90-day period on the hospital sicklist was mandated, and a 400-page Initial Medical Evaluation Form was prepared for each PW to help guide his evaluation and document his medical and psychiatric status.

The information gathered in that form, as well as in the hospital record, is currently being analyzed in preparation for a detailed report of the medical status of the Vietnam PWs at the time of repatriation. The present paper is a preliminary report which attempts, in a general fashion, to describe some of the more common or significant medical problems of captivity and repatriation. It also attempts to show the context in which these medical problems occurred, as well as providing a perspective for evaluating their significance.

There are three general points which should be kept in mind in considering the medical aspects of captivity and repatriation. First, the PW experience does not constitute a specific medical disease, or even a syndrome. The diseases and injuries the men suffered are a combination of some or all of the following quite familiar medical entities:

    a.   Malnutrition: Both protein-calorie and vitamin deprivation

b. Infectious diseases: Including malaria, intestinal worms, and various types of diarrhea

c. Trauma due to torture and physical abuse

d. Trauma due to either ejection injuries or gunshot wounds

e. Dental problems: Including caries and periodontitis

f. Psychological stresses: Including pressures for cooperation with captors; pressures from long periods of small group-living in confined quarters; pressures from maintaining a somewhat artificial peer group in an alien environment; and pressures from worrying about wife and family.

Second, the ill-health a man may have experienced in captivity depended in part upon his individual attitude, abilities, and unique situation. Some men were finicky and starved themselves, whereas others ate everything, including worms, rats, maggots and insects in bread, sewer greens, or anything that could remotely be considered as food. Some men did 300 pushups a day, whereas others exercised little or not at all. Some men were injured severely during ejection and may or may not have received treatment, whereas others were not injured at all, and may not have suffered much physical abuse. It is necessary in any attempt to describe this group to be wary of generalizations and to be alert to individual differences.

A third factor to be kept in mind in evaluating a returnee's well-being in the future, is the man's own perception of his health. Prior to capture many of these men tended to be deniers of ill-health. They had to be because most of them were fliers, and ill-health was a threat to their flying status. On the other hand, the literature on the captivity experience (Ballard, 1973; W. Miller, personal communication, 1973) indicates that the typical PW develops a hypochondriacal attitude. Extreme attention to any real or potential threat to health, and ultimately life, is probably necessary to survive in captivity; however, whether this hypochondriasis will continue after repatriation is not predictable. It is possible that some PWs may feel that since they have survived tremendous psychological and physical stresses, they can survive almost anything, with a resultant neglect of their health after their return.

Conditions in Captivity

It has become obvious since repatriation that there were two quite different types of PW experiences in Vietnam. The northern experience was endured, almost exclusively, by Navy, Air Force and Marine

96

fliers. The southern experience was shared by Army and Marine infantrymen, a majority of whom were enlisted men. (About 100 of the men held in the south were moved into the northern prison system in the period 1969-1971.) In both cases, however, the PWs' lives were intimately related to their geographical and social environments.

PWs in the north were held in conventional prisons, or buildings that had been converted to prisons, in or near metropolitan areas. Although the men might be manacled to their beds for months at a time with their hands handcuffed behind them, this restraint was used as a form of punishment rather than as an additional confining device. The prisons provided shelter, although they were usually chilly in the winter and hot and often stuffy in the summer. A few prisons had toilets, but the usual facility was a "honey pot" which the PW emptied daily. Drinking water was usually provided in the form of a bucketful once each day. Although the quantity was often inadequate, particularly in the summer, the water was boiled to purify it. Food in the north was better quantitatively and qualitatively than in the south. There was a late morning and a mid-afternoon meal, each of which consisted of a half loaf of French bread and a bowl of thin vegetable soup. Outside Hanoi proper, rice was usually substituted for bread. After late 1969 the quantity of food increased, side dishes with an occasional piece of meat were more frequent and an early morning meal consisting of bread and sweetened milk was added.

In the south PWs were held in small groups accompanying guerilla bands as they travelled in the mountain jungle or wet, swampy areas. Shelter consisted of bamboo and thatch "hootches" or sometimes bunkers dug in the soil. If the area was sufficiently far from American troops, and the jungle or swamp sufficiently difficult to travel through, the men would not be restrained; otherwise, they were chained or manacled inside their cages. In addition to having to endure whatever extremes of weather that were present, particularly the monsoon rains which flooded the hootches, southern prisoners lived in an endemic malaria area. The PWs shared the guerillas' fate of being at the tail end of the supply chain, which usually meant inadequate amounts of food, medicine, and other vital supplies. Rice was eaten almost exclusively, although sometimes manioc (a tuberous plant similar to a yam) was substituted. The PWs also ate whatever greens, fish, small animals or reptiles they could scavenge, with opportunities being better for this the further south the men were held.

Hygiene in Vietnam is poor in general, and in the north limited medical equipment, drugs, and personnel compound the problem (Halberstam, 1973; Scrimshaw, 1973). In such a situation a rather pragmatic philosophy of preventive medicine and health care delivery develops. The populace was taught by rote to boil their drinking water, and use alternating privys to kill parasites in night soil. The unfortunate limitations of rote learning of health care practices were observed by several of the PWs. Guards would frequently expectorate in the halls, and it was not unusual to see a guard spit the rinse water back into the water bucket after brushing his teeth. The scarcity of physicians meant great reliance had to be placed on paramedics, or "assistant doctors" as they were known to the PWs. It is not known however, how much medical training such personnel may have had. Paradentists were also available, and after 1969 frequently placed temporary fillings in the PWs' cavities. At least a few of the PWs had serious injuries treated at hospitals in North Vietnam, although their stay there was seldom longer than a day or two. Many common medicines were available in the north, but these were sometimes outdated, notably the tetracycline. PWs in the north also received immunizations for cholera, typhoid, and polio, and perhaps other diseases.

Judged by American standards, health care in the north was inadequate, with the most prominent deficiency being the failure to continue treatment for more than a day or two. By Vietnamese standards, however, the care may have been superior to what the general populace received since the PWs represented a valuable commodity with which to bargain and, thus, had to be kept alive and at least in reasonably good health. Nevertheless, it was not uncommon for the North Vietnamese to use the withholding of medical treatment as a ruthless and very effective weapon to force cooperation from the PWs.

Medical care for PWs held in the south was much more limited than in the north. Although in some secure areas the Viet Cong had set up field hospitals, no American PWs were treated there. The one American physician PW, held in the south his first few years, was not allowed to treat his fellow PWs although he was able to do so covertly. Medical care was provided by the guerillas themselves, who sometimes had a soldier attached to their unit who functioned as a corpsman. Although medications were usually available, including vitamin B_1 for beri-beri and quinine for malaria, their quantity was always extremely limited. Moreover, use of medicines to treat a PW might mean that none would be available if one of the guerillas fell ill.

PWs rarely received medication until they were desperately ill, and than might receive far too little, too late. To counter this treatment, the PWs would attempt, sometimes successfully, to fake illness in order to obtain medicines which could then be hidden until real illnesses struck.

The North Vietnamese attempted to make the PWs more cooperative by isolating them in small cells. Communication with other PWs was absolutely forbidden, and activities such as emptying the honey buckets were conducted one cell at a time to avoid any opportunity for communication. The PWs did no work, except for a few minor housekeeping chores. Any outside exercise was a rarity, always done alone or in twos or threes. As a result the PW's existence was a lonely, monotonous and incredibly boring one.

The PWs vigorously fought against this monotony with two powerful, covert weapons: a PW military organization based upon seniority or rank, and communication using the tap code to pass messages between walls. Communication and organization were crucially important in the four years from 1966 to 1969, when the North Vietnamese were determined to exploit the PWs for propaganda purposes by torturing them to make audiotapes and write letters and biographical statements denouncing the war and praising the "humane and lenient" treatment that they were allegedly receiving.

The fact that they could be "broken" and forced to cooperate with their captors against their will was quite unexpected by the men and a powerful source of intense and long-lasting feelings of depression and guilt. The psychological reactions to being forced to cooperate were by far the most difficult and emotionally painful liability of captivity. Communication—bringing the word to a "broken" PW that he was not alone, that everyone had been forced to cooperate, that his fellow PWs understood—provided a tremendous morale boost and helped to place the episode in proper perspective.

As time went on, the covert PW organization was able to issue guidelines as to what would be acceptable behavior under the circumstances. The basic dictum was to adhere to the Code of Conduct as much as possible, divulging only name, rank, serial number, and date of birth and to "take torture" rather than give out additional information. Torture was to be endured, however, only to the limit of "danger of permanent mental or physical damage," although even then information released was to be limited as much as possible in quantity and usefulness. After late 1969 conditions in North Vietnam improved greatly. Torture stopped except for serious violations of camp rules. The PWs were brought together in groups of 20 to 50 in a single camp, Unity, at the end of 1970. In January 1971 the Fourth Allied POW Wing was formally organized.[1]

In contrast to the enforced inactivity of the prisoners held in the north, PWs in the south were usually made an integral part of the camp work force. They helped to raise or catch food, acted as porters for supplies brought to camp, chopped and gathered firewood, and prepared most of their own meals. They also frequently helped build the camps and hootches. Under these circumstances prisoners mingled freely and communicated readily. In a few instances a PW was isolated in an individual cage, thus, resulting in total isolation from other PWs.

Attempts were also made to exploit the PWs in the south for propaganda purposes, but the efforts were far less frequent than in the north. Seemingly, much of the day to day activity in the south had to be devoted to surviving under generally harsh conditions. On the other hand, the military bureaucracy of North Vietnam, in addition to providing medical care, quarters, and better food for its PWs, was also under more constraints to account for its PWs and to keep them alive. PWs held in the south represented a considerable liability for their captor's sometimes meager supplies of food, limited manpower, and requirements for mobility. There was a lesser requirement in the south to account for PWs held, and PWs were shot escaping, if they could not keep up on the trail, and in retaliation for the execution of Viet Cong terrorists. These factors combined to produce a mortality rate of 20.7 percent among PWs held in the south, compared to only 4.8 percent among the PWs held in the north.[2]

Common Ailments in Captivity

The highest rate of trauma occurred at the time of capture, and represents injuries received when ejecting from a damaged plane, from

1. *The prisoners almost immediately established an informal covert resistance organization. When conditions improved, this organization was formalized into an actual military command structure, complete with commanding and executive officers, a chain of command, as well as policies and directives. It included all allied POWs, with the men being organized into several smaller squadrons, each with its own commanding officer. Additional prisoners were placed in staff positions in the command structure and assigned responsibilities such as, "Welfare and Morale", "Chaplain", and "Memory Bank".*

2. *Five hundred and three persons were held in the North; this number included 6 non-Americans and 12 men who were released prior to 1973. Out of these 503 individuals, 24 are officially reported as having died in captivity. One hundred and ninety-eight men were held in the South, including 29 who were released or escaped prior to 1973. Out of these 198 individuals, 41 are officially reported as having died in captivity.*

100

a firefight, or from the ire of the local populace. After settling down to a captivity existence, and after the injuries had healed in one fashion or another, the PWs faced a variety of illnesses and diseases. In the north these were mostly annoying and discomforting, but not usually life-threatening. Southern PWs, however, also had to endure repeated attacks of malaria which in some cases were fatal. No matter what the problem, the PWs tried to find ways to alleviate it. Diarrhea and dysentery were extremely common, particularly in the south. The PWs would eat banana peels in an attempt to stop the diarrhea, and soak their buttocks in water to reduce the skin irritation produced by the diarrhea. In some cases diarrhea seemed to be attributable to certain foods, particularly large quantities of pork fat or underbaked bread. All PWs assumed they had intestinal parasites, based on observations by the majority of men of worms in their stools. Some of the prisoners had had the distinctly unpleasant experience of pulling large ascaris worms out of their noses or mouths. The favored remedy for this problem was to chew and swallow tobacco. Gastric acidity was another common complaint.

The skin was perhaps the single organ most plagued by disease, especially in the south where hot, humid conditions promoted a variety of skin infections. (Allen, Taplin, Lowy & Twigg, 1972, noted that skin infections were the chief medical cause of combat non-effectiveness among infantrymen operating in the wet lowland terrain, accounting for more man-days lost from combat than all other medical causes combined.) The key challenge was to keep the skin clean and dry. PWs in the north would insert rag pads in their armpits to soak up sweat when exercising or, on hot days, to prevent chaffing, and rub pork fat on chapped lips. Vietnamese toothpaste or saltwater were used as antiseptics on wounds. Fungus infections in both the north and south were treated with iodine or mercurochrome, if available, and exposure to sunshine, if permitted. Fungus infections in the south were more frequent and more extensive, sometimes spreading over nearly the entire body. Cellulitis (bacterial skin infections) and boils were also prevalent in the south, but seemed to occur with particular viciousness in the north. Each summer many PWs would suffer large crops of extremely painful boils.

In the north exercise was considered a vital part of preventive medicine, and nearly all PWs had at least a minimal daily exercise program. Some PWs extended this to 100 or more pushups and and several hundred situps each day. Men who, prior to captivity had injuries requiring physical therapy, would recall those techniques and apply them to similar injuries suffered by their fellow prisoners.

Dental problems were also an extremely common affliction among the PWs, perhaps involving as many as half of the men. The most common problem was old fillings being broken by biting down on small bits of rock in the rice or bread. This often led to toothaches and painful abscesses persisting for so many months at a time that some PWs felt that they were the most difficult stress of all. So serious was the physical and psychological debilitation which could be produced by "bad teeth" that in the opinion of one PW no military man should go into combat without having his teeth in the best possible condition. A second common dental problem was periodontitis (pyorrhea), an inflammation of the gums. This condition was usually asymptomatic, except for minor transient bleeding of the gums occurring immediately after toothbrushing. It can eventuate in serious tooth loss if not treated. This bleeding was sometimes confused with the classic "bleeding gums" of scurvy. In actuality, however, scorbutic pathology is different, and true scurvy was rare among Vietnam PWs if it occurred at all. In the north the PWs were provided with tubes of toothpaste, which had to last several months, and toothbrushes, which usually broke after a short period of time.

Some serious illnesses occurred in captivity. Although only a few of the PWs had asthma, perhaps due to local allergens, when this occurred it was often severe enough to prompt the Vietnamese to initiate treatment with injections. One Army PW was thought to have had a heart attack in captivity, although this diagnosis was later changed to a pulmonary embolus. One Army and one Navy PW were each felt to have had cerebrovascular accidents (strokes) in captivity, both of whom recovered quite well.

PWs in the south suffered repeated attacks of malaria, which were sometimes fatal. Only the most desperate cases were treated, and then only with one or two doses of quinine. Repeated attacks gradually resulted in a form of immunity, manifested by progressively milder clinical episodes. Wet beri-beri, a vitamin deficiency disease, was sometimes seen in the south. Severe cases were usually treated with injections of vitamin B1 by the Viet Cong corpsman.

Medical care for PWs in the north improved after 1969. Routine immunization became more frequent, and medication as well as physicians became somewhat more available. Paramedics and paradentists visited the PWs much more frequently, sometimes every few weeks, and guards were now empowered to dispense simple medication such as aspirin at the request of a prisoner. The prisoners were allowed to receive packages from home which provided a shared source of vitamin tablets almost daily. The improved care, however, was sometimes a mixed blessing. In 1971 an epidemic of conjunctivitis (pink eye) broke out. The majority of PWs feel the epidemic was actually spread by contaminated antibiotic eye-drops administered to all the PWs in a prophylactic effort to prevent additional cases from developing. In 1970 and 1971 there were several minor epidemics of jaundice, presumably due to infectious hepatitis. In several cases the disease could be traced among a group of men, each of whom was immunized by the same dull, bent, non-sterile needle which had simply been boiled in water.

Residual Illness and Injuries

Whatever illnesses and injuries the PWs had suffered in captivity, the tally at the end of Operation Homecoming was a total of 1,528 formal diagnoses for the three services, Army, Navy, and Marine Corps. These represented medical problems requiring treatment or at least evaluation. Most were still active problems, but some, such as old well-healed fractures, were only noted historically. The list excludes a number of trivial self-limited problems, such as upset stomach due to overeating or minor head colds, which presumably had nothing to do with the PW experience, per se.

The average number of diagnoses per PW was 5.0 for the Navy, 5.6 for the Marines, and 8.9 for the Army. The matter has not been studied in detail, but the much greater number of diagnoses for the Army PWs probably can be explained on the basis of two factors: more of the Army PWs were held under the adverse conditions of the south, and Army medical records reflected some of the problems which were not enumerated by the other services.

The list of problems is a surprisingly variegated one, with numerous diagnoses listed only once or twice. In addition to dental problems, which bothered about half of the PWs, parasitosis is the only other prominent diagnosis, i.e., involving more than one-quarter of the men. On the average 76 percent of the PWs had at least one intestinal parasite.

Because of this variety, the following discussion will be limited to four categories: injuries, infectious and parasitic diseases, malnutrition, and psychiatric and adjustment problems.

Injuries. The majority of significant injuries, particularly ortho-pedic injuries and injuries with residuals occurred during the events surrounding capture. Aviators were sometimes injured when their plane was hit. Almost invariably they had to eject from their plane at high speed, frequently with both themselves and their plane in considerably less than optimal position for a safe ejection. These circumstances produced shrapnel wounds, lacerations, mild burns, fractured bones, spinal compression fractures, and dislocated joints. The orthopedic injuries were often severe ones producing open, comminuted fractures and severe dislocations. Several Army and Marine PWs were helicopter crewmen, who received similar orthopedic and burn injuries when their craft crashed. The local populace was sometimes another source of injury and one that was entirely unpredictable. Some fliers were treated kindly, even having wounds dressed. Others were beaten, shot at, or stabbed.

The most common fracture was compression fracture of the vertebrae involving 19 Navy, 9 Army and 2 Marine PWs. Compression fractures were a notorious side effect of the ejection procedure used to evacuate high performance aircraft, and the majority of these fractures sustained by fliers were obtained in this way (Ewing, 1966; Hirsch & Nachemson, 1961; Jones, Madden & Leudman, 1964; Shannon & Munson, 1973). Others were sustained during hard parachute landings or helicopter crash landings. In most cases compression fractures respond well to a few months bed rest, a condition obviously not present in captivity. Nevertheless, although some of the PWs suffered pain, nearly all of these injuries are now asymptomatic. The next most common fracture involved the humerus (11 Navy PWs), followed by fractured tibia and/or fibula (8 Navy and 1 Army PW). Fractures of the radius and/or ulna involved 5 Navy and 2 Army PWs, and fractures of the femur involved 2 Navy, 2 Army, and 1 Marine PW. In some cases these fractures have healed well, often in spite of quite limited treatment. Other fractures never healed, or healed in bad positions producing deformed limbs with limited usefulness. This was particularly true for fractures involving the joints.

Army and Marine infantrymen usually received their serious injuries in fire-fights prior to their capture. The gunshot and shrapnel wounds of these men occurred in nearly every part of the body and "scar" (21 percent) and "residual metallic foreign body in tissue or bone" (10 percent) are the ninth and eleventh most frequent diagnoses, respectively among Army PWs. An unfortunate characteristic of the ordnance, both crude and sophisticated, of the Vietnam war was its tendency to produce severe permanent neurological damage (Whelan, 1969). Reflecting this, three of the Army PWs incurred severe neurological residuals from their wounds.

A third source of injury was the physical maltreatment meted out in an attempt to force cooperation and enforce camp rules. In spite of the extensiveness of this maltreatment, the North Vietnamese and the Viet Cong were usually skillful enough to inflict great pain without causing permanent damage. Beatings included the use of fan belts and strips from tires, as well as clubs. PWs were also forced to undergo "self-punishment" for hours to days at a time by standing at attention, kneeling with arms raised straight upward over the head, sitting on a low wooden stool, or leaning against the wall balancing themselves with their hands. The favorite method used by the Vietnamese was "the ropes", which consisted of tightly binding the PWs with ropes or nylon straps into distorted and uncomfortable positions for as long as the PW could endure the pain — usually no longer than a few hours.

"The ropes" resulted in several types of injuries. Since the elbows were usually bound tightly together behind the back, dislocated shoulders were not infrequent. Rope burns and lacerations often became infected, producing festering sores, and, not infrequently, the entire arm or leg would become infected. Eventually the wound would heal, leaving a scar. As they became more sophisticated, the captors attempted to minimize this complication by allowing the PWs to wear clothing and binding ropes over their clothing. A third effect was prolonged nerve damage of the extremities which, in a few cases, was permanent. This, along with the resultant swelling, was sometimes sufficiently severe that the PW could not write, shave, or even feed himself for several weeks. In one group of Navy PWs, 13 percent still had some residual neuropathy of the extremities, in the form of a faint feeling of numbness, at the time of repatriation. However, 33 percent of this group had had paralyzed extremities at some time during captivity, and 80 percent had had peripheral neuropathy (numbness, feelings of pins and needles or burning); all were attributable to the rope treatment. Skin infection and sometimes nerve damage also resulted from the manacles and handcuffs used to restrain the PWs. This was particularly true for the ratchet or "torture cuffs" which could be tightened to a very small diameter.

Infectious and Parasitic Diseases. Table 1 indicates the frequency of the most prevalent of all PW medical problems, intestinal parasites. Over three-quarters of the men returned with at least one parasite, and many had several. The most prevalent worm, the ascaris, is about a foot long in its adult length and was frequently seen in PWs' stools. Hookworm infestation was quite low among Navy PWs, reflecting the largely indoor conditions in which these men were held. (The hookworm's favored mode of entry is through the skin; it is usually acquired by people walking barefoot on infected soil.) Hookworm can be a particularly serious infection under conditions of low food intake since a heavy infestation can absorb up to ten percent of the food consumed by its host. Whipworm infestation is often associated with rectal prolapse; however, only one percent of Navy and Marine PWs, and none of the Army PWs had this complication. Although 11 percent of the PWs had amoebic parasites, these were not causing amoebic dysentery at the time of repatriation, and no cases of amoebic liver abscess, usually a fatal complication, were seen. Pinworm, seen in 9 percent of the PWs, is characterized by an intense itching around the anus. This intestinal parasite, unlike the others, crops up from time to time even among otherwise hygenic middle-class American families; it is highly contagious and pesky to eradicate.

TABLE 1. *Incidence of Intestinal Parasites in Vietnam PWs**

Parasite	Percent of Repatriates			
	All Services	Navy	Army	Marines
Any parasite	76	74	74	88
Ascariasis	41	41	38	54
Ancylostomiasis (hook worm)	18	6	34	35
Trichuriasis (whip worm)	38	42	27	50
Enterobiasis (pin worm)	9	7	6	27
Amebiasis	11	12	10	8
Giardiasis	1	1	3	0

*Repatriates: Navy = 138, Army = 77, Marines = 26; Total = 241

Navy, Army: One each strongyloidiasis
One clonorchis sinensis

The PWs were very concerned about their worm infestations, both in terms of implications for their future health and the possibility that they might spread the parasites to their families. Fortunately, the men could be reassured on both counts. Millions of people around the world have a chronic worm infestation, usually without adding any great burden to their system. Intestinal parasites can, however, exacerbate serious underlying illnesses or states of malnutrition. All of the men with evidence of infestation were treated at Operation Homecoming and, for most, treatment was successful. A very few cases of amoebiasis and ascariasis have persisted and were evidenced at the follow-up examination a year later. Several men still have asymptomatic whipworm infestations, primarily due to the fact that no drugs licensed in this country are really effective for this worm. Fortunately, after a few years the infestation dies out.

Table 2 shows the incidence of malaria among Vietnam PWs. On a world wide basis, until recently this disease was responsible for more deaths per year than any other transmissible disease (Young, 1966). Reflecting the fact that malaria is considered endemic only in South Vietnam, Cambodia, and Laos, no Navy PWs had malaria. However, at least a few Navy PWs had elevated malaria antibody titres, possibly indicating that the disease does exist in North Vietnam. The majority of infections in Army and Marine PWs are due to unknown species of the malaria organism, and represent historical diagnoses based on the PW having been told, usually not by a doctor, that a febrile illness he had had at some time was malaria. The degree to which the description of these illnesses matched the classical pattern of malaria attack varied considerably; therefore, some doubt must be expressed as to the accuracy of these diagnoses. Nevertheless, a high incidence of malaria among PWs held in the south was expected.

TABLE 2. *Incidence of Malaria in Vietnam PWs*

Species	Army	Marines
Unknown	29	11
P. vivax	8	1
P. falciparum	3	0
Mixed	8	0
Totals	48	12
Percent of total repatriates by service	62%	46%

Nineteen Army and one Marine PW had clinical evidence of malarial infestation at Operation Homecoming and several Army PWs showed the classic symptomatology of the disease. At one Army hospital, half of the nine PWs treated for the disease subsequently developed recurrences of it; in one case, nearly a year later. This probably represents not a highly resistant parasite, but rather an intestinal malabsorption syndrome on the part of the PW. The latter would sufficiently inhibit absorption of medication to prevent

107

adequate blood levels of the drug. In accordance with standard military medical practice, all PWs without clinical evidence of malaria were nevertheless given prophylactic antimalarial medication because they had served in an endemic area.

A variety of mild respiratory infections occurred in 14 percent of the Navy and Marine PWs and 20 percent of Army PWs. These were due to several factors: a flu epidemic was present in Hanoi just prior to repatriation, resistance to American viruses was relatively lower, and cigarette consumption increased dramatically within a few weeks after repatriation, from six a day to one or two packs a day in many cases. Unlike World War II and Korean War PWs, active tuberculosis was not seen in any of the Vietnam PWs. This is fortunate because tuberculosis was a leading cause of death in the former groups in the first few years after repatriation. However, six Army and two Marine PWs did have positive tuberculosis skin tests at repatriation, presumably indicating exposure to the disease during captivity.

Malnutrition. Historically, malnutrition in the form of protein-calorie and vitamin deficiency has been one of the greatest scourges of a PW's lot (Anderson, Boysen, Esenten, Lam & Shadish, 1954; Biderman, 1963; Jacobs, 1970; Kantor, 1955; Nardini, 1962; Reed, 1947; Todd, 1946; Walker, 1944). The nutritional status of the Vietnam PWs is still under intensive study at the Letterman Army Institute of Research, Department of Nutrition, which is analyzing detailed dietary histories obtained by registered dietitians from each of these men. Eventually each of the several different captivity diets will be compared to recommended minimum daily nutritional requirements.

Preliminary findings indicate that malnutrition was not common in the north but did occur to some degree in the south. Medical textbooks list numerous signs of vitamin deficiency, but many of these, for example cheilosis or dry, chapped lips, are non-specific and have many possible causes. Others, such as night-blindness, have an element of subjectivity to them. Mere weight loss, even 20 to 40 pounds, does not necessarily indicate malnutrition. Many PWs, particularly the fliers, were well above their ideal weight at the time of capture. On the reduced rations of captivity, they fell to their ideal weight and remained at that level unless serious illness or injury intervened to produce further weight loss. Moreover, the PWs in the north were, for the most part, physically inactive which further reduces both caloric and vitamin needs. (Even PWs who did large numbers of sit-ups or push-ups did not increase their caloric needs since only exercise which moves the entire body requires large amounts of energy.)

Table 3 gives the incidence of vitamin deficiency in Army PWs, the group which endured the worst nutritional status. Beri-beri is a disease due to vitamin B_1 deficiency, which can take either of two forms: wet beri-beri or dry beri-beri. Wet beri-beri, a form of congestive heart failure, begins with swelling and fluid accumulation, or edema, in the feet and ankles. If not treated, the swelling gradually spreads up the legs eventually involving the whole body, with fluid accumulating in the lungs. In advanced stages the disease can rapidly be fatal, but adequate treatment with B_1 completely reverses the process. There is evidence, however, that prolonged deficiency can permanently damage the heart (Benchimal & Schlesinger, 1953; Smith & Furth, 1943; Wenger, 1974). Dry beri-beri is a type of neuritis, most commonly of the lower legs, and takes the form of paresthesias or feelings of numbness, burning, tingling, or pins and needles. It can be quite painful. If the deficiency persists, eventually muscle weakness develops, characteristically taking the form of experiencing difficulty when rising from a squatting position. Dry beri-beri is also much more likely to become a permanent problem. Both types were well known to Americans held by the Japanese (Jacobs, 1970; Nardini, 1962; Todd, 1946); dry beri-beri went by the name of "happy feet" or "burning feet" (Cruickshank, 1946; Glusman, 1947; Lewis, 1950). Many of these World War II PWs now maintain that they are having a high incidence of heart attacks directly attributable to having had beri-beri as a PW (G. Anloff, personal communication, 1972). The evidence is anecdotal but somewhat impressive and worthy of further study.

TABLE 3. *Incidence of Vitamin Deficiency in Army PWs*
(Number of Repatriates = 77)

Diagnosis	Number of men	Percent of Repatriates
Wet and Dry Beriberi	12	16
Dry Beriberi only	11	14
Wet Beriberi only	6	8
Nutritional Amblyopia	13	17
Vitamin A Deficiency	5	6

The problem with diagnosing these potentially serious diseases among the Vietnam PWs is that the diagnosis has to be made on the basis of historical evidence remembered by the PW and interpreted by his Homecoming physician. Unfortunately, the most common symptoms usually considered indicative of beri-beri—swollen extremities and peripheral paresthesias—can have other causes and different prognoses. Simple protein deficiency can produce a similar swelling, which then goes by the term "hunger edema" or "famine edema". Both the swelling and the paresthesias can be, and often were, produced by "the ropes" or manacles used to bind the PWs. Although at least some episodes of true beri-beri undoubtedly occurred, it is difficult in retrospect to make the diagnosis with certainty.

Nutritional amblyopia is a visual defect characterized by fuzziness or blurring of vision usually starting in the center of the visual field and spreading outward. The permanent visual defects, which may be produced, are generally accepted as objective evidence of nutritional deficiency. Only 17 percent of the Army PWs have this diagnosis, but the visual changes seem permanent; one Army PW is almost blind. Night blindness is the classic symptom of vitamin A deficiency, again usually a subjective and retrospective diagnosis.

There is no good evidence of scurvy occurring among any of the PWs. Although many of them had "bleeding gums", a classic sign of vitamin C deficiency, this seems to have been due to periodontitis rather than scurvy.

Psychiatric and Adjustment Problems. Historically, the greatest morbidity and mortality among ex-PWs reflects a high incidence of psychiatric problems. Cohen & Cooper, in their V.A. study in 1954, found an incidence of accident, homicide, and suicide among the PWs half again as great as in a group of control subjects. From the European literature (Eitinger, 1964; Eitinger & Strom, 1972; Strom, 1968) has come the term "KZ Syndrome" describing a persistent, incapacitating complex of nervousness, insomnia, irritability, depression, difficulty concentrating, defects in short-term memory, increased startle reaction, social isolation, difficulty finding and holding a job, and a feeling of chronic ill health, which is seen in survivors of Nazi concentration camps. Beebe (in preparation), in a 20 year follow-up study of World War II PWs, found the rate of psychiatric problems to be 11 times greater among the PWs than in a control group and attributed it to a permanent loss of ego strength.

Psychiatric exams were an integral part of the medical follow-up evaluation given the Vietnam PWs. Table 4 gives the formal psychiatric diagnoses found among this group. Most of these were neuroses. Therefore, the prognoses were felt to be good. Five PWs, all enlisted men, were diagnosed as schizophrenic, however. In each of these cases there was evidence of some pre-captive morbidity. It should be noted that Table 4 represents only those cases in which the pathology was sufficiently overt to warrant the psychiatrist making use of a formal diagnostic label.

TABLE 4. *Formal Psychiatric Diagnoses at Homecoming*

Diagnosis	Number of Repatriates*			
	All Services	Navy	Army	Marines
Situational Anxiety	10	3	6	1
Depression	6	1	4	1
Schizophrenia	5	0	3	2
Other	7	3**	4***	0

*   *Repatriates: Navy = 138, Army = 77, Marines = 26; Total = 241*

**   *3 = Alcoholism*

*** *1 = Psychosis*
       1 = Sociopathic personality
       1 = Dissociative reaction
       1 = Alcoholism

All the POWs, however, went through an adjustment process at repatriation. In the typical pattern, during the first few days the men were hyperactive; they were excited, euphoric, and voluble. They slept little, and bounced rapidly from topic to topic and activity to activity. Then there followed a few days of relatively subdued activity. This period quickly merged into a period where the men were all desirous of return to active duty as soon as possible; impatience was the order of the day—the medical evaluation, catching up with the family, and all other business had to be finished quickly in order to free the ex-PW for the desired immediate assignment. Finally, after realizing he did not have to "prove himself", the PW settled down to appreciate his mandatory prolonged convalescence.

Another aspect of the psychiatric evaluation, the role taken by psychiatrists, goes beyond the subject matter of this paper but is discussed in greater depth in a paper by Dr. R. E. Strange (see Consultant's Viewpoints).

Table 5 outlines the personal readjustment problems experienced by the PWs. Depression, anxiety, and hyperactivity were emotional states noted during the psychiatric examinations but these were not of sufficient intensity to warrant a formal diagnosis. A major concern of nearly all the men was their future career. Most were resolved to stay in the military, but worried about their ability to catch up with technological advances and were concerned about their opportunities for obtaining a challenging, stimulating assignment in which they could prove their abilities and maximize their changes for advancement. They expressed fear that they would become charity cases, carried along in dull, unimportant billets. These fears took on added significance with the realization that their very repatriation symbolized the end of the war and, therefore, a reduction in opportunity for military advancement. Adjustment to permanent injuries was a problem for ten of the PWs; and for aviators, there was the fear that injuries might prevent a return to flying status.

TABLE 5. *RPW Readjustment Problems – Personal**

Problem	All Services	Number of Repatriates		
		Navy	Army	Marines
Career	23	16	4	3
Depression	22	11	5	6
Anxiety	18	13	4	1
Adjustment to injury	10	7	2	1
Hyperactivity	6	5	1	0

*As noted by psychiatrist
Number of repatriates: Navy = 138, Army = 77, Marines = 26; Total = 241

Considerations for the Future. In many respects the medical experiences of captivity have presented some fascinating problems. Numerous abnormal laboratory findings appeared during Homecoming, only to disappear in a few weeks. Liver enzymes such as SGOT and SGPT were mildly, transiently elevated in many PWs. This type of finding is compatible with liver damage, such as might occur in a mild case of hepatitis. Probably the most likely explanation is that this abnormality represented a period of adjustment to increased alcohol in the diet after years of almost complete involuntary abstention. The kidneys showed a similar phenomenon with a mild, transient elevation of the BUN (blood urea nitrogen), a measurement of nitrogen waste products in the blood. This probably represented an adjustment to increased daily protein in the PW's diet. Similarly, the pancreas demonstrated an abnormality of carbohydrate metabolism for a few weeks. A number of the men had glucose tolerance tests which, under other circumstances, might have classified them as mild diabetics, but this disappeared when the pancreas adjusted to more carbohydrates in the diet. Thus, these transient abnormalities probably represented nothing more than an adjustment to an American diet. However, similar changes (except for the liver) also occur in older men, and, therefore, these changes may be indicators of decreased ability to handle metabolic stresses and maintain homeostasis.

Another abnormality appeared in the X-rays of some PWs. Their bones showed thinning or demineralization, another change characteristic of old age as well as decreased calcium intake. In a few PWs this was marked. Repeat X-rays, several months later, showed that the bones of most of these men had returned to normal. A very few, however, remained demineralized, thereby raising the possibility of an alteration in bone metabolism beyond that merely due to dietary calcium deficiency. To date the significance of these changes is not known. Although the bones look weak, there is no evidence that this is actually so. A speculative concern is that this demineralization might appear again as the PWs get older, but perhaps at a younger age than a similar group of non-PWs.

Another intriguing finding was the fact that a majority of the PWs appeared to be five to ten years older than their chronological age would suggest. This may be simply a superficial phenomenon, but it may also be a manifestation of deeper, more fundamental physiological changes. It seems obvious that the captivity experience has greatly stressed these men, yet, in most cases, extensive laboratory tests, X-rays, and physical examinations are within normal limits. In other words, it is difficult, if not impossible, to measure aging with present examination techniques although some procedures, such as measurement of subtle cellular deficiencies, have been proposed. If, in fact, these men have aged at an accelerated rate, will the process continue? Unfortunately too little is known about the aging process to make any reliable predictions, and treatment will probably have to be limited to such preventive measures as weight, blood pressure, and lipid control, and adhering to sound health practices such as the elimination of smoking.

Coronary atherosclerotic heart disease is considered the leading medical cause of death in the western world (DiGirolamo & Schlant, 1974). Interestingly enough, from that perspective, the captivity experience had some good points: the PWs were on a diet low in cholesterol, saturated fats, and carbohydrates, they came down to their ideal weight and did at least some exercising every day, and cigarette consumption among smokers was reduced to a few per day. All these represent reduction of several risk factors associated with coronary heart disease (DiGirolamo & Schlant, 1974). Perhaps these few years in captivity will make a small positive contribution to these

PWs' cardiovascular health. In the same vein, it was noted by dental officers that PWs who had no periodontitis at the time of capture did not seem to develop it in captivity. This disease is also related to a high carbohydrate diet, which promotes plaque formation at the gumline. Overall dental health may also have benefitted slightly as a result of the captivity experience, since periodontitis is the leading cause (20 million people) of complete loss of teeth in the American population (Glickman, 1971).

The suicide of two Vietnam PWs, and the death in an auto accident of a third, immediately calls up unsettling memories of the Cohen & Cooper (1954) study showing high mortality rates in the first two years after World War II and the Korean Conflict. Unfortunately, the small number of Vietnam PWs makes it impossible to determine if these deaths are the beginning of a trend or merely isolated events. Preliminary results from a one-year follow-up study of Navy PWs indicates psychiatric problems overall are running somewhat lower than what would have been predicted on the basis of evaluations made at the time of repatriation.

Another factor which makes predictions difficult is the dissimilarity between American PWs from Vietnam and those from former wars. A majority of the Vietnam returnees—three quarters—are officers, and most of these are fliers. They are older, better educated, and more mature, and they were originally selected for flying because of their physical and mental fitness, stability, and adaptability. All of these factors are assets for surviving as a PW (Nardini, 1962) and should also aid these men in shedding the deleterious effects of the stressful captivity experience in the years which lie ahead.

Conclusion

In general, the returned PWs from Vietnam were in fairly good health at the time of their release from captivity. From the beginning, they have fared better than any previous PWs with respect to post-captivity medical care. All were immediately placed on the hospital sick list for a minimum of 90 days and given comprehensive and extensive medical evaluations. So far as is known, few physical or psychiatric problems went undetected, untreated, or undocumented. The Assistant Secretary of Defense for Health and Environment has mandated that all Vietnam PWs be offered complete medical care by the military services for a period of five years. To maximize the benefits of this, the services are conducting extensive annual follow-up exams using a detailed protocol patterned on that used in Operation Homecoming. The information from all these examinations is being compiled and studied to uncover any evidences of pathology and to provide feedback for the further improvement of care. Unlike the unfortunate post-captivity medical experience of PWs from former wars, everything possible is being done for the Vietnam POWs to insure that no problem will go undetected and no treatable problem will go uncorrected. This is being done even though there is evidence that this particular group of PWs may fare somewhat better, as regards to future physical and mental health, than did former PWs. At this point, however, it is a matter of watching and waiting, hopefully in vain.

9

Dilemmas And Conflicts Specific To The Military Returned Prisoner Of War

WILLIAM N. MILLER

Introduction

Evaluating the residuals of imprisonment is a difficult task. This paper represents a compilation of findings, both factual and intuitive, growing out of ten years of personal experience studying the wide variety of physical and psychological stresses to which Americans are subjected in foreign prisons. Intensive interviewing of returned prisoners of war and detailed analyses of debriefing data were conducted in order to develop an in-depth understanding of the prison experience. After personal interviews with large numbers of prisoners, both military and civilian, as well as a study of reports of the experiences of many others, it became apparent that the military prisoners faced pressures very different from their civilian counterparts. A recent study of the experiences of the Navy prisoners of war from Indochina confirmed these impressions of the past decade.

The military man, unlike the civilian, receives training with respect to his responsibilities as a prisoner. This training may vary from a cursory reading of the Code of Conduct to hours or even days of lectures, combined with simulated prison situations. All military prisoners are aware that their behavior will be closely scrutinized, that their actions while in captivity will affect their future careers, and that they could be subjected to military discipline upon release. The impact of this knowledge is profound and may result in a number of related dilemmas and conflicts.

The purpose of this paper is to discuss several areas of conflict which are unique to the military prisoner of war. These dilemmas range from situations in which the enemy's behavior did not fit a pattern that the prisoner was led to expect, to the problems faced by senior ranking officers with implicit command responsibilities. Such a discussion will perhaps be of particular use to personnel seeking a deeper understanding of the returned prisoner of war (RPW) and his problems.

The Dilemmas of the Military Prisoner of War

Consequences of "un-heroic" actions immediately prior to capture. Prominent among the many emotions which a man experiences at the time of capture is the anger he feels for having gotten himself into the situation in the first place. He immediately curses himself for those actions which might have been avoided, but which in actuality were those responsible for his having been captured. In addition to the usual second-guessing, he may have to face the fact that immediately prior to capture he was perhaps performing in a manner not consistent with the heroic military image. Despondency over capture in this case is apt to be unusually severe and, therefore, such individuals begin their prison careers with a significant handicap. Since they begin their confinement with a sense of guilt with which they must deal, it becomes extremely difficult for them to face the enemy with strength and confidence. Such a situation will not only affect the posture and attitude with which such men face the enemy, but will likely cause them to distort the true story regarding both capture and captivity upon return.

Capture directly or indirectly attributable to another's action or error. In order to understand another conflict some prisoners may have to face at the outset, it is necessary to consider the state of mind of the individual who finds himself a victim through no fault of his own. A prisoner would be acutely aware of where to point the blame if he were captured because of faulty equipment, an erroneous mission brief, or abandonment by his unit. How would he handle this? Would he pass it off as just bad luck or the fortunes of war, or would he brood and harbor a growing resentment or hostility towards all those whom he felt were responsible for his being in this predicament?

The psychological impact of a significant variation between enemy behavior and the prisoner's preconceptions. In the whirling fear, despondency, and hopelessness of the early hours and days of capture, the prisoner usually expects the worst. His mind fills with fleeting remembrances of comments from buddies, statements of briefing officers, bits and pieces from his survival training, scenes from old movies, and horror stories passed on through training films and briefing documents. He desperately seeks some kind of security, and searches to find behavior, actions, or situations that he can predict or that fit patterns he had been led to expect from past guidance.

If at this point he is, in fact, treated as he was led to believe he might be, and his captors appear and behave as he had expected, he is likely to maintain full faith in the system responsible for preparing him for this situation. If, on the other hand, the captors' behavior differs from his images, particularly if he has been led to believe that the enemy is always insidious and inhumane, he will have some very strong props pulled out from under him. If, for example, the captor risks his own life to shelter the prisoner from artillery or aircraft fire, or transports the captive to a hospital area with high risk to himself, or ministers immediately to his captive's wounds, or shares his food equally, or gives his last water to him, the prisoner may find himself in a severe quandary. His expectations are not congruent with his experiences. No matter how hard he may try to convince himself that this is a trick, he often becomes more impressed by the similarity between what he is observing and "normal" behavior. Even the smallest demonstration of compassion by a captor or by a member of the local populace can have a shattering effect on preconceptions. In this, one of the most insecure of all situations, the prisoner desperately seeks security and the "truth"; he finds he is considerably more impressed by what he is observing than by what he has been told. On the other hand, it is also possible for the prisoner to be treated far worse than he had been led to expect, and in that case doubts would also arise as to the adequacy of his prior training.

There is no need to expand greatly on the implications of this kind of situation — they are obvious. The man feels uninformed at best and misled at worst. In the apathetic, hopelessly depressed state which often follows capture, it is very easy for this disparity between what the prisoner has seen and the treatment he had been led to expect to cause him to doubt the totality of his prior beliefs. He may feel "used" and sense a growing hostility towards his military service, his government, or perhaps towards specific individuals associated with training or briefing programs.

This kind of reaction by no means happens to everybody. A number of prisoners retain an attitude of unremitting hatred for their captor that no amount of compassion on the part of the captor can change. Men who believe this strongly may feel themselves so genuinely and consistently mistreated that everything negative they have heard about their captors tends to be confirmed.

Probably the most severe psychological dilemmas beset those men who, while in prison, come to view the captor as essentially "human"; i.e., as an individual carrying out the difficult job of caring and feeding for foreign prisoners generally disliked by the population, and trying by his standards to follow orders and do his job. The prisoner who develops this attitude toward his captor finds himself upon his return, greatly at odds with the established stereotypes of the enemy. If he vocalizes these feelings, he may risk branding himself as a weak individual who has been brainwashed. The chances are very good that he may find himself at odds with his debriefers, his superiors, and even his friends and colleagues. Thus, he may find it easier to distort or invent a story of brutality and mistreatment to conform to popular images. How the man resolves this disparity is an individual matter, but the potential for conflict is great.

Conflict resulting from "persuasive" enemy statements. There are few things as calculated to instill puzzlement and a lack of confidence in the military prisoner's own values as finding the enemy talking "reasonably". This is particularly hard on the soldier who has been led to believe that all enemy statements are untruths or fabrications. It is obviously difficult for a military man plagued with this problem to admit that he found himself agreeing with enemy statements and now actually needs help in proving to himself that such statements were false. Here, then, is another area with potential for long-term problems.

Inability to follow orders. Perhaps the most common cause for guilt while in prison is the captive's realization that he could not live up to what he considered (correctly or not) to be a mandatory demand upon him to divulge to the enemy no more than Name, Rank, Serial Number and Date of Birth. This paper is no place for a lengthy discussion of this topic, but one should realize that guilt feelings can result from this problem. The more the individual believed that it was his unfailing duty to hew to this line, and the more he was impressed with the punishment which would result if he failed in this respect, the more traumatic the depression and guilt can be for his almost inevitable failure.

Some men were fortunate in having the opportunity to communicate with other prisoners who were able to boost their morale by giving them added assurance in the knowledge that all were in the same boat. Others, however, were deprived of this reassurance and became so debilitated and depressed by their inability to hold to the letter of their guidance, as they saw it, that upon capitulation — alone and in the throes of depression — they found all of their resistance sapped, and ended up complying with demands to an extent which they later found inexcusable. Such guilt was difficult, if not impossible, for some to assuage. Not only did many men spend the bulk of their imprisonment flagellating themselves for their behavior throughout their captivity, but many have continued to do so long after imprisonment.

Reactions of the prisoner of war, of course, run the entire gamut of human defense mechanisms. Many became 'super heroes' in camp to atone for having been broken initially, urging fellow prisoners to great heights of resistance with an evangelical desire to prevent them from doing the same thing. Others built up feelings of hostility toward those who put them in the situation and completely denied they had ever engaged in such behavior.

The dilemma of the senior man. Senior ranking men (SROs) are faced with particularly thorny dilemmas that may result in residual psychological problems. If they have been trained to take command of all those junior to them, they face some unique and trying situations in prison; not all SROs will handle the ensuing problems in the same manner. Outside of prison one has options; he can choose not to take command if he believes he is a better administrator, engineer, or flier, than he is a leader. In other words, under ordinary circumstances, men are able to avoid leadership assignments or remove themselves from such positions as expeditiously as possible; they may even choose to resign from the service. This is not true for the prison experience.

Among the many unique problems of leadership in the prison situation are those caused by the inability to transmit complete orders, the inability to know with certainty how subordinates are behaving, and the inability to know with certainty to what degree subordinates are physically and psychologically debilitated. If, while in prison, the senior ranking officer for some reason feels he should not exercise command, he runs a high risk of being branded a shirker. This can occur even in circumstances where he might feel that assuming command could hurt morale rather than help it. Considerably more painful, however, is the constant feeling of helplessness and rage the SRO may experience. He may believe it is his duty to alter the captors' treatment of his men, but his actual ability to do so is minimal. There have been instances where junior men have misinterpreted resistance instructions from their seniors and suffered permanent damage or death. The senior ranking officer suffers right along with each man; the more rigid, demanding and resistive he becomes over the years, the greater is his risk of retaliation for all. Yet, the more passive and non-harrassing he becomes, the more he appears to be failing in his leadership role. Rank may be sought after in the normal military career, but, in prison, it can have severe disadvantages.

Disagreement with orders from senior ranking prisoners. Although this represents a controversial area, it is one that must be understood. Not all captivity situations allow for an organized chain of command; a formal organization is not always found, even in situations where it is theoretically possible. There are several reasons for this. First, it is unlikely that all men in the same prison would have received prior training emphasizing the importance of the chain of command while in captivity. If, in addition, there is no common identity among the men, by branch of service or occupation (i.e., all combat soldiers or all fliers), it is not easy for a senior man's authority to be recognized, no matter what his rank. Combat experience of any kind makes men cautious about automatically accepting orders from those not connected with his particular combat skill or responsibility. Furthermore, if the men are separated in individual foxholes or hootches so that only occasional visual contact is possible with fellow prisoners, as was the case in South Vietnam, a leadership hierarchy is even less likely to arise.

If, on the other hand, all prisoners in the group have received training which puts emphasis on maintaining a chain of command in those situations where some degree of communication is possible, one could assume that prisoners would be receiving specific guidance from the senior men with respect to acceptable degrees of resistance behavior. In some cases, this guidance is excellent and attuned to the realities of the situation, but differences of opinion as to appropriate guidance and behavior are bound to exist.

It is obvious that men go into prison with varying ideas as to what is reasonable behavior in the face of the captor. Individual differences alone will breed differences of opinion. Outside of prison, a man who disagrees with a superior officer has some alternatives; if he feels justified in his stand, he can appeal to higher authority, ask for a transfer or resign his commission. However, none of these options is open to the prisoner. Some of the greatest conflicts have arisen when orders emanated from the prisoner senior in rank, but not senior in prison experience. Imagine the plight of the long-term prisoner in the following example:

> *He has been a prisoner for two years. He started out trying to hold to Name, Rank, Serial Number, and Date of Birth, but found he could not. He feels that over the*

*months and years he has finally made an accommodation
which allows him peace of mind. He has complied with
some demands of the captors, and, yet, he has learned to
avoid behavior which he feels would be damaging to his
country or to other prisoners. Upon the arrival of a new
prisoner who is senior, however, he receives instructions
to cease some activity which he himself is convinced is not
only harmless but necessary to keep his captors from
applying even greater pressure.*

*He is now faced with a severe dilemma. He must either
irritate his captors by a sudden change of behavior or dis-
obey his senior officer. The first choice may bring an unpleasant reaction from the captor; the second alternative
may result in disciplinary action upon release. The problem
is compounded if he is in marginal physical condition and
convinced that following the senior man's orders could in-
vite punishment or duress which might further debilitate
him. How he handles this is going to be extremely important for his long-term mental health. Should this prisoner
decide that he will not obey the orders of his superior, he
must fully recognize the consequences within the military
setting. No matter how well he can justify it, he is well
aware of the fact that he has pitted himself against military
tradition. In the loneliness and paranoid-prone prison existence, he has no reason to believe that he can even muster a
good defense for his action. He has no way to appeal and
no way to escape. Thus, it is not difficult to imagine that a
man can begin to feel embittered toward the system that
allowed him to be faced with this type of dilemma.*

The necessity to protect a military career. For civilians, there is no
implication that their performance in a foreign prison will be related
to the furtherance of their careers. For the military man, however,
this relationship is implicit and can lead to profound psychological
implications. Many who have engaged in intensive interviews with
returned prisoners of war are convinced that, for some prisoners, the
complete and candid revelation of all their thoughts, fears, and actions in prison are necessary for good psychological catharsis and
rehabilitation. A number of men have a strong desire to "tell it like it
was". At the same time, the career military men are aware of what
they must project in order to earn a reputation of having maintained
a posture of maximum resistance and strength in the prison situation.

It will take an exceptional career man to divulge behavior at variance with this model.

The result of this dilemma is that many men are considerably less than candid, deny certain behaviors, omit others, and generally, paint their experiences in the best possible light. Whether they can live comfortably with this deception for the rest of their lives is an individual matter. A related area of bitterness may occur if the prisoner divulges behavior which tarnishes his reputation, and then watches others, known to have behaved no differently, earn heroes' reputations.

Increase in self-criticism as prison reality fades and traditional military concepts are reinforced. It is impossible for one who has not undergone a prison experience to understand completely the debilitating effects of being totally removed from guidance or support. On top of this, few men have experienced the psychological effects of malnutrition, dehydration and prolonged diarrhea that often accompany the prison situation in an emerging nation. Of particular interest, however, is the fact that after repatriation it is often impossible for the prisoners to resurrect the level of debilitation which they had reached. They sometimes find it difficult in retrospect to understand their own behavior under those circumstances.

Even while still in prison, after having learned to handle both the environment and their captors to some degree, many prisoners tend to flagellate themselves for earlier behavior. Self-flagellation and feelings of guilt are frequent and become worse as time passes. This, then, represents still another area that some returnees find difficult to handle and, over a long time period, may lead to serious problems.

Feeling that the experience was meaningless. It is important, for many reasons, that a man feel that the years spent in prison were not wasted. Prisoners will often spend thousands of hours contemplating what they have done with their lives and what they intend to do with them if they are lucky enough to survive their imprisonment. This kind of contemplation often results in very positive philosophical changes in a man's attitude, value system, and philosophy of life. The value of remaining years increases with each one lost. It is not uncommon for military men to realize that one of the most direct contributions they can make will be to insure that any possible deficiencies in their own preparation for the prison experience not be repeated for the next prisoner of war. Even those returned prisoners who shun public-speaking engagements, conferences, and conventions are often more than willing to talk with people involved in training programs.

Dilemmas and Conflicts Specific to the Military Returned
Prisoner of War

If the returnees feel that others are benefiting from their experience, they are indeed fortunate. If, however, events give them the impression that their advice was not listened to, or that the Services are not doing their utmost to update training programs, they may feel robbed of the one possible value of all their wasted years and, thus, become subject to a growing bitterness.

Conclusion

A number of areas of conflict arising from the prisoner of war experience which present unique dilemmas for the military prisoner of war, but not for the civilian are set forth in this paper. Since the manner in which the military man approaches and copes with these dilemmas determines to some extent the level of his psychological adjustment following release, it seems important for personnel dealing with the military returnee to understand what significance these dilemmas may have for the future.

10

Psychiatric Residuals of Prolonged Captivity Experience

RICHARD C.W. HALL

PATRICK T. MALONE

Introduction

Since the release and repatriation of American PWs from Indochina, various attitudes have prevailed among those charged with the responsibility of aiding these men and their families. Attitudes of optimism and pessimism have been evident among various segments of the planning community. Central questions have been: can those responsible for the re-entry program realistically make assumptions that are useful in promoting the successful readaption of the returned PWs, or is such intervention necessary? One concept is that maladaptation is an individual phenomenon predominately based on premorbid personality factors and directly related to specific individual stresses. This model suggests no framework for the correction of difficulties other than traditional psychotherapy, and further assumes that planned intervention is inefficient until symptoms appear. The alternate position asserts that the captivity experience itself initiates predictable reactions which can be treated prior to the onset of disabling psychiatric symptoms.

Our clinical impression of a small sample of PWs suggests that the stresses of prolonged captivity are specific and should be treated before symptoms appear. Our position is that, although captivity stresses are specific, they are not unique and consequently that information previously obtained about man's reactivity to stress can be applied (Archibald et al, 1962; Asch, 1951; Berle, 1957; Biderman, 1957, 1960; Chodoff, 1963; Engel, 1962; Farber et al, 1957;

Friedman, 1949; Grinker & Spiegel, 1945; Group for the Advancement of Psychiatry Symposium, #3, 1956; Hinkle & Wolfe, 1956; Kardiner, 1959; Kinkead, 1959; Klein et. al, 1963, Kral, 1951; Lifton 1956; Meerloo, 1956, Miller, 1957; Santucci & Winokur, 1955, Schein, 1956; Schein et al, 1961; Segal, 1954; Solomon & Wynne, 1954; Tas, 1951; West, 1957, 1964).

The purpose of this paper is to present data obtained from individual interviews with returned PWs and their families in relation to the gross stress model of behavior. We hope this will provide a useful framework to facilitate their re-entry, reintegration, and treatment. The model is neither new nor original to us; it relies heavily upon the work of Weiss and Payson (1967). The contribution we hope to make is to relate specific data to its principles, and to elucidate behavior patterns which may herald incipient decompensation or interfere with successful readaptation. The reader should note that the data is clinical and based on a sample of six PW families. Therapy with these men was unorthodox and initiated at the wives' insistence.

The Gross Stress Model

Gross stress reactions are defined as emotional changes secondary to forces perceived as threatening to the individual or group. They represent attempts to defend or restitute the personality or group from disorganization.

The breakdown of adaptive capacity during stress is most likely to occur when performance of a task essential to an individual's integrity is in conflict with other of his vital needs. For example, a soldier under fire may act to save himself by taking cover while the rest of his unit advances. Such action prevents him from being injured, but places him outside his peer group. Subsequent group rejection and guilt may produce psychiatric symptoms.

Each man's reaction to stress is dependent upon his age, personality, physiologic integrity, nutritional state, degree of physical and mental preparation, exposure to similar situations, and the expectations of his peer group governing his performance. Fatigue, ambiguity of role, unreasonable expectations of others' performance, infections, injury, social isolation and inability to plan a method of response are known to predispose to untoward stress reactions.

Stress reactions consist of four overlapping phases: the anticipatory or threat phase, the impact phase, the recoil phase, and the post-traumatic phase.

The anticipatory phase is characterized by future orientation and contingency planning. It is aided by the illusion of invulnerability. Mental work is confined to action oriented successful future models. The carrier pilot, for example, may plan a series of actions, should his plane ditch on take-off, such as blowing the hatch, inflating the life raft, and waiting for pick-up. He is unlikely to plan for being trapped in the aircraft or for shark attack. Denial during the anticipatory phase minimizes the impact of future stress; for example, the combat soldier fully realizes men will be killed in action, but maintains the outlook that death occurs only to others.

Excessive awareness of danger may turn the anticipatory phase into a prolonged impact phase contributing to progressive disorganization and maladaptation. Futile worry, fear of isolation, and anticipatory panic all tend to increase the individual's sense of hopelessness, dependency, and isolation. An anticipatory phase in which tolerable productive worry occurs is salutary for successful psychological adjustment to stress.

The impact phase persists for the duration of the stress. The focus of attention is on the immediate present. Initial physiological reactions to this phase are increased vasomotor response, epinephrine and nor-epinephrine release, muscular tension, ADH and ACTH secretion, alertness, improved attention and increased memory span. The pupils dilate and gluconeogenesis is increased. If the impact phase is prolonged, adaptive mental changes rapidly deteriorate and are superseded by a state of diminished alertness, concentration and cognition, numbness, dulling of the sensorium, narrowed attention span, obliteration of memory function, disorganization of thought content, and the suspension of affective awareness. Behavior rapidly becomes automatic and passive.

Effective leadership and the opportunity for effective action inhibit the decline of mental function. Without these alternatives panic reactions and regressed behavior increase.

The recoil phase begins at the end of impact. It is characterized by the incomplete return of emotional expression, self-awareness, memory processes, and behavioral control. Memory screening permits only limited and distorted recall of the stress. The individual moderates his increased anxiety by seeking dependency relationships.

Self-concept is enhanced if performance during stress is adaptive. Conversely, awareness of maladaptive or unacceptable behavior during stress tends to damage self-esteem and erode self-confidence. Individuals who perceive their behavior during stress as deviant experience severe guilt or inadequacy upon reassimilation into the group.

When group and individual perception of an individual's conduct vary, reassimilation may be more anxiety provoking or impossible due to group rejection.

The post-traumatic phase begins when the individual's sense of self has been maximally reconstituted. Orientation, psychomotor function, and affective control are re-established at this time. A fixed modified recall of the stress and one's response to it are available to consciousness. Successful resolution of this phase involves group reassimilation by the sharing of emotionally charged experiences with others. Group sharing clarifies distortions and diminishes guilt.

Unsuccessful resolution results in unfavorable self-concepts, chronic anxiety, depression, fatigue states, recurrent catastrophic dreams, guilt, anger, diminished frustration tolerance, and aggression. Survival guilt may be of different types, e.g., "others died for me and I was unworthy," "I'm glad that others I was close to died, so I might live". When present, such guilt is often dissipated into phobias, defensive ceremonial rituals, tics or the constriction of interpersonal relations. Successful resolution of this phase is contingent upon the presence of adequate time before exposure to further or new impact phases.

Tyhurst (1951), in studying individual reactions to community disasters, found that for a single short term anticipated stress, only 10-25 percent of the population functioned in what he termed a "cool and efficient" fashion; 75 percent of the population acted stunned and bewildered but followed instructions; and the remaining 10-25 percent became severely confused, aggressive, panic stricken, catatonically rigid, or anxious to the point of immobility. This latter group showed a markedly restricted ability to recall the events of the disaster or their own conduct during it. Tyhurst interpreted this memory loss as a device which permitted the individual to relinquish responsibility for his unacceptable behavior. If such behavior develops during the relatively short impact phase of a natural disaster, what might one reasonably expect to see as residuals among even the healthiest of men exposed to a prolonged impact phase?

The Men and the Model

Premorbid personality characteristics. The six PWs were all career military pilots with certain common personality features. They were aggressive, assertive, competitive, competent, emotionally suited to flying, action oriented, idealistic, patriotic, role dominant, system-oriented men who rejected passivity and minimized their own dependency needs. They viewed themselves as absolute patriarchs of their households and were markedly invested in clearly defined male and female roles. All actively participated in physical conditioning activity and expressed great body awareness.

The captivity experience. The events occurring during each phase of stress described below are those reported by the men interviewed and are illustrative, but not inclusive, of the rather complex pattern of demoralization strategy to which these men were subjected. All of the men herein reported were captive for more than five years. The following is a short composite of this group's experience and the men's reactions to it.

The anticipatory phase of captivity. This phase began shortly before actual capture. Two men anticipated dying when their planes were down, the others during pick-up or escape on foot. All of the men initially expected death upon capture. The anticipation of escape was brief in all instances as capture quickly followed impact thus limiting the opportunity for denial. Rapid capture prevented anticipatory mental work by obliterating future orientation, contingency planning, and the illusion of invulnerability. Worry was now directed towards the captivity experience. All men, instead of being killed, were immediately and summarily beaten or ridiculed. By the time of their arrival at "the Hanoi Hilton" they had formulated escape plans and felt convinced they would be able to honorably withstand treatment similar to that which they had already experienced by maintaining a belligerent attitude. All reported surprise at being placed in solitary confinement and being senselessly beaten immediately upon arrival. They anticipated that if physical punishment was inflicted, it would be for the purpose of gaining military information. When they were beaten, isolated, and further tortured without any specific attempt to gain information, the anticipatory phase broke down. The men experienced bewilderment and feelings of panic at not being able to predict future events. Their captors purposely disrupted routine, deprived them of sleep, food and medical care. Isolation warped their time sense and severed their concept of group identity. Four of the six men reported a last ditch anticipatory attempt at control; they would provoke their captors into killing them. Provocation yielded total physical restraint of prolonged duration and close observation. A sense of personal helplessness began to develop and the anticipatory phase of captivity merged into a prolonged anticipatory-impact phase. Self-concept was based upon the fighting man's Code and deviance from this pattern, although protective, served only to erode their sense of personal identity and self-worth.

Richard C. W. Hall, Patrick T. Malone

The Impact Phase of Captivity

This phase crystalized when the PW joined his group of other captives. Impact involved the difficult assimilation of previous unexpected group behavior patterns.

New prisoners were startled by the "zombie like" appearance of their colleagues, as previously described by Segal (1973) and Chodoff (1966). The behavioral norm of the group consisted of anxiety, passivity, subservience, and passive-aggression directed toward the captors. Attempts to preserve self-identity and military bearing consisted of activities such as developing secret communications systems, lecture programs, organizing a chain of command, and periodic sabotage. Over time, camp routine became the expected sum of life experiences. The potential for action and the effectiveness of leadership prevented panic reactions from occurring when the man remained identified with the larger group. Fear of future separation, solitary confinement, torture, bodily injury, disease, and group rejection now constituted the major anticipated stresses. The men interviewed all talked with blunted affect of the guilt they experienced when separated from the larger group. Panic reactions occurred and information concerning other men was often given when sensations of helplessness became intolerable. One PW wept while recounting a three-day period of torture saying he felt worthless because he "talked" to get them to desist. "They tortured (another PW) for a week and he didn't tell them anything." Five of the six PWs felt they had betrayed their comrades by preserving their own physical and psychological integrity. They most feared that the North Vietnamese Army (NVA) would reveal to the group what they had said under torture. They were unable to share their panic experience for fear of group rejection and consequently internalized their conduct as a unique personal weakness. The lack of a group corrective experience resulted in five of these men subsequently developing repetitive catastrophic dreams, guilt, selective memory deficits, anxiety, or depression. The fear of deprivation of group identity, the only sustaining force available, constituted the major control exerted by the NVA.

Over time a traditional stress reaction developed. Alertness and cognition were dulled; numbness, disorganization of thought, memory deficit, and increased suggestibility appeared. Data suggests that this mental attitude was maintained by the periodic and irregular induction of panic while the individual was separated from any supportive group structure. Following the disintegration of the panic experience, the only available model for reintegration was the passive model provided by the group. Direct anger, being non-adaptive, was

132

internalized. Prison roles were gradually incorporated into the men's personalities through a normal maturational process.

The impact phase changed during the last year of hostilities, because of differences in the way later captives were treated. In these cases the stresses more nearly approximated those envisioned during the anticipatory phase. These differences in treatment led to some disorganization of group process.

The impact phase persisted through re-entry. The additional stress of release, evacuation, physical examination, debriefing, return to the Continental United States (CONUS), family reunion, resumption of military roles, and hero status all prevented recoil from previous stress. All of the men viewed the stress of re-entry as significant.

A persistent fear that four of the six men shared, related to how they would be viewed by the military and civilian population upon their return. Their behavior during periods of panic evoked feelings of shame. Re-entry, medical examination, and debriefing represented a threat of discovery and subsequent group rejection. Group discussion of panic experiences, therefore, did not occur during re-entry. When charges of cooperation with the enemy were filed against several other PWs, these four men experienced a resurgence of guilt, anxiety, and insomnia. These additional stresses disrupted the recoil phase of the previous stress that was essential if conflict resolution was to occur.

The Recoil Phase

We believe that five of the six returned PWs are currently in the recoil phase of their experiences. Only one of the six has reached the post-traumatic phase. A case history format, or longitudinal data presentation, although useful, has been rejected so as not to identify any of these men. Data represents a group composite at their request.

Symptoms present during the recoil phase were viewed with different perspectives by the men and their wives. Table 1 represents the data on cognitive function. No attempt has been made to factorially weigh or statistically interpret this data. It represents the clinical impressions of the evaluating physicians, the PW, and his family.

Confusion was inferred from flooding of awareness and indecisiveness of action relative to everyday situations such as the ability to shop and calculate. Time disorientation refers to perception of time passage and the planning of activities to fit a structured schedule. Diminished visual motor perception was inferred from reports of inability to properly drive a motor vehicle and was considered present when men reported being unable to park their cars, straying over the centerline, striking curbs repeatedly, or having accidents. Diminution of memory function and assessment of concentration span data were obtained by self report, the reports of spouse, and mental status testing.

TABLE 1. *Cognitive Function*

Symptom	No. of men in which present	PW Only	Wife Only	Both	Physician
			Perceived as Significant by		
Confusion present past date of re-entry:					
1. One month	4	0	2	2	2
2. Two months	3	1	2	0	1
3. More than two months	2	0	0	2	1
Disorientation to time:					
1. One month's duration	4	1	2	1	1
2. More than one month	2	0	2	0	1
Diminished visual motor coordination inferred from difficulty with driving	5	0	4	1	3
Diminished memory function	5	2	1	2	4
1. Recent memory	4	1	0	3	3
2. Remote memory	1	1	0	0	1
Diminished concentration span	4	2	1	1	3
TOTAL	34	8	14	12	20

This data indicates that significant though often subtle changes in cognitive function are present in the returned PW. Improvement in cognitive function was steady in most men and was pronounced after sixty days at home. Confusion cleared early; time sense was well integrated in all of the men by eighty days post return. Concentration span has increased but is not fully returned to normal, and memory remains somewhat impaired. Visual motor coordination, though better, still constitutes a significant problem.

Changes in cognitive function were more apparent and disconcerting to the families than to the men. Concerns centered on possible accidents, or the occurrence of embarrassing incidents. The wives felt it necessary to protect the men by screening data and, in most cases,

TABLE 2. *Emotional Function*

Symptom	No. of men in which present	PW Only	Perceived as Significant by Wife Only	Both	Physician
Marked mood shifts	2	0	2	0	2
Paranoid ideation	1	0	1	0	1
Aggressivity	2	0	2	0	2
Depression	3	0	1	2	3
Fatigue	2	1	1	0	0
Guilt	4	4	0	0	4
Phobias	0	0	0	0	0
Defensive rituals	1	0	0	0	1
Anxiety episodes	3	1	1	1	3
Flashbacks of camp experiences	3	3	0	0	3
Intrusions into awareness	3	3	0	0	3
TOTAL	24	12	8	3	22

were very helpful in organizing schedules and limiting exposure to external stresses. Our impression was that little recoil took place during the period when cognitive function was most impaired. Role behavior did not constitute a problem for the first six to eight weeks post return as both the men and wives realized the value of her organizing function.

It is important to emphasize the subtle quality of the cognitive changes present. None of these men appeared grossly incapacitated. The picture was not one of organic brain syndrome but rather of adaptive slowing, manifested primarily by reduced rates of cognitive processing and impaired ability for the assimilation of new material.

Table 2 represents the data on emotional function. Emotional symptoms were recognized and considered important by both husband and wife in fewer cases than cognitive symptoms. However, the recognition of these symptoms by one or the other spouse was high. We believe that emotional symptoms were more affectively charged and anxiety producing to the couple than cognitive symptoms, and; therefore, were handled by mutual avoidance. The fear that such symptoms represented significant mental illness was expressed by either the husband or the wife in five of the six families. The PWs tended to be more concerned about intrapsychic processes while the wives expressed more concern about symptoms affecting interpersonal behavior. The couple could easily relate cognitive symptoms to captivity but were unable to view emotional symptoms with the same perspective. We were impressed that in cases where wives were advised to openly discuss their feelings about such symptoms with their husbands, they were unable to do so. Wives seemed to feel that cognitive function would return with time but clearly desired assistance in dealing with emotional disturbances which they perceived as more devastating. Three of the six wives set definite time schedules for improvement and saw divorce as a solution to interpersonal difficulties if this schedule was not met. The time limits, clearly communicated to the men, were of less than one year's duration in all cases. The changes necessary to fulfill the wives' expectations of improvement, however, were not clearly communicated.

The mood shifts appearing in two of the men were somewhat unusual and represented bipolar emotional-cognitive swings. One pole of the axis was characterized by purposeful "doing" activity coupled with enthusiasm and future planning, increased family participation, and emotional closeness between family members. The other pole was represented by withdrawal from the family, disassociation from group activity, a pessimistic future orientation, and increased hostile and accusatory behavior directed at family members. Both men who experienced these symptoms could move from one position to the other in a matter of minutes. The swings were in many instances triggered by what the men perceived as rejection by their wives. The wives responded to the swings with initial caring, then with anger, and finally by emotional withdrawal. As the wives increased their emotional distance, the children also withdrew from their fathers and paired with their mothers.

Paranoid ideation, in the classical sense, was present in only one PW, and was well encapsulated in his personality. As best we can ascertain it represents a trait present prior to his captivity. It pervaded his lifestyle and was difficult for his wife and family to deal with. For example he would meticulously total purchases as he felt all people were out to swindle him. He demanded written explicit contracts for simple transactions and interfered in his children's normal play with other youngsters whom he felt were attempting to capitalize on his own "community status".

The physical aggressivity present in two men occurred at times of frustration and in no case seemed premeditated. It was directed, as best we know, only towards family members and usually in circumstances where their inaction was interpreted as "defiance". Behaviorally, except for one slap which produced marked guilt feelings in the man, shoving was the most common form of physical aggressivity.

The wives stated that such behavior did not occur in their husbands prior to captivity.

The symptoms of depression observed in three men were reactive in type and mild-to-moderate in severity. Depression symptoms included intermittently depressed mood, cyclical thinking, episodic tearfulness while alone, which was controllable, and feelings of inadequacy. In no case did a picture of endogenous or agitated depression develop. Suicidal ideation was not present in any of these men. Two of three men experiencing these symptoms were able to actively discuss them with their wives who responded in a supportive fashion. Although all men reported fatigue to varying degrees, excessive fatigue for which no apparent physical basis could be found occurred in only two men. These two both reported the depressive symptoms described above and perceived their fatigue differently than the other men. Our opinion was that the fatigue took on a clearly adaptive function which prohibited the men from engaging in stressful social events.

Guilt was pronounced in four of the six men. It remained unstated to the families but was openly discussed with the authors after a relationship of trust had developed. Wives seemed totally unaware of its presence. The guilt centered on reactions while in the camp. The guilt arising from self-perceived shamefulness made post re-entry group cohesion difficult. It enhanced each man's sense of isolation and blocked acceptance of his new role. The authors feel that there is a direct relationship between the guilt expressed and the currently present memory deficits which impede progress into the post-traumatic phase. Attempts to bind this guilt in three of the men have resulted in anxiety episodes while the fourth man evolved an almost delusional system to explain his behavior. None of the men are able to emotionally relate their behavior to that of their fellow captives. The guilt engendered during the phase of family reintegration, to be discussed later in the paper, seemed entirely different in both its severity and psychic import.

Although no phobias, per se, were present, one man did develop the defensive ritual of formally pledging allegiance to a small American flag every day upon arising and retiring. Anxiety episodes occurred in all of the men but were deemed significant in only three. One man, who clearly understood the relationship between his own sensations of guilt and the development of subsequent anxiety, did not reveal its presence to his family. One man denied anxiety, yet his wife reported his suddenly developing tremulousness, an apprehensive facial appearance, and wet hands. The third man was able to openly discuss his anxiety with his family and sought help in understanding its origin.

Three of the men reported both flashbacks of camp experiences and intrusive thinking similar to that described by Horowitz and Becker (July 1971, November 1971) and Horowitz et al., (1972). The flashbacks were episodes during which the men felt as if they were physically still in captivity in North Vietnam. These were short term and followed by cognitive awareness of the misperception. The intrusive thinking was characterized by the sudden appearance in consciousness of previous events which were recognized as having occurred in the past. One man found himself suddenly attempting to pick up grapefruit juice, which he spilled on his kitchen floor, and drink it from his hands. He felt he was back in his cell and that the juice was essential to his survival and not to be wasted. He was relatively complacent emotionally to the flashback and merely said, "they (NVA) really get to you after a while". Another man reported intrusive recall of interchanges with an interrogator, while driving his automobile. He refocused his thinking on reality only after his wife yelled that he was straddling the centerline of the highway. These phenomena occur most frequently in settings physically similar to those experienced during the imprisonment. Small white rooms and concrete floors seemed to be the most evocative stimuli for their appearance.

TABLE 3. *Social Function*

Symptom	No. of men in which present	Perceived as Significant by			
		PW Only	Wife Only	Both	Physician
Deterioration of social habit	2	0	2	0	2
Verbally aggressive inappropriate social behavior	1	0	1	0	1
Fear of crowds	4	2	0	2	4
Anger aroused by sight of Orientals	1	0	1	0	1
TOTAL	8	2	4	2	8

Table 3 represents data on social functioning. Two men exhibited marked disregard for conventional social customs. They ate with great rapidity, scraped food from the plates of other family members, walked about the house in underclothing, left bathroom doors open, etc. They did not initially perceive their behavior as unusual and made no apology for it. The wives at first remained silent, but within a period of two to three weeks confronted the men about this behavior. The situation improved dramatically in one case and somewhat in the second. It remains an issue with the latter couple and now seems to represent a passive aggressive weapon the man uses to diminish his wife's social expectations of him.

One man exhibited markedly aggressive verbal behavior directed toward any female friend of his wife. He deeply resents her having any close friends and has expressed concern that she has been involved in lesbian relationships while he was away. This same man exhibits grossly inappropriate social behavior when stressed. On one occasion, while attending a party, he loudly announced he didn't want to be around a group of "freaks" and left.

Four of the six men are still apprehensive in crowds. In two cases, this fear has served the useful function of permitting the wife the opportunity to support the PW. In only one case did the fear initially prevent group activity upon return.

One PW reported the sudden emergence of anger upon seeing certain Orientals. The reaction was not common to all Orientals encountered but seemed specific to those with facial features or mannerisms similar to those of one of his captors. The anger was never directly expressed and resulted in no confrontations.

Disordered social function was viewed as significant by the wives more frequently than the PWs and was not usually an area of mutual concern or discussion. Persistent disruption seemed to represent an area for expressing other marital conflicts.

Table 4 represents data on family relations. Readjustment difficulties seemed most manifest in family relationships. Five of the six returnees, after a short period of dependency, rapidly reassumed their dominant roles. For an interval of two to three weeks they relied on their wives to reorient them to changes which had occurred, then suddenly reasserted strong control over the family. Wives who had previously handled finances, made decisions about the children, purchased houses, etc., were now expected to turn "executive function" over to their husbands. Three of the wives expressed resentment at the husband's control of the children, "as if an outsider had come in and begun ordering them about". The maleness and femaleness of tasks became an important issue. One wife, for example, was forbidden to garden because it was "man's work". Her liking for the activity was not considered a relevant issue by her husband. The men assumed control of the male children, but often left the female children to their mothers.

TABLE 4. *Family Relations*

	No. of men in which present	PW Only	Wife Only	Both	Physician
			Perceived as Significant by		
Family role of PW					
1. Dominant	5	0	0	5	0
2. Passive	1	0	1	0	0
Marital Relations					
1. Viewed as satisfactory	2	0	0	2	2
2. PW jealous of spouse	2	0	2	0	2
3. PW suspicious of spouse	2	0	2	0	2
4. PW excessively controlling of spouse	1	0	1	0	1
5. Conflict with children	2	0	2	0	2
6. Hoarding behavior	1	0	1	0	1
Communication					
1. Language skills	1	1	0	0	1
2. Interpersonal	4	2	2	0	4
TOTAL	21	3	11	7	15

One man remains dependent on his wife for decision making. He has had no difficulties with his children, and there seems to be little tension between the couple. He seems quite happy with his role in the family, and plans to assume more responsibility when he has "caught up". Although his present role is different from his previous one, it appears adaptive to him at this time.

Only two of the six couples viewed their marital relationship as currently satisfactory. Two wives felt that their husbands were excessively jealous and suspicious of them. Mileage checks on odometers, phone calls to stores, and repetitive interrogations pertaining to simple business communications with male store personnel, exemplified this behavior. One of these men became totally controlling of his wife's behavior and refused, for several months, to let her out of his sight. He bought her clothes, sat at the hairdresser with her, and forbade individual social contacts. His wife has responded by totally abandoning her previous role, developing migraine headaches, and gaining forty pounds. These same two men are having marked difficulty with their children who have either paired with their mothers or acted out their emotional difficulties.

One man evidences severe hoarding behavior which initially developed during his captivity. He refuses to discard objects, saves string and tinfoil, and is writing his memoirs on the backs of small scraps of paper.

The choice of suitable words constitutes a problem for one man, his difficulty is more cognitive, i.e., the naming of objects, than interpersonal. Four of the men are having difficulty with interpersonal forms of communication. The difficulty lies primarily in their inability to understand the affective content of language and to process its nonverbal component. Their responses are concrete and directed only to words actually spoken. For example, one man was asked by his wife if he would like to walk along a beach as they had early in their marriage. She saw the moment as romantic and had often fantasized this stroll during his absence; he simply responded, "no, too many mosquitos". She became sad and withdrew. Several weeks later he still was perplexed by her sudden change in mood.

The wives attached far more importance to family difficulties than the men, who were often unable to perceive that they even existed. The wives ranked the problems in the following descending order of severity:

1. Emotional isolation from their husband.
2. Inability to feel important to their husband.
3. Their husband's emotional deafness to them.
4. Difficulty in sharing control of their children.
5. Role reversal from their previous pattern.
6. · Social isolation.
7. Fear of emotional breakdown in their husband, children, or themselves.

The magnitude of these emotional issues may shed some light on the increased divorce rate of PWs previously reported.

One man, shortly after his return, acquiesced to his wife's desire that he have a vasectomy. Later he became quite upset about his sterility and equated her request to involuntary castration. "She finished the job they (the NVA) had been trying to do on me for years." This couple was able over time to resolve this issue in a satisfactory manner.

Concerns about work are presented in Table 5. Three of the men expressed apprehension about not being able to perform well at their present jobs. Perhaps the general concern was best expressed by one man who said, "I understand a jet manual but all this paperwork about people really throws me". The strangeness of the new task, lack of previous experience with such duties, difficulty with memory and concentration, and the fear of failure all focused on the issue of job performance. All of the men spent long hours "studying" the new job and continually assessing their performance. Therapeutic efforts were directed toward getting them to go home at reasonable hours. Four men were unsure if they were able to return to work, and two felt their indecisiveness would preclude satisfactory adjustment. The men were much more concerned with this aspect of their lives than their wives. Except for two cases where self-imposed evening work supplanted family life, all of the wives were helpful and supportive toward their husbands. Work represented the first external assessment of their functional capacities, which they viewed as being synonomous with self-worth.

TABLE 5. *Work*

	No. of men in which present	PW Only	Perceived as Significant by Wife Only	Both	Physician
Ability to function at present job	3	1	0	2	0
Able to return to work	4	2	0	2	0
Indecisiveness	3	2	1	0	0
TOTAL	10	5	1	4	0

One man elected to return to college rather than a military role. He experienced additional difficulties as his group identification with college students was practically impossible. Except in this one case, all of the men performed their work function satisfactorily. Only one of the six men seen has returned to flying status. He was the one individual whose wife's role had not changed during his absence and who was considered by the author's to have reached the post-traumatic phase.

Depressive symptomatology is presented in Table 6. As previously stated, three men were felt to have reactive depressive symptoms. Initial insomnia tended to abate during the first month of return. One man experienced sleep disrupting nightmares clearly related to his captivity experience, while two others experienced non-sleep disrupting catastrophic dreams centering on themes of punishment, or subservience. For example, one man reported dreaming of a partially edentured captor who "laughs at me while I'm asleep". The absence of diminished sexual function or clear psychophysiological disorders at this time should be noted. Depressive symptoms were readily apparent to both husband and wife.

TABLE 6. *Depressive Symptomatology*

	No. of men in which present	Perceived as Significant by			
		POW Only	Wife Only	Both	Physician
Insomnia:	5	0	1	4	5
1. Early AM awakening	1	0	1	0	1
2. Sleep continuity disorder	2	0	1	1	2
a. with nightmares	1	0	0	1	1
b. without nightmares	1	0	1	0	1
3. Difficulty falling asleep	2	0	1	1	0
4. Catastrophic dreams	2	2	0	0	2
Disturbance of Appetite:	2	0	2	0	2
1. Hyperphagia	1	0	1	0	1
2. Hypophagia	1	0	1	0	1
Diminished sexual function	0	0	0	0	0
Suicidal ideation	0	0	0	0	0
Clear psychophysiological reactions	0	0	0	0	0
Significant physical disability	1	0	0	1	1
Identification with aggressor	2	0	0	0	2
Intermittently depressed mood	3	1	0	2	3
Cyclical thinking	3	1	0	2	3
Episodic tearfulness	3	1	0	2	3
Feelings of inadequacy	3	1	0	2	3
Excessive fatigue	3	1	0	2	3
TOTAL	36	7	9	18	34

The Post-Traumatic Phase

We believe only one of the men seen has at this time reached the post-traumatic phase of his stress reaction. Several factors distinguish him from the other PWs. He had read extensively about the captivity experience because his father had been a PW during World War II. He and his wife were both raised in the town to which he returned. He returned to an extended family system which had permitted his wife to maintain her previous role in his absence. His only child, a son, had several relatives who functioned as surrogate fathers and who possess value systems similar to his own.

His insight, gained from his father's PW experience, permitted him to correctly anticipate the stresses of captivity and thereby maintain his internal controls. He did not feel guilty over his behavior and conduct in camp, even though it was basically similar to that of the other PWs. His perception of captivity seemed more accurate than the others and he did not feel obliged to be a hero. When one of the men stated in the media that he would return to captivity if necessary, this man's reaction was, "he must be crazy". He was able to share his experiences with his wife and parents and had a father who could relate to them. His cognitive, psychomotor, and affective control have all returned to normal.

Conclusions and Recommendations

The reactions of this group of PWs and their families may provide guidelines which will be of use in evaluating other PW families. Superficially, they seem to have made a good re-entry. On initial contact at this time, the majority would appear no different than the population at large. However, cognitive deficits become apparent as the length of contact increases. The early confusion has abated, but memory deficits, diminished attention span, and visual motor incoordination persist.

We believe thorough evaluation or early psychotherapeutic intervention will be difficult because of the suspicion, distorted self-concept, lack of trust, guilt, and fear of insanity that these men harbor. In our experience, contact with the wives has provided the best means of reaching the men and aiding their families. None of the men we have seen would have "submitted to psychiatric interrogation" were it not for the sense of trust their wives evidenced in the authors. In any future re-entry program, contact with the wives should be actively established prior to the men's return.

Psychiatric symptoms in the returning PW were not readily apparent to casual observation and were not initially available through the self-report of the men. Many of the men actively tried to conceal painful reactions from the psychiatric teams who initially saw them. Their symptoms persisted and the men became amenable to treatment only because of the manifestation of the symptoms in marital and family relations. Behavioral symptoms which we believe best indicated significant intrapsychic distress in the returned PW were: jealousy of spouse, cyclical mood swings, physical aggressivity, defensive rituals, anxiety episodes, deterioration of social habits, verbally aggressive or socially inappropriate behavior, excessively controlling behavior, marked conflicts with children, hoarding behavior, and catastrophic dreams.

Intrapsychic conflicts such as survival guilt, feelings of worthlessness, depression, and fear of insanity were expressed only after a relationship of trust developed with the physician.

Psychotherapeutic strategies which seemed useful were all directed towards permitting the men to move through the recoil into the post-traumatic phase.

Wives were encouraged to communicate directly and patterns of miscommunication were explored with each member of the couple separately. The men were encouraged to work through their feelings of humiliation, guilt, and shame. Initially the therapists took a directive role which provided structure for conflict situations. Later they were able to move toward a more non-directive supportive position.

Clarification of role and self-image distortions, passive-aggressive anger, fear of dependency and inability to trust, survival guilt, and fear of insanity were important therapeutic issues for the men.

Clarification of role deprivation, inability to share children, feelings of uselessness and inadequacy, social isolation, distortions of communication, and unrealistic expectations were important therapeutic issues for the wives.

Direct therapist involvement in work situations and questions pertinent to job performance were considered useful by the men.

The nature of the therapy contract was most unorthodox. When the men refused to come to the psychiatric clinic, they were seen in restaurants at lunch or in their offices. No official psychiatric records were kept and home visits were often made. The therapists rapidly found themselves deeply and directly involved in the men's family lives.

Although several attempts to initiate group therapy or group discussions were made, no group formed. Only the man who had reached the post-traumatic phase of his adjustment was willing to talk in a group setting about the things that troubled him. The other men flatly refused group therapy but were desirous of maintaining "limited"/"social" contact with each other. Each of the men, however, told the therapist that he could share information about himself with the others provided his identity was not divulged. Thus, a group process "in absentia" was created.

Retrospectively, these particular men and their wives felt that the return of the PWs to CONUS was too rapid and that reunions were too abrupt. The men wished to know more about what their wives had experienced and the women felt that assurances of their husbands' health by receiving hospitals had made their appreciation of the men's emotional problems difficult. Both regretted that no group structure was initially implemented and both were desirous of information concerning the total group's progress after re-entry.

Our impression is that the suggestions previously made by Chodoff (1966) and Segal (1973) would have been useful for these men.

We believe the data presented indicate that the following assumptions, programs, and actions would be useful in the creation of future re-entry programs:

1. Psychiatric symptoms will be present in most of the returning men.
2. These symptoms are directly related to the gross stresses of captivity.
3. Symptoms are best viewed as normal reactions to abnormal situations.
4. The returning men will have difficulties in seeking psychiatric help.
5. Marital and family difficulties post re-entry are likely to occur and may represent the best opportunities to engage the PW in treatment.
6. Severe intrapsychic distress may be externally unapparent but can be readily inferred from those prominent behavioral patterns previously mentioned.
7. Close therapeutic alliance with the wives and children prior to the return of the men greatly facilitates the post re-entry use of helping agencies by the families.
8. Homecoming should itself be considered a significant stress and planned for accordingly.
9. Re-entry groups prior to family reunion, though difficult to initiate, are essential and should deal with the sharing of prison experiences, description of panic reactions, and the clear acceptance of in-camp behavior by authority figures. Opportunity to ventilate anger should be provided. Such group interaction will increase both self-concept and group identity and diminish survival guilt.
10. Information to diminish cultural shock and the briefings on current family status given prior to re-entry were viewed as helpful by these men.
11. The confidentiality of psychiatric records is a major factor in obtaining the trust of these men.
12. Men should be oriented to their new jobs and have a non-threatening liaison person to whom they could turn for information.
13. Medical and dental treatment programs, should be well underway prior to family reunion.
14. Sponsors for the man upon his return to duty greatly diminished re-entry fear.

The cardinal principal of any re-entry program must remain *primum non nocere.*

Readjustment and Reintegration

11

Families Of Returned Prisoners Of War: Some Impressions On Their Initial Reintegration

PHILIP J. METRES, JR.
HAMILTON I. MCCUBBIN
EDNA J. HUNTER

Introduction

Historically, the prisoner of war experience has usually been viewed retrospectively, with interest focused primarily upon the returnee's physical and emotional adjustment and, in particular, mortality and morbidity rates (Beebe, in preparation; Cohen & Cooper, 1954; Nefzger, 1970). Still other investigators have examined the occupational and educational adjustment of returned prisoners of war (Schein, Singer & Cooley, 1960). However, none of these studies has explored the dynamics of post-repatriation adjustment of families of the returned prisoners of war and the role of the family in the returnee's adjustment.

The few studies which have examined family adjustment after wartime separations have been limited to adjustments following World War II (Boulding, 1950; Reeves, 1947). Family adjustment to separation and reunion in World War II was examined in depth in a landmark study by Reuben Hill (1949). Hill observed that readjustments during reunion were problematic for both the husband and wife, as well as for the children.

Although these studies pointed up difficulties which emerged after long periods of separation, they did not make specific reference to the returned prisoner of war (RPW) and his family. Only recently with the return of American prisoners of war (RPWs) from Southeast Asia has there been an opportunity to gain any knowledge of these families. After such an unprecedented and prolonged period of family separation with its concomitant stresses, it seems probable that readjustment problems would occur when the families were reunited.

147

Philip J. Metres, Jr., Hamilton I. McCubbin, Edna J. Hunter

Predictions of family difficulties following prolonged absence of a husband or father who has been held prisoner during wartime have been reported in the recent literature. Hall and Malone (1973) on the basis of their continuing work with PW/MIA families, predicted that "marital and family difficulties post re-entry are likely to occur". They emphasized that this readjustment period "... may represent the best opportunity to engage the POW in treatment". In a larger comprehensive study of the adjustment of PW/MIA families prior to reunion, McCubbin, Hunter and Metres (1973) pointed out that any formula for reunion must include the complex adjustments and stresses which the families experienced during the separation period. They went on to predict that the probability of major adjustments in family roles would be high and that these role readjustments, as well as the families' expectations for the reunion, would affect the quality of the readjustment.

The Vietnam RPW family's readjustment process may be more complex than that of the typical World War II serviceman's family primarily because of the unprecedented duration of the separation, time during which the families, their members, and society had changed. These factors made reunion somewhat unique and, therefore, increase the importance of understanding the process of reintegration, as well as the importance of evaluating the potential services needed to assist these men and their families. The specific focus of this paper is the initial readjustment of RPW families of the Vietnam conflict following reunion. It is assumed that the manner and speed with which the families adjusted during the homecoming period and during the initial months of reunion would, to some degree, aid in the prediction of the long-term adjustment of the individual returnee and his family.

Procedure

One opportunity to view the initial stages of family adjustment was offered to the Center for POW Studies staff through attendance at a series of retreats held during the summer of 1973 for families of servicemen missing in action (MIAs), listed prisoners of war (PWs), and returned prisoners of war (RPWs). These retreats occurred approximately four to six months subsequent to the returnees' homecoming and came at a juncture in the RPW's family readjustment—when the intensity of public demands upon the RPW had begun to subside. This was a time when many RPW families were taking stock of their situations; it was a prelude to a return to military and family duties after long periods of confinement and hospitalization.

Families of Returned Prisoners of War: Some Impressions on Their Initial Reintegration

Information for this study was gathered through informal interviews and group discussions with 21 returned prisoners of war and their wives. The couples were in attendance at one of five week-long religious retreats sponsored by a non-profit organization. A total of 26 returnees, 21 of whom were married and five of whom were single, came to the retreats. These men represented all three military services; civilian returnees were also in attendance.

Interviews and discussion groups were conducted or led by three or four members of a team of behavioral scientists, consisting of a psychiatrist, three psychologists, two social workers, and three ministers, and supported by three youth counselors. The leaders provided structure and general direction for the group, with an emphasis upon two general themes: (1) What the families had experienced in the last six months since reunion, and (2) What the families were planning for the future.

Findings

Initial Reactions. At the outset, the returnees were only superficially willing to discuss their personal experiences; they appeared unsure as to how open they ought to be within such a group and were clearly hesitant to share any very personal or private experiences. The wives, on the other hand, at the start were more willing to discuss their personal situations. As the discussions progressed however, the wives became conspicuously quiet, allowing their husbands to voice their thoughts and feelings. It appeared as if the wives felt that they had had their say many times during their husbands' absences and wished now to allow the men to carry the responsibility of the discussion. The wives primarily provided non-verbal cues of acknowledgement to the topics being discussed.

With assurances from the group that adjustment difficulties after separation were seemingly "normal" or commonplace experiences among returnees and wives, the couples were more willing to explore what seemed to them to be highly sensitive and personal areas. A few indicated that they were having extensive adjustment problems but were determined to resolve them on their own; a few felt that marital counseling was necessary and had decided to seek it. In one case a couple came to the group feeling that they had grown too far apart in their personal goals and values over the years; they questioned the potential for reconciliation of their differences but still appeared motivated to discuss their problems with the goal of seeking solutions.

Philip J. Metres, Jr., Hamilton I. McCubbin, Edna J. Hunter

Dual Responsibilities: Public vs. The Family. As the discussions proceeded, the men seemed to welcome the opportunity to focus their attention on personal matters. This became most evident as they discussed the tremendous pressures they had been under to make numerous public appearances. Most of the returnees noted that they felt an overwhelming sense of duty to report to the American people what took place in the prisoner of war camps. More importantly, they felt a commitment to the American people who had done so much to bring them home and to give them a warm homecoming. They felt obligated to respond to the public clamor for appearances and speeches. Many of the returnees reported feeling "swallowed up" by the tremendous demand for their attention, and indicated that it had taken several months for them to learn to say "no" to such requests without associated feelings of guilt for having "let someone down" or for having "hurt" someone's feelings. While it is not difficult to understand the intensity of the returnees' sense of obligation, it also appeared that this feeling of moral obligation was in part based on their perceived unproductivity during the many years of their confinement. They seemed to feel that the public appearances offered them the opportunity to make up, in part, for their "lost time", and represented the initial step towards becoming once again respected and contributing members of the community.

This emotional attachment to the public seemed to lead to feelings of detachment from the families. Many of the wives reported feeling somewhat dismayed by, and resentful of, the numerous demands placed on their husbands, who, in some cases, reported having spent only two or three evenings alone with their families since their return. After the extended enforced separation due to captivity, many of the wives felt these demands to be more than they wanted to tolerate. Several of the returnees revealed that their conscientiousness toward pleasing the public became a legitimate excuse for setting aside the necessary family readjustment issues which demanded their attention. Many of the men viewed the retreats as an opportunity to change this situation and refocus their attentions on their personal and family lives.

Praise for Operation Homecoming and the Military Assistance Programs. As a group, the returnees and their families expressed praise for the manner in which Operation Homecoming was handled. Prior to return, the men had viewed repatriation and reunion with their families as potential problem areas since many of them did not know what to expect. However, for the most part, they were pleasantly surprised. After years of deprivation and longing to return home, the men were overwhelmed by the warm and generous welcome they received and by the thoroughness and the efficiency with which their return was planned and executed. They felt the medical evaluation program was comprehensive and that every effort was made to assist them in their planning for the future.

The majority of the returnees also expressed appreciation for the continued efforts of the casualty assistance and family assistance programs on behalf of the families during the men's absences. These programs, established by the individual services, were designed specifically to provide continuous service to and liaison with the families of servicemen missing in action or prisoners of war. Although there were some notable exceptions to the generally adequate level of assistance by the military, the group members, by and large, thought the families were relatively well cared for.

Role Readjustments. The wives described how difficult it was for their husbands to adjust to their spouses' new-found independence. Many of the wives described their own personal growth in response to the requirements which were inherent in their husbands' absences: such as dealing with family finances and legal matters pertaining to the family, learning how to negotiate and transact all business in behalf of the family, and single-handedly raising the children. Some of the husbands reported that they had initially felt "unneeded" because their households had been managed so well in their absences. A few wives struggled to hold on to their role as heads of the households, and where this occurred, the returnees continued to feel left out and "unimportant" as fathers and husbands. One wife, representative of those few who did not wish to give up her control of the household, expressed her ambivalence about her husband's return; she was not sure she wanted him back. In this situation her husband viewed himself as the intruder in a family that seemed to function without him.

More typical of this group's experience were the families who reported the renegotiations which occurred and the movement towards sharing responsibilities equally between spouses. Husbands, more than ever before, began to accept their wives as "equal partners." In acknowledgement of the wives' independence and autonomy which developed during their husbands' absences, the returnees expressed a greater awareness of and respect for the wives' capabilities.

Concern for Their Children. In the discussion groups the couples expressed their concern for their children's adjustment and questioned what impact the whole experience would have upon their children's futures. For example, a number of the couples with boys expressed their concern over the absence of a strong male model during the father's captivity, even though for many of these families there had been a male figure with whom the boys could identify: a grandfather, uncle, coach, scout leader, pastor or neighbor.

Some specific criticisms were voiced by several returnees in regard to their children. While many were very pleased with their children's development, a few expressed disapproval of the seemingly questionable behaviors acquired in their absence. The lack of respect for authority shown by their children was high on the list of the returnees' complaints. Several mentioned the conspicuous absence of "sir" and "ma'am" as a means of formal address. Although some mentioned the long hair and unusual mode of their children's dress, these did not appear to be serious criticisms. The exposure of their children's behavior was defensively challenged by the mothers as undue criticism of their own performance as disciplinarians.

Many returnees reported that after initial minor conflicts were resolved, they were gradually able to resume the role of father and head of the household. One mother, recalling the reaction of her son who felt relieved by his father's resumption of authority, quoted her son saying, "I'm glad I no longer have to negotiate everytime a decision is made around the house." On the other hand, a few wives discussed how difficult it was for them to have to share the discipline of the children and accept father's authoritative role. These wives had functioned as the sole parent for so long that some resented their husbands' efforts to intrude into an area that the mothers had defined as exclusively their own.

Sensitive Issues: Dealing with MIA Families, Suicide, and Divorce. One area of particular difficulty for the returnee and his family was facing and responding to the questions and concerns of families whose husbands and sons had not returned. The returnees expressed feelings of discomfort in dealing with MIA family members. The returnees sought support from the group; they wanted to know how they should behave and, "What can we say to them?" Facing the MIA family was difficult because the returnees had to respond to questions of whether they felt there were any prisoners of war still remaining in Southeast Asia. They did not want to build false hopes among those who were trying to accept their husbands' or sons' absences as final nor deter those who felt strongly that their husbands or sons might yet be alive. Underlying the returnees' apprehensions in dealing with these families' concerns was a questioning of their own survival: "Why me and not your husband or your son?" This phenomenon of "survivor guilt" has been noted in previous studies (Chodoff, 1966; Niederland, 1968).

On the other hand, the plight of the MIA families held special meaning for the wives of returned prisoners of war. The RPW wives felt a strong degree of empathy with MIA wives and desired greater communication with them. It was not long ago, they recalled, when they were members of that group and shared similar, if not identical, feelings and experiences. Like their husbands, the RPW wives pondered over their own good fortune. They, too, appeared to experience a kind of "survivor guilt," which could, in part, be resolved by sharing these feelings with the MIA wives.

The suicides of two returned prisoners of war shortly after repatriation brought sharply into focus the anxieties that many of the returnees felt. Many asked, "Why did these particular men commit suicide?" The implied concern was "Who is next?" A number were worried that they might also have similar tendencies that they were unaware of. Discussion of the suicides produced strong feelings of shock and disbelief. In one group, when this subject was introduced for discussion, it was tactfully avoided in favor of a less threatening one. The topic of self-destruction was one which was either "taboo" or more appropriate for individual contemplation rather than group discussion; it was too sensitive an issue to be discussed at this point in time.

The subject of divorce evoked similar expressions of shock and disbelief. The divorces which the returnees and their wives had read and heard about caused them considerable anxiety. On the one hand, they expressed anger toward "those women" who did not wait for their husbands. On the other hand, they could intellectually grasp what it meant to be separated for five to eight years without a word to indicate that their spouses were still alive. They were aware of how such a situation might reasonably affect the viability of a marriage.

The Future. Most of the families seemed to feel that the separations had actually served to bring them closer together. They felt that both husband and wife, as well as the children, no longer took each other for granted. They perceived their marriages as having been given renewed life and their family relationships as having been given a new start. The future, however, represented an enigma. Many returnees questioned their own self-confidence after having spent long periods of non-productivity. For many there were the uncertainties of whether or not to complete their careers in the military or begin anew in a civilian career. In either case, uppermost in their minds was the desire "to make up for the lost time".

Philip J. Metres, Jr., Hamilton I. McCubbin, Edna J. Hunter

Most of the returnees saw themselves returning to educational pursuits. The majority wanted to get back into training or schooling so that they could update themselves prior to assuming additional responsibility. A few wanted to get back to a meaningful operational assignment as soon as their convalescent leaves were completed. Most felt that the sooner they could rid themselves of the label "ex-POW", the better off they would be. As a group, they feared that people would not accept them for their own abilities and accomplishments, but rather for their notoriety as "ex-POWs". They wished to be thought of as productive individuals, not Olympian heroes.

Discussion

The emergence of family difficulties, as well as personal growth on the part of the wives after prolonged wartime separation, which have been noted in the literature, were further supported by the group discussions among RPW family members reported on in this study. The development of the wife away from dependence towards autonomy as head of the household, which was reported by Hall and Malone (1973), Hill (1949), McCubbin et al. (1973), and Reeves (1947), was also seen among the wives in this study.

Our observations did not either confirm or refute Hill's (1949) hypothesis that wives who had assumed the husband's role in his absence had a more difficult reunion. Although some wives in this study who became "head of the household" in their husbands' absences experience a comfortable transition, others found the shifting of roles more difficult.

Boulding's (1950) conclusion that families returned to their prewar patterns of family behavior was not totally confirmed by this study. In fact, there are indices that the families would establish new patterns of interaction. The husbands' increased respect for the wives' capabilities and greater willingness to accept their wives as "equal partners" would seem to indicate a trend away from Boulding's findings. It would seem reasonable to assume that this trend, in turn, would be supported by changes in modern American marriage patterns where wives are more frequently viewed as having equal status.

Summary and Conclusions

Discussions held in the setting provided by a retreat, away from the public fanfare, proved to be a valuable tool in gauging the RPW families' readjustment progress. The discussions provided an opportunity for the returnees to talk over many of the concerns and anxieties that the families were experiencing at that particular point in time. Putting readjustment problems in the context of normality, not pathology, helped these families view their differences with greater equanimity, and, thus, gave them greater confidence that they might eventually find resolutions to their conflicts. The group process also afforded the families an opportunity to observe their own concerns repeated in other families. Through discussing their common concerns, they could seek support from others in a similar situation and solicit solutions which might have relevance to their personal conflicts.

The returnees' concerns for their families, the care provided the families in their absences, and the services extended to their families since reunion, seemed to loom uppermost in the men's minds. The men's shifting of priorities away from involvement with the public toward involvement with their families and their careers was quite evident. The returnees' intense desire to meet all public commitments was now being placed in perspective, and their energies directed toward their families' adjustment and continued development in their own professional careers.

Opportunities to discuss plans and feelings appeared to be strongly needed at this transition point in their readjustment. Given this opportunity again, it appeared that many returned prisoner of war families would take advantage of the offer. They seemed to realize that readjustment after long separation is accompanied by certain normal adjustments, and that these can be ameliorated by similarly structured individual or group discussions led by mental health professionals.

One interesting outcome of the groups was the fact that discussions of the difficulties of readjustment were often tempered with apologies. The men and their wives wanted it known that while they were experiencing difficulty, they were not complaining—"Our families are united, the military did a fine job with my homecoming, and I am in good health as is my family; who are we to complain about our problems? Is coping with family adjustment problems any more difficult than what my wife and I have already been through?" Questions such as these present an interesting challenge to mental health professionals and need to be explored in greater depth at some future time in a more extensive study on the adjustment of these families. Only time will tell.

12

Waiting: The Dilemma of the MIA Wife

DOROTHY BENSON
HAMILTON I. MCCUBBIN
BARBARA B. DAHL
EDNA J. HUNTER

Introduction

The emotional adjustment of wives of servicemen missing in action (MIA) during the Southeast Asian conflict has become a topic of considerable concern in recent literature (e.g. Hunter and Plag, 1973). Such sources have emphasized the difficulties these wives have experienced not only because of the prolonged period of husband absence, but also because of the unended grief caused by a situation in which there is no conclusive evidence as to the husband's fate. Hunter and Plag (1973) also found that the wives felt unable to plan realistically for their futures. How could they be sure if their men were dead, alive or ever going to return? Some additional information as to whether there was still a possibility that these men might return, became available with the signing of the Peace Agreement[1] and the return of American prisoners of war. Although, in most cases, the information available was not conclusive, the return of American prisoners of war, the reports by some returnees as to the improbability that servicemen still remained in Southeast Asia, and the activities by the Joint Casualty Resolution Center to account for those servicemen still missing meant that families had to evaluate the available evidence and, thus, arrive at some decision as to whether or not the missing husband would return. This was a critical time for most wives. For some it signaled an inevitable change in official status: a reclassification of the missing husband to "killed-in-action"

1. *Signed in Paris, France on January 27, 1973.*

157

(KIA) or to "presumptive finding of death" (PFOD), based on the best available information. In either case, a reclassification meant modification in the family's financial status, a restructuring of the wife's social role, and a decisive placement of responsibility upon the MIA wife for the planning of the family's future. For other families the events meant continued waiting and hoping until final word was received.

Studies regarding the adjustment of wives of servicemen still missing in action following "Operation Homecoming" are virtually non-existent. The one study conducted after the return of American prisoners of war focuses on the children (McCubbin, Hunter & Metres, 1974). Any references to the wives' adjustment have been in relation to the children. In view of the paucity of information and because the period immediately subsequent to the prisoners' release might be a critical time of re-evaluation and readjustment for these women and their families, it was believed important to examine in greater depth the adjustment of these wives whose husbands' fate still remained uncertain.

Problem

Ruth Lindquist (1952) in her study of Air Force families reported the deleterious effects of frequent separation on family life. Findings of that study indicated that family stability was endangered by fear of philandering, assumption of the matriarchal role, and/or reliance on relatives for emotional support and protective functions. In addition, other studies (Dickerson & Arthur, 1965) have emphasized the harmful nature of separation during critical stages of development in both boys and girls — stages that require a father figure in order to proceed satisfactorily. The study of father absence by Baker, Cove, Fagen, Fischer and Janda (1968) emphasized the mother's difficulty in maintaining family controls and consequent child behavior problems. Social introversion and associated feelings of loneliness by the children were common in their particular study group. Their work also indicated that separation had an enduring impact on the lifestyles of the family unit.

Although other military wives adjust to their husbands' absences, there is a vital difference between routine separations among military families and separations in which the husband is declared MIA. Wives whose husbands are declared missing-in-action are placed in a considerably more stressful role. All of the routine problems confronting the military wife who is separated from her husband are further aggravated, in the MIA situation, by the uncertainty about whether or not her husband will ever return, or if he is even alive.

For many of the MIA wives there has been a constant struggle with problems of self-esteem. Forced to make substantial adjustments to the community and its social networks, frequently the MIA wife has had to adjust to a life pattern that is totally different from the one she had previously known. Although Eliot (1946) reports that when a young woman loses her husband, it is easier for her than for the older widow to go on with her life, this does not appear to be the case for the MIA wife whose loss is not yet certain. For this latter group of women, anxieties and depressions have fluctuated month after month, and in many cases year after year, in a cyclical rhythm which has defied resetting into an ongoing pattern of adjustment.

Normal grief can be regarded as a disease specifically caused by object loss, possessing well-defined and specific symptoms, and in uncomplicated cases, running a predictable course towards recovery (Engel, 1961). But complications arise when grief is prolonged or delayed. When grief is held in abeyance and prolonged by no closure, the normal stages are aborted or blocked and the denial stage is protracted and mourning is stalled. In such cases, readjustment to the loss cannot be made, because the loss is not finalized. Even if some forward movement is made, the expectations of others can cause turmoil. How can these women get on with their lives when children, parents and society as a whole expect them to wait?

Purpose

The purpose of this paper is to describe some of the findings that grew out of a series of group discussions with wives of servicemen missing in action. Because it has been established that people sharing similar situations are often able to help one another in practical ways by offering emotional support, these discussions were arranged in an attempt to understand what this unique population was experiencing during the period immediately following the return of the American prisoners (RPWs) from Southeast Asia. What had the return of the PWs meant to these women and their children?

Procedure

Discussion groups were an integral part of five, week-long religious retreats sponsored by the High Flight Foundation in the summer of 1973. Although group participation was strictly on a voluntary basis

Dorothy Benson, Hamilton I. McCubbin, Barbara B. Dahl, Edna J. Hunter

for the MIA wives, approximately 160 women, representing all branches of the Service, availed themselves of this opportunity. Group meetings were held two times daily for two hours each. Since members from the professional staff of the Center for Prisoner of War Studies acted as group leaders in only three of these retreats, the findings reported in this study are limited strictly to data collected during those retreats.

Findings

Pre-established sub-groups. Two sub-groups of wives had been established prior to the retreats and these groups carried over into the discussion groups held at the retreats. The sub-groups were an outgrowth of previous participation by many of these same women in counseling groups held in two different geographical locations in the United States. This pre-established "group dynamic" proved to be an enhancing stimulus. These wives, as a result of prior interchanges among themselves, appeared more open and willing to deal with very sensitive issues; thus, they legitimated the open discussion of personal matters for the other members. In this way, they also enabled the group discussions to reach quickly a stage of development which under other circumstances may have taken a longer period to attain. These sub-groups brought into focus many sensitive issues never before touched upon by many wives. For example, an open discussion of the prospects of dating and involvement with men other than their husbands was introduced matter-of-factly and discussed by the group. Although such topics might have emerged eventually, the fact that they were brought out in the early stages of the groups' development set a precedent for "safe" discussion of other sensitive subjects, such as concern for children, anxieties about their children's futures, anxieties about their future remarriages and preparation for a possible change of status. Perhaps of greatest importance, it created an atmosphere which permitted the sharing of deeply felt emotions.

Some wives initially attempted to control the group experience by demanding that the group follow a set protocol and focus on very specific topics. One wife, in particular, felt that the group discussion should approximate that of the National League of Families. In other words, she wanted the discussions to focus on political issues. The group leaders, with the support of some group members, however, emphasized the importance of discussion topics of personal concern to all the wives, so that each could benefit from this experience.

Since the groups were held as part of a religious retreat, an atmosphere conducive to the discussion of religious values was provided.

The wives varied in terms of their feelings regarding the importance of religion. Although a few women had found that religion provided a source of strength which enabled them to cope with their position, the majority of the wives focused on the "here and now"; that is, they were concerned with their immediate problems of depression, frustration, etc. and were not dependent on religious interpretations of "why" this was happening to them. Thus, the majority of wives in the groups turned toward either the behavioral scientists for insight or became dependent on the experiences of other wives; they did not look toward religion.

Three Types of Wives. Among the wives, whose average age was 31 years, there appeared to be three "types" participating in the groups. First, there were the "old-timers" epitomized by those women who had played an active role in the National League of Families and had taken it upon themselves to represent the MIA wives' concerns by traveling overseas and by going to Vietnam, Laos, and Paris. These women gave speeches, wrote letters and performed their role as an MIA wife to the maximum of their abilities. They felt a real sense of pride in their activities. These were the women who took leadership roles in the retreat groups. Their years of experience, the waiting, the coping with the hardships attributable to husband absence, and their newly found fund of confidence and independence all contributed to their willingness to discuss issues as candidly and openly as possible. Compared with the other wives, they appeared to have more clear-cut opinions about what they had been through and about whether or not their husbands were going to return. They also seemed to be making some decisions as to their futures. Many had already adapted totally new lifestyles from those which characterized their lives in earlier years.

The second group of women, probably the more typical, was epitomized by the MIA wife in transition. For her, things were just becoming clear. That is, she was beginning to display more confidence in coping with the dual father-mother role and in adjusting to absence of her spouse. Her husband had been gone for at least two years, but she was still in the process of experiencing numerous hardships in struggling with new ways of responding to unexpected difficulties; she was "in limbo". She expressed to the group her frustrations over having to wait for a husband who might not return. She seemed to be more ambivalent about her position than the "old wife". However, at times during the discussions, she emphasized her need to make some commitment as to whether or not her husband would return. This second group seemed to be struggling with the preparation necessary to establish a new life for themselves independent of their husbands, but as yet, had not embarked upon a new lifestyle.

There was yet a third group that appeared to differ substantially from the two groups already mentioned. This third group of wives could be classified as "the new shootdowns", as they called themselves. Many of them had only recently been classified as MIA wives, their husbands having disappeared within the year prior to the signing of the cease-fire agreement. This group also included MIA wives of long-standing who had fervently committed themselves to waiting and maintaining hope for their husbands' return. For the most part these women were experiencing severe depression and frustration. They could not fully understand, yet respected, the views of those wives who had begun to date, and of those who had committed themselves to the belief that their husbands would not return. These wives sensed that they were different from the others and expressed themselves accordingly. One wife noted, "I don't have anything in common with the rest of you, because I still believe my husband is alive and located somewhere in Laos." Another wife, within the same "new group", was much more emotional in her reactions: "How can you possibly give up on your husbands when there is still hope that some of them may return? I don't see how you can date without feeling guilty or feeling that you've let your husband down."

The "old wives" had already been through the shock period and had recovered somewhat from the bitterness and the anxiety about starting new lives for themselves. In a sense, they had said "goodbye" to their old lives and "hello" to a new life. In this new life they no longer held out serious hope that their husbands were alive and would return. Thus, occasional and serious dating were considered appropriate by that group. The "new wife", on the other hand, was characterized by a strong belief that her husband might still be alive and might return. This belief was usually based upon casualty or intelligence reports, but was also based on religious faith, dreams, or even upon a belief in their husbands' omnipotence. Many of them felt that a suitable period of time during which to gather information concerning his casualty had not yet passed. By and large, these women did not date because they could not seriously accept the possibility that their husbands were dead. Their inability to accept this possibility may have been related to a fear that they might never meet a man as good as they had fantasized their husbands to be.

Operation Homecoming. Many of the wives from both the "old" and the "new" groups were deeply affected by Homecoming and the return of the American prisoners from Southeast Asia. They felt a

162

sense of happiness for those women fortunate enough to have had their husbands return and, for themselves, felt that this event was a turning point. The fact that the American returnees had reported that it was doubtful that any other prisoners remained in captivity indicated to many of the women in the group that it was finally time to face the reality of their situation. They began to move forward in planning their futures. The wives who were not in accord with this position also seemed to have a legitimate basis for their beliefs. They were, for the most part, wives of servicemen who were shot down over Laos, a country that still refuses to give an accounting of prisoners. These wives believed that they did not have enough conclusive evidence to indicate that their husbands were dead. This viewpoint was accepted by the other group members without disagreement.

Concern for the Children. The group as a whole was unified on one major concern. They were extremely sensitive and perplexed as to the fate of their children. Concomitantly, they questioned whether or not they had been good mothers during their husbands' absences. With a brief introduction by one of the wives on the subject of child adjustment, the women were pleased to have the opportunity to discuss their children's welfare. Even with the differences among the three types of MIA wives mentioned previously, there seemed to be a common bond and a common concern as to whether or not their children would be able to survive and endure. They were not concerned, necessarily, about their own welfare, as much as they were about their children's welfare. The wives felt that they could cope and do well for themselves, but their children's futures were less predictable. To these women the children represented the future, especially in those cases where there was a son who could carry forth the husband's identity, his values, and his aspirations. For others, the children represented their absent husbands. These were *his* children and the only meaningful representatives of *him*. Children also represented a problem. Some mothers expressed concern about specific incidents of truancy or misbehavior on the part of their children. Greater emphasis, however, was placed upon the adolescents and on coping with the problems of this particular stage of development. One woman expressed extreme concern about her daughter who was overreacting to her father's absence and who was eventually treated in a psychiatric setting for an attempted suicide. The woman believed that her daughter's problems were attributable to the loss of her father, and she wondered whether or not the other children would be affected in much the same way. Although the group gave her some encouragement and took note of the fact that her daughter had also

163

recovered and was doing well in college, they, too, emphasized this concern as to the long-range impact of father absence. They were eager to have the leaders examine the possibility of including their children, as well as themselves, in some longitudinal study. As one wife expressed it, "we may not be able to help our children by this type of research, but I would be willing to participate in it in the hope that we can help other families who may be faced with the same situation". There was unanimous agreement among the participants that such research should be conducted, and all appeared willing to participate.

Discussion of a topic as sensitive to these women as child adjustment also brought forth other reactions. For one woman, her child's adjustment was interwoven with her own future. It was her belief that her youngest son would be the carrier of the family banner. She was adamant about her son's resemblance to his father both in appearance and behavior and, thus, felt the only logical thing to do was have him follow in his father's footsteps. Her description of the home situation and her aspirations for this child were carried one step further. It was her belief that she should reallocate all of her husband's awards and decorations to each of her sons as a step towards drawing closure to the whole issue. Having done so, she would then plan to date and seriously consider remarrying. Finally, she made it clear that under no circumstances would her sons ever be adopted by her future husband. The family name was to be maintained by her sons. The group reacted strongly to this situation. They questioned her motives and whether or not she was really concerned about meeting her own needs or those of her children. When the group questioned her as to her sons' personal desires, she quickly avoided the subject, which was set aside temporarily but later returned to by the group. As discussion proceeded, she became more accepting of comments about her personal situation and actually seemed to be enlightened by the concern of the other wives about her need to idolize her husband and her expectations that her second son be his spitting image.

Another area of discussion related to the children was the concern many wives felt for the children's grandparents on their father's side. Even the wives who had little relationship with the husbands' parents believed that some thought had to be given to the continuity of the relationship between the children and their grandparents. Many wives felt that with time this situation could be worked out, but others were afraid that once they remarried, the grandparents would withdraw from the children. Most of the women expressed a need for help with this concern.

Establishing a New Identity. Socializing appeared to be a very difficult area of adjustment for these women. One of the problems confronting those who wanted to progress from "marking time in place" was that they were handicapped by not finding a proper social outlet or a comfortable new role. Typically, the MIA wife eventually reached the conclusion that, although she held some small shred of hope about her husband, she had to make some attempt to socialize. When she did, however, she often felt like a "fifth wheel". Although she would occasionally attend some "safe" social function with couples she and her husband had known prior to his casualty, she frequently got the message that the other wives were watchful of her behavior, and perhaps, even resented her presence.

Many of the MIA wives indicated they had received much social and emotional support from other prisoner of war and MIA wives. When they were together, it was acceptable to be without a husband and, more importantly, within that group the wives did not have to explain where their husbands were. Often having to explain to outsiders what "MIA" meant was the beginning of the end of an evening out. Thus, MIA groups sometimes formed the basis for meeting other adults of both sexes. One group, for example, joined a mixed bowling league. Other individuals reported joining political groups, returning to college, or commencing or resuming graduate studies as a means of normalizing their social contacts.

Dating for these women often resulted in both guilt feelings and feelings of frustration. Some wives openly discussed what one woman called the "rat race" of dating other men. Their major concerns seemed to fall into two areas. One was a reaction to their personal concerns over becoming emotionally involved. After all these years of postponement, of waiting, and of avoiding the question of whether or not they were able to become fully and emotionally involved with another man, they ironically discovered it was difficult to become involved again. Those who had successful experiences offered much encouragement to the others in the group, based on their experiences. Others described their frustrations with their expectations as to what their future husbands might be and the quality of men that they had dated. They frequently reported finding that none of the men compared with their idealized memories of their husbands. Although they verbalized that this might be unrealistic on their part, they still wanted the men to meet these expectations. Interestingly enough, the wives emphasized how they, in all likelihood, would prefer to marry another career military man. This did not come as a surprise to the other group members and was strongly endorsed and elaborated upon by all present. As one Army wife said, "I believe that only a military man would understand what I have been through and would be able to comfort me in the manner in which I feel I need to be comforted. He would understand me. The civilian man would not, although he might try to be compassionate and understanding."

Dating, in the absence of conclusive evidence that the husband was dead, invariably appeared to induce some degree of guilt. Even though the wives expressed a firm commitment to the belief that their husband would not return, dating itself and the prospects of becoming involved created a situation that was guilt-provoking. The wives felt uncomfortable about this; they felt dishonest, and were reluctant to become emotionally involved. Serious dating meant coping with the inability to make any permanent contracts of marriage while still in their present status as MIA wives. There was also a great fear, on the part of some of the women, of being exploited by men they were dating; they expressed a desire to harden themselves so as not to become vulnerable again.

Preparation for a Change in Status. Preparing for a change in status was extremely difficult for most wives. Even though verbally expressing their apprehensions concerning a possible change in status, the prospect of the change provoked a great deal of emotion as to their futures. The wives had a difficult time comprehending the full implications of a change in status. The loss of a continuous income, burial ceremonies, and the change in identity from wife to widow were all perplexing issues. One wife, who immediately prior to the retreat had received a change of status, matter-of-factly discussed the pros and cons of this experience. "I thought I had everything all worked out and resolved in my mind. The memorial service brought it all back, and I found it very, very difficult to work through. It was like being notified of my husband's casualty all over again. I cried and thought I would never stop." Another MIA wife, in speaking of the change to KIA wife, said she felt abandoned and betrayed; she still did not believe that her husband was dead, and she had been unable to move forward in her adjustment even after the change in status was accomplished. For many of the others whose husbands had not yet been reclassified, the statements of these two women were responded to by a sense of fear — a fear of having to go through an unanticipated period of re-grief. Many had believed that they would be able to handle with ease the "rituals" made necessary upon actual declaration of death; they had not expected the accompanying emotions.

Another issue that faced the wife in relation to this predicament was her concern over her in-laws' adjustment to a change of status.

She understood and was sympathetic toward their position; for, she knew how very difficult it would be for them to draw closure on their situation. She could start a new life for herself, but for them no such outlet was available.

Conclusion

For many of the wives of men who did not return from Southeast Asia a myriad of problems still exist. Some may yet undergo the problems faced by the wife whose husband was originally classified as killed-in-action. These difficulties, described by psychiatrist Zunin (1969) in his work with groups of KIA wives at Camp Pendleton, California, are the realities that must be faced by the widow — the difficult process of saying "goodbye" to her old life and removing such outward signs of "holding on" as the wedding ring. Others may yet face the residuals of anticipatory grief, the sense of guilt or feeling of shame that Spolyar (1973) describes as frequently occurring if the bereaved person has previously worked out the grief process prior to the actualization of death.

In most cases, however, as time passes the wives appear to be developing the insights which are vital in enabling them to go forward. Most MIA wives in these discussion groups reported feeling they had matured emotionally through their experience of suffering. Their increased independence promoted a belief that they could now do anything that they had to do. Although some of the wives had not yet accepted their loss, they were acutely aware that life must go on.

13

Maintaining Hope: The Dilemma Of Parents Of Sons Missing In Action

HAMILTON I. MCCUBBIN

PHILIP J. METRES, JR.

Introduction

Following the repatriation of American prisoners of war from Southeast Asia early in 1973, nearly 1300 servicemen remained unaccounted for, being listed as missing in action (MIA) or prisoners of war (PW) by the military departments. For most of the servicemen, their unresolved status had been prolonged due to a paucity of information as to the events surrounding their casualties and a dearth of information upon which unequivocable determinations of death could be made. Because most of the public's attention had been focused upon the end of the Southeast Asian conflict and the return of the prisoners of war, the family members of those MIA men still unaccounted for remained in the background; seemingly few in the public arena were deeply sensitive to and fully aware of their personal suffering and emotional needs during this protracted period of waiting.

While the adjustment problems of wives and children of servicemen missing in action or prisoners of war have been the subject of a few studies, the adjustments made by parents of sons missing in action have drawn less attention (Benson, McCubbin, Dahl & Hunter, 1974; Hunter & Plag, 1973; McCubbin, Hunter & Metres, 1973; McCubbin, Hunter & Dahl, 1974; McCubbin & Hunter, 1974; Spolyar, 1973).

Interviews conducted by the Center for Prisoner of War Studies with a select sample of 17 dependent parents of servicemen missing in action or prisoners of war prior to the return of the PWs led the

169

writers to believe that these parents were experiencing severe emotional difficulty in coping with the unresolved status of their sons. This highly tentative but noteworthy finding suggested the importance of a more careful assessment of the parents' reaction to this situation. The purpose of this paper, then, is to discuss observations made of parental adjustment based on group discussions with a subsequent sample of some of the parents of MIAs following the 1973 PW release.

Parents under Stress. Parental reaction to the separation and possible death of a son missing in action or a prisoner of war is relatively predictable with the onset of what is commonly referred to as "the work of mourning" or the "grief cycle". Grief is defined as those emotions which follow the loss or anticipated loss of a loved one. Physical symptoms such as anorexia, insomnia, and fatigue, as well as psychological reactions such as preoccupation with the image and memory of the missing son are predictable characteristics of parental grief. Lindemann (1944) and Engel (1961) emphasized that normal grief reactions precipitated by a loss include these well-defined and specific symptoms and proceed through a normal cycle towards recovery.

The work of mourning has been clearly described in the literature with varying degrees of emphasis placed upon stages of adjustment depending upon whether reference is being made to the individual facing death or to the surviving family member. Bowlby (1961), in viewing grief reactions from the point of view of the dying person, emphasized three general stages of the grief cycle: (a) protesting and denial of the possibility of death, (b) despair and disorganization, and (c) reorganization. Kubler-Ross (1968), on the basis of extensive experience and research, elaborated upon the concept of the grieving process as constituting five definite stages of adjustment: (a) denial and isolation, (b) anger, (c) bargaining, (d) depression, and finally (e) acceptance. Futterman and Hoffman (1973), in an attempt to move away from these more traditional psychological-reactive and defensive descriptions of grief work, and in an attempt to focus upon the grief work of the surviving family members, suggested an adaptation theory of family adjustment. Family adjustment was considered a necessary and adaptive process involving: (a) anticipatory mourning, (b) the maintenance of confidence and the struggle for mastery of the situation, (c) participation in activities designed to reconcile the situation, (d) maintenance of personal and family equilibrium, (e) affirmation of the value of life and of the family, and (f) reorganization.

170

Maintaining Hope: The Dilemma of Parents
of Sons Missing in Action

The work of mourning, a normal and vital process, is intended to free the survivor from the intense emotional attachment to the absent person or family member. This has been described by Freud (1957) as the painful and necessary work of readjustment to the loss. The normal outcome is that deference to reality wins out. The process of facing the facts is not uniform for all persons, however, but rather is accomplished step by step, at the individual's own pace. When mourning is completed the surviving family member is freed to pursue new and vital relationships both outside of and within the family unit.

Method

Observations presented in this paper are based on a study conducted at a religious retreat[1] for families of servicemen missing in action or prisoners of war, as well as for families of returned prisoners of war. A total of 79 parents participated in a series of group discussions which focused upon parents' feelings and adjustments to the seemingly irreconcilable and personally threatening PW/MIA situation.

Members of the professional staff of the Family Studies Branch of the Center for Prisoner of War Studies, as well as volunteer pastoral counselors, a psychiatrist, a social worker, and youth counselors functioned as discussion leaders. The staff provided a minimum degree of structure to the group discussions, allowing the parents at each of the five, week-long retreats to express their feelings about their sons, their experiences during the waiting period and their predictions for the future.

Observations

Understanding the Loss. Although for these parents there could not be any completely satisfactory explanation for their sons' loss, they believed that some understanding of the absence was very necessary. This resulted in discussions of the possible meaning of their sons' casualties among themselves. A few parents felt that the war was totally unjustified and, therefore, their sons' casualties could not be reconciled by reference to the "traditions of our country" and "the price of freedom". For others, however, the tragedy could be explained by reaffirmation of their beliefs in these patriotic values.

1. *High Flight Foundation sponsored an all-expense paid religious retreat program for families of returned prisoners of war, missing in action, and listed prisoners of war. The retreats were held in Estes Park and Granby, Colorado during the period of 16 June through 27 July 1973.*

Although listening to other parents in a similar situation express and restate the values underlying the war appeared to be reassuring to some parents, most appeared hesitant about revealing their innermost feelings. Fathers, as a subgroup within the larger group, in general adopted a more quiet and unassuming manner than their spouses during the discussions. In a few cases, sudden outbursts of angry feelings by the fathers about specific incidents revealed what appeared to be their basically unspoken frustrations with the MIA situation. Unlike their wives, most fathers did not appear to be willing to express their feelings nor discuss the meaning of their sons' casualties.

From the start of the group discussions, there appeared to be a covertly communicated group feeling that it was not acceptable to discuss the possibility that their sons had died in Southeast Asia. Inadvertantly, the brief discussions of the meaning of their sons' casualties did, however, lead to revelations by some parents that they had already reconciled their sons' loss and had presumed that they had died in captivity or in battle. A few of these parents emphasized the importance of looking at this entire situation through "their sons' eyes". "He loved the military and wouldn't have been happy doing anything else." "He was proud of his uniform and what the military stood for." "He knew the risks and was willing to accept them, because he believed in what he was doing, even if it meant the possibility that he would die in combat." Other parents acknowledged this to be true for their sons also, but still found it difficult to accept the situation. For some, affirmation of faith in their sons' commitments to the military appeared to be reassuring in these parents' struggles to reaffirm and preserve confidence in their sons' lives and life in general.

Most parents recounted the value of religion in helping them cope with their situation. For some parents reference to their beliefs and religious teaching was the only possible way to explain the casualty and the hardships and pain they had endured over the months and years. Through prayer they sustained hope; through their beliefs they gained understanding.

Recalling the Past. Recalling memorable times spent with their sons, the parents seized opportune moments in the discussion to share these personal feelings and memories. They described positive and heartwarming memories: "[He] and I were very close and we did so many things together." "[He] was always close to his father and they were so alike in so many ways." "[He] always knew what he wanted and went after it."

Memories of disturbing conflicts or unhappy incidents were also mentioned but were always qualified: "but he made up for it by ... " " ... but this was really a minor incident." Any indepth discussion of unresolved conflicts and associated feelings of guilt appeared to be too painful and sensitive to be discussed in the context of the group. One parent, however, was compelled to tell her story; memories of her son were disturbing to her and precipitated feelings of guilt and self-doubt. She recounted how her son, having already served a tour in Vietnam, could have been awarded a compassionate reassignment because of his father's illness, but because she had not asked for his reassignment, she saw herself as being responsible for his casualty. In her opinion her negligence in not taking action was the basis of the problem. "If I had acted as a responsible parent, this might not have occurred. I feel guilty for letting him go." In allowing her to discuss her feelings further, the other parents in the group were able to encourage her to begin to put these feelings into perspective. The group as a whole was understanding of her dilemma. One parent asked her, "How did your son feel about going again?" The mother's reply had meaning for all parents in the group—"My son wanted to return to Vietnam because he felt it was his duty and felt he could do more for the Vietnamese." By adopting their sons' points of view, the parents, and this mother in particular, seemed to gain some consolation as well as a more realistic outlook on the situation.

Trust versus Mistrust. Several parents expressed reservations about their relationship with the government and, in particular, the military. They questioned whether the government would continue to do "everything" in its power to seek a full accounting of those still missing. They were fearful that the government, because of political expediency, might settle for what they considered to be the imperfections of the Paris Peace Agreement with the North Vietnamese. In the face of what appeared to these parents to be inconsistencies and contradictions in the information they had received, they expressed reluctance to depend totally upon the government and the military for resolution of the situation. This mistrust between parents and the government seemed to have evolved over the years; parents remembered and related numerous specific events which deepened the roots of mistrust. They remembered the extensive efforts on the part of the National League of Families and what they saw as an intense struggle with the military; they remembered the seemingly extensive amount of information about men in Southeast Asia which came through non-government agencies and contacts, as a result of efforts by concerned citizens; and at the time of the retreat, they appeared frightened by the possibility of change in status to presumptive findings of death or killed in action — a change in status without additional information confirming death. The parents expressed how difficult it was for them to dismiss the stories and rumors that emerged over the years about men surviving immeasurable hardships; these had kept their hopes alive. After all these months and years of waiting and hoping and living on faith, it was difficult, they felt, to accept a change in status without "new" information. "After all" a parent noted, "I have built hope on this information; now they plan to say that he is dead without adding any new piece of evidence." These parents were unsure of how the government would pursue this "change of status" issue. Would the government pursue a full accounting of these men and take the necessary steps to accomplish this end, or would it write their sons off as having been killed? To them, of course, there was no real choice; they felt that it was the government's responsibility to leave "no stone unturned".

The greatest fear expressed by the parents was that the missing men would be forgotten or cast aside because of other more important political issues and because the American populace seemed to want to forget the Vietnam war. Someone, they felt must ultimately be responsible to act on behalf of the men still unaccounted for, and they, as parents, should carry their share of the responsibility.

Regaining Control of the Situation. Had they done enough on behalf of their sons? Most parents felt they had been doing their best and as much as seemed reasonably possible to help bring their sons home, and they planned to continue their efforts. To some it was comforting to hear during the discussions what others had done and to realize that each, in his own way, had contributed to the cause. Parents described their efforts to obtain information about the casualties. Some discussed their trips to Paris and North Vietnam, while others focused on their plans to travel to Laos.

Their search for information also appeared to be helpful in providing themselves, as well as others, with a means of gaining some control over this enigmatic situation. Given their knowledge of the casualties, they were able to discuss and question more critically and judiciously the policies and discrepancies in the information provided by the military, foreign governments or the press. Through questioning and critically evaluating information they received regarding their sons' casualties, these parents felt they were able to influence policies, both directly and indirectly, which in turn might affect their future or that of their sons. They were proud of their ability to make specific recommendations to the military departments, the Department of Defense and to the Congress, and expressed their views with confidence.

For a few parents the struggle to gain some control over the situation had virtually become a way of life. A few mothers and fathers described their total involvement in local and national activities relating to the PW/MIA situation: letter writing, campaigning and talking to local civic groups. Although for most of these parents there appeared to be no limits as to what they felt they could be doing, a few did question the value of their activities. "Where do I stop?" "It has gotten so that I feel guilty when I am not involved in some PW/MIA activity." "I feel like I am letting my son down by not doing more, yet I feel I am neglecting my husband and my other children."

Thus, parents found themselves in a double bind. On the one hand, they felt responsible for their sons' loss and in turn obligated to do everything possible to bring them home; while on the other hand, they did not want to forget their duties for caring for a spouse and/or other children. Balancing these tasks was extremely difficult and, for some, virtually impossible. Something had to give!

Some Resolution. Despite convincing expressions of commitment to the belief that their sons had not died and were in captivity somewhere in Southeast Asia, some parents expressed an underlying expectation that evidence would eventually come forth confirming death. Interwoven with these feelings there appeared to be a wish by some that a decision would be made even if it meant that their sons were dead. Thus, in this way they might draw closure on an issue which had lingered for so many years; at that time they, as parents, could then avoid the pain and frustrations which seemed to have no apparent end. One mother, in describing a progressive realization that her son's death would eventually be confirmed, indicated that with the return of the PWs, she then felt a deepening awareness that her son would not return and, therefore, felt a natural narrowing of hope.

Feelings such as these were usually repressed because of the guilt they aroused. A few parents actually felt that their constant and never-ending preoccupation with thoughts of their sons' survival was, in fact, the very force which might be keeping him alive. They, therefore, believed that any decreases in thoughts or efforts devoted to his safe return might actually be the deciding factor in his death.

As one parent described it, "I have often felt guilty for not having thought about my son every moment."

The Future. Most of the parents found it difficult to discuss their plans or their perceptions of the future; for so many years they had focused upon their sons' return that it was difficult to plan ahead and inconceivable to talk about the future without them. When asked by another group member, "What would your plans be should your son not return?", a mother, who expected her son to return, replied, "My mind is made up; don't confuse me with the facts."

Even for those parents who were willing to discuss their thoughts about the future, the picture they painted was filled with concerns and apprehensions. This was most apparent among parents who had daughters-in-law and grandchildren—their sons' families. These parents, who wanted to maintain their identity as grandparents, felt they had reason to be concerned: "What will happen to me if my daughter-in-law eventually remarries; would I still be able to see my grandchildren and would they see us as grandparents?" Many described a strain in their relationship with their daughters-in-law; having been critical of their behavior during their sons' absences, their apprehensions were even greater.

The impact of the casualty and the years of waiting and hoping were not in all cases without some positive attributes. Although the situation brought about numerous hardships for the family, most parents, and mothers in particular, felt that they had changed and grown as a result of the total experience. Most felt that they had gained self-confidence and matured in their ability to relate to the public and to stand up for what they believed in. Their exposure to public officials and the sincere interest and concern expressed by congressmen, cabinet members, the Vice President, and the President of the United States, contributed significantly to their sense of well-being.

Summary and Conclusions

From the observations made possible by discussion groups held at a religious retreat, the adjustment of parents of men still classified as MIA appeared to be a process of coping with a number of major interrelated dilemmas. For each dilemma it became apparent that parents needed to work out an equitable and personally satisfying balance between conflicting sets of tasks: between acknowledging and accepting the ultimate loss of a son and maintaining hope for his eventual return; between concentrating on commitments to other family members and devoting greater energy toward reconciliation of the MIA situation; between pursuing a personal, active and unrelenting cause for obtaining a full accounting and demanding more from government agencies; and between moving forward with their lives and remaining committed to a life centered around their absent sons.

Grieving was just one facet of their total adjustment process and some aspects of the grieving process were not totally evident in the group discussions. Grieving appeared to fluctuate with other life stresses. Although they reported experiencing depression, anger, and preoccupation with the memories of their sons at varying points in time, experiences of these MIA parents were not constant and were influenced or precipitated by other life events. For some parents the grieving process appeared to be either regulated, delayed, limited or channelled into other relationships.

The normal work of mourning appeared to be modified by many factors, including the personality of the parent, the nature of the relationship between the parents and their sons, the social and communication climate in which the losses occurred and by the ambiguity of the situation which left these parents in a state of limbo as to the finality of their losses. In this situation the work of mourning had been aborted or suspended and might, over time, cause psychological complications more commonly referred to as prolonged grief reactions (Barry, 1973).

Unfortunately, because of the relatively small size of the study sample and the possibility of bias in the sample of parents who were motivated to attend the religious retreat, it is impossible to make any cross comparisons of responses to a son's absence based on differences in religious orientation, length of absence, or number or age of other siblings. It did seem that the losses of their sons, irrespective of these variables, appeared to be an equally difficult experience for the parents.

It appears necessary to have more complete data collected at this critical moment of awaiting word of the fate of their sons to determine whether the observed reactions were predominantly normal or in some ways, pathological. However, it can be said that some parents had difficulties with which they could have benefited form professional counseling.

All parents did not react the same way, and therefore, should not be approached in the same way. In dealing with these families the clinician must be sensitive to the undercurrents of conflict between father and mother and between parents and daughters-in-law. Furthermore, he must be skilled enough to judge the stage of individual reaction and sensitive to which issues can be handled at each stage. Our experience with MIA parents, however, would suggest that as a whole, mothers especially needed to talk about their experience, grief, frustrations and aspirations; whereas, fathers needed help in expressing their feelings and getting in touch with the anger and frustrations that lie hidden beneath their facade of understanding silence. During the period of awaiting word from the casualty division of the armed services regarding the fate of the men, the clinician should make himself available to help in the processes involved in the alleviation of anxieties and feelings of guilt concomitant to "accepting" the outcome. After years of maintaining hope in the face of overwhelming odds, and keeping alive the active search for some answer as to their sons' fates, any inclination towards "giving up" brings on feelings of guilt and self-condemnation. Since helping parents to understand and accept the outcome may simultaneously increase their guilt and frustration, it is necessary that clinicians be sensitive to the ambiguity of the situation.

14

Differential Viewpoints:
MIA Wife Versus MIA Mother

EDNA J. HUNTER

HAMILTON I. MCCUBBIN

DOROTHY BENSON

Introduction

The return of American prisoners of war of the Southeast Asian con-flict[1] early in 1973 heightened the concern and anxieties of families of servicemen who did not return and who still remained as missing in action (MIA) or possibly as prisoners of war (PW). These families were naturally concerned about the fate of their husbands or sons and anxious about the possibility of a change in their official status to killed in action (KIA) or to a presumptive finding of death (PFOD). The future, once filled with hope, was now clouded with uncertainty. Certainly, this was a critical period for families of servicemen who did not return, and they sought some explanation for these events and some answer to the loss of their husbands or sons.

In the euphoria of Homecoming, numerous MIA families, although elated by the fact that the other prisoners were home, tended to feel somewhat ignored. For some of the MIA wives and mothers, acute grief symptoms resumed when the release came. Moreover, after years of maintaining hope, they now faced the very real possibility that their men might *never* return. However, too many questions still re-mained and some of these families were not yet ready to make the permanent adjustments imposed by death until they could obtain some satisfactory answers.

1. *566 military prisoners of war were released by North Vietnam during the 60 day period following the signing of the peace treaty on January 27, 1973.*

Benson, McCubbin, Dahl, and Hunter (1974) pointed out that for the MIA wife, the return of the PWs "signaled an inevitable change in official status . . . which meant modification in the family's financial status, a restructuring of the wife's social role, and a decisive placement of responsibility upon the MIA wife for the planning of the family's future." For the MIA mother it meant none of these changes, unless, of course, she was dependent upon her MIA son's income. Nothing really changed for most mothers; they learned nothing new which shed light on the fate of their sons, and they continued to wonder if there was a possibility their sons might still return.

Religion has often been mentioned as a potential, if not real, source of strength in explaining and understanding the loss of a family member (Spolyar, 1973). For some PW/MIA families, religion was a major source of consolation, and the church, as an institution, a reference point in time of need. In other cases, families had reported the feeling that religion, in general, had not supported them, and that religious beliefs had not been a source of comfort and understanding (Hunter, McCubbin and Metres, 1974).

Our observations (McCubbin, Hunter and Metres, 1973) have led us to the proposition that wives and parents in the PW/MIA situation experienced different type of stresses, perceived the situation differently, and had varying approaches to coping with the exigencies of the situation. For the wives, the prolonged absence of their husbands meant facing many of the day-to-day traumas of coping with loneliness, depression, the rearing of children, and planning for the future. At times they appeared overwhelmed by the demands of daily living. Their husbands' absences were real and the impact was felt on a daily basis. Consolation and some satisfaction came from resolving daily problems and planning for a future. For the MIA parent, the stresses of daily living were not as apparent as those experienced by the wives. Parents seemed to concentrate more upon their personal grief and loss and devoted much energy in attempting to explain their loss and in understanding their personal feelings about it. The parents, more than the wives, appeared to be groping for some philosophical, yet consoling explanation for their loss. These observations have led us to hypothesize that religion would have greater value for the MIA parent than it would have for the MIA wife.

Purpose

The purpose of this paper is two-fold: (a) to focus upon the role religion played in assisting the MIA family find answers and come to terms with inner feelings and beliefs, and (b) to examine further differences between the MIA wife and the MIA parent, specifically the MIA mother. Through confirmation of our impressions, we might then be better equipped to plan for continuous services to these families and afford them the differential type of care the situation might demand.

Methodology

During the summer of 1973, less than five months subsequent to the return of the PWs from Southeast Asia, staff members of the Center for Prisoner of War Studies[2] attended three of five one-week religious retreats for PW/MIA families to observe and document how these families were responding and adapting to a critical period of transition. The retreats gave the staff an opportunity to explore with both the MIA wives and the MIA mothers their needs and concerns and to assess the value of the religious retreat for both populations.

In attempting to evaluate the value of the retreats and to document aspects of family adjustment, information was gathered through questionnaires, personal interviews, and through participation in both religious-type group discussions and the more traditional discussion groups which focused on the problems of adjustment and on the feelings and responses to the stresses of being an MIA wife or parent. The wives' and parents' groups were usually held separately, although, on a few occasions, the groups were combined. The traditional discussion groups were monitored by psychologists, a psychiatrist and social workers, with ministers also in attendance. The religious groups were headed by the members of the retreat staff, who were primarily members of the clergy. The families had the opportunity to attend either or both types of groups, depending upon their particular interests and concerns. Given the fact that both behavioral science and religious inputs were available at the retreat and that both types of service were to be afforded, it is assumed that the way in which the families distributed themselves between the services which were offered would be an index of which type group experience they valued most. Our primary sources of data for this paper were threefold: (a) a pre-retreat questionnaire which attempted to measure expectations and interests, (b) a post-retreat questionnaire to measure satisfaction or fulfillment of expectations, and (c) group discussions. Completion of the forms by participants was on a voluntary basis and, therefore, not all attendees completed both questionnaires. The findings from the questionnaires reported in this paper are based upon the responses of the 148 MIA wives and mothers who completed *both* the pre- and the post-forms.

2. *Staff members who attended the retreat were Dr. Edna J. Hunter, Dr. Hamilton I. McCubbin, Dorothy Benson, and Philip J. Metres, Jr. Two staff members were present at each of the three retreats attended.*

Profile of the Family Members

During the five one-week retreats, approximately 1300 PW/MIA family members, representing about 400 families, attended the sessions. Of those MIA family members attending sessions 1, 3, and 5 and completing both pre- and post-questionnaires, 83 (56.1%) were MIA wives and 65 (43.9%) were MIA mothers. All branches of the military service, as well as civilians, were represented. There were 76 (51.4%) wives and mothers representing Air Force families, 41 (27.7%) from Army families, 19 (12.8%) from the Navy families, and 2 (1.4%) from civilian families. On the average, these families had experienced long separations extending over a period in excess of four years. For the MIA mothers, their sons had been missing for an average of 58.4 months, and for the MIA wives, the average absence had been 49.1 months.

Results and Discussion

Reasons for attendance. Did wives and mothers come to the retreat for the same reasons? Their responses on the pre-retreat questionnaire

TABLE 1. *A Comparison of the Reasons Given by MIA Wives and MIA Mothers for Attending the Retreat*[1]

Reason	MIA Wives %	MIA Mothers %	χ^2
Vacation	74.7	41.7	15.9 ***
Chance to get away and think	73.5	73.0	NS
Opportunity to work on personal feelings and concerns	62.2	72.9	NS
Meet and talk with other PW/MIA families	60.2	86.9	12.2 ***
Get family closer together	44.1	50.0	NS
Obtain counseling	41.5	71.0	12.4 ***
Obtain answers to unanswered questions	36.6	58.3	6.6 *
Opportunity to plan future	32.1	36.4	NS
Chance to talk about own personal experience	31.3	47.4	NS
Opportunity to work out adjustment problems of other family members	26.3	33.3	NS

1. *Based upon responses given at the time of registration, prior to participation in retreat activities.*

*** $p < .001$
* $p < .05$

indicated that, for the most part, both groups came for many of the same reasons – for a vacation, for a chance to get away and think, for an opportunity to work out personal feelings and concerns, and for a chance to talk with others in similar circumstances (see Table 1). Certain reasons, however, were given more emphasis by one group than by the other. For the wife, the opportunity for a vacation appeared to be significantly more important than it was for the MIA mother. The mothers, on the other hand, attached much more importance to the opportunity for talking with others, obtaining counseling, and finding answers to unanswered questions.

Perhaps the wives, who had to cope with the practicalities of raising the children, pursuing a new career, or establishing a new lifestyle, had already come to terms with themselves and their future plans, while mothers were still struggling to come to terms with their feelings about their loss. In other words, wives were asking, *"How* do I cope since it appears he will not return?"; while mothers still asked *"Why* did it happen and what are the chances of his return?"

TABLE 2. *Differences in Expectations of the Retreat*[1]

Statement	MIA Wives %	MIA Mothers %	χ^2
I believe this experience may affect my future	47.0	77.1	13.2 ***
I expect this to be a religious experience	50.0	74.2	8.6 **

1. *Based upon responses made at the time of registration.*

*** $p < .001$
** $p < .01$

Expectations of the retreat. From the responses given at the very beginning of the retreat, the wives and mothers appeared to differ significantly in their expectations about what impact the retreat would have upon their lives (see Table 2). The MIA mother, more than the MIA wife, expected the retreat would be a religious experience and that the experience would indeed have a profound effect on her future.

The reasons the groups gave for attending the retreat and their expectations concerning the retreat could be expected to affect their desires to participate in the various activities offered there. This was found to be true. The groups differed significantly on their expressed

183

TABLE 3. *A Comparison of Interest Shown in Various Activities by MIA Wives and MIA Mothers*[1]

Activity	MIA Wives %	MIA Mothers %	χ^2
Recreation for self	92.4	90.6	NS
Recreation for children	92.3	51.4	24.9 ***
Discussion with other persons in same situation	91.5	91.2	NS
Discussion with other family groups	84.0	94.7	NS
Spiritual counseling	72.7	78.7	NS
Family counseling	70.7	60.0	NS
Legal counseling	70.7	44.2	8.0 **
Opportunity to be alone	70.0	62.8	NS
Personal counseling	69.7	62.0	NS
Financial counseling	68.8	41.9	8.3 **
Child counseling	68.0	13.9	28.5 ***
Career counseling	59.7	28.2	10.3 **
Educational counseling	58.4	30.8	7.9 **

1. *Based upon responses given at the time of registration, prior to actual knowledge of what activities might be available.*

*** $p < .001$
** $p < .01$

interest in particular activities, as shown in Table 3. Both expressed a high degree of interest in recreational activities, group discussions, and spiritual and personal counseling. Of course, the wives more frequently reported interest in recreational activities for children and child counseling, as might be expected, since few of the MIA mothers had young children with them at the retreat. The largest differences between the groups were with respect to the MIA wives' significantly greater interest in legal, financial, educational, and career counseling. These differences seem to reflect the wife's emphasis upon the "here and now" and preparation for the future. She wanted to know "how?", not "why?". One particular wife commenting on why she chose to come to the retreat stated, "I hope to be able to take stock of my situation as an MIA wife and formulate some concrete plans for my future." This statement was in sharp contrast to the MIA mother who answered the same question with, "I want to be given an answer to my family's concern about why God has seen fit to take a wonderful man, our son, away from us. My only response thus far is to tell them we can never question God's ways, but I need more convincing answers."

Group discussions. The group discussions confirmed many of our earlier observations. For the MIA wives, the prolonged absence of their husbands meant coping with constant loneliness, and they reported being frequently overwhelmed by the vicissitudes and demands of day-to-day living. Consolation and support seemed to be directly related to the assistance they needed to cope with the demands of life stresses and the realities of the absence of their loved ones. The MIA parents, rather than emphasizing the struggles with daily living, dwelt on their attempts to cope with their personal grief. They reported spending hours recalling the past, and the severe emotional shock about their son's casualty seemed heightened by their efforts to recall his growth and development, their interactions with him, guilt over things not done, with an overall pattern of reminiscing about the times they had spent together.

Family participation. As the retreats came to a close, the families were questioned to see if the activities they had previously indicated interest in were the same ones they had actually taken part in during the retreat. For the most part, this was true. As could be expected, from pre-retreat expressed interests the wives took significantly greater advantage of recreational activities for themselves than did the MIA mothers. When the retreat began, the wife group had also shown a much higher degree of interest in legal, financial, educational and career counseling than the mothers had. However, the expected differences between the groups did not show up in the post-retreat

TABLE 4. *Activities Participated in by MIA Wives and MIA Mothers*[1]

Activity	MIA Wives %	MIA Mothers %	χ^2
Recreation for children	85.7	20.4	45.6 ***
Recreation for self	85.7	66.7	5.5 *
Opportunity to be alone	73.0	55.6	NS
Spiritual counseling	71.4	57.1	NS
Family counseling	49.2	26.7	5.5 *
Child counseling	47.6	9.3	17.2 ***
Personal counseling	34.9	28.6	NS
Legal counseling	14.5	17.8	NS

1. *Based upon responses given at the close of the week-long retreat.*

*** $p < .001$
* $p < .05$

TABLE 5. *Differences in Feelings about the Retreat Experience*[1]

Statement	MIA Wives %	MIA Mothers %	χ^2	
I felt completely free to discuss my problems	76.9	87.8	NS	
I made new and lasting friendships while here	64.1	87.8	8.2	**
It was a deeply religious experience for me	55.4	79.2	6.9	**
Most of the questions I came with have been answered	47.5	64.3	NS	
I feel this has been the start of a new life for me	32.8	53.3	4.6	*

1. *Based upon responses given on the last day of the week-long retreat.*

** $p < .01$
* $p < .05$

reports. This finding is perhaps a function of the fact that in some instances these offerings were not available, or not adequate, and not necessarily because the wives did not participate in them.

A comparison of the responses of MIA wives and MIA mothers showed that the two groups did indeed have varying reasons for attending the retreat, as well as different expectations of what such an experience might offer to them. Moreover, their expressed interest in activities differed at the start of the week, and those differences were reflected in the activities they had actually participated in during the week. It appeared that a "fulfillment of prophecy" phenomenon may have been operating. In other words, what a wife or mother "expected" to derive from the experience in some way affected the way in which she felt she had benefited from it (see Table 5). Two of the more important reasons for coming to a religious retreat for MIA mothers were to meet and talk with other PW/MIA families and to obtain answers to unanswered questions. By the end of the week the MIA mother, more than the MIA wife, felt she made new and lasting friendships, and that most of the questions she had come with had been answered.

It seemed from the discussions that the mothers had been more isolated socially than the wife group since the casualty of their family member. Therefore, the retreat was a more unique situation for them, since it offered an opportunity they did not ordinarily have — a chance to meet and talk with others, in a similar situation, who understood their needs and feelings. As the retreat drew to a close, one MIA mother stated, "I came with no particular problem — just heartache and some frustration — frustration stemming from conditions I cannot change. I carry away some new friendships and a renewed acceptance to let the Lord work in his own mysterious ways."

The MIA mother expected that the experience would be a religious one, and that it would have an effect on her future. Post-retreat responses did indeed show that the retreat experience had been perceived as a deeply religious experience for the MIA mother, and that she felt it was the start of a new life for her more often than did the MIA wife. The MIA wife, on the other hand, came to the retreat seeking recreational activities for her children and herself and the opportunity to be alone; thus, for her, it served as a much-needed vacation. Her responses showed that she was more interested in personal counseling than was the MIA mother, especially counseling services which would perhaps aid her in coping with everyday affairs and taking practical steps for the future. The practicality of the MIA wife is perhaps reflected in the departing statement of one who said, "We will never be the same as when we came if we remember a little and practice a little of what we have been given," adding that her goal was "to go forth and live a fruitful and giving life."

It should be pointed out that because these particular wives and mothers chose to attend a religious retreat they may not be representative of the entire MIA mother-wife group. However, since attendance did not depend upon financial commitments on the part of those who attended, and because the sponsors emphasized to the families the retreat experience was there "to do with as their desires commanded", perhaps those who attended were more representative than one might have expected.

The information derived from both the questionnaires and the discussions seems to indicate that the MIA wives were not necessarily looking for philosophical or religious explanations of the loss of their husbands. Rather, they sought guidance in coping with the stresses of daily living. Conversely, the MIA mothers were really asking a fundamental question: Why my son? Such a question could be answered through religious reference. For both the MIA wife and the MIA mother, the experience had offered the opportunity to discuss freely their personal problems and frustrations in a setting that provided an emotional climate which allowed them to do so. The combined expertise of religious leader and behavioral scientist made it possible to approach both the "how" questions of the MIA wives and the "whys" of the MIA mothers with guidance which seemed to offer alternatives and benefits for both groups.

Conclusions

The findings in this study in terms of the participants' evaluations of the retreats, appear to support the views of Westling (1973) and Berger (1973) that religious retreats with competent clergy and behavioral science personnel can provide valuable assistance for the PW/MIA families in coping with their unusual situations. Chaplain John W. Berger in a presentation entitled, "A Pastoral Concern for POW/MIA Families" (1973), pointed out that the retreats for PW/MIA wives in which he participated during the years 1971 and 1972 "served a purpose, benefiting those attending at a time when there was a need." The period during the summer of 1973, in the months immediately following the release of prisoners, also appeared to be a critical time of need for these same families. Chaplain L. L. Westling, Jr. (1973), in a manual for those who minister to PW/MIA families, also pointed out the value of retreats for these families, stating:

> *Chaplain-organized retreats which included competent psychological leadership of the staff were commendable in dealing with and in some cases interrupting anticipatory 'grief work.' Hostilities were allowed to surface and to be examined for what they were and guilt and self-accusation were reorganized. Rage was redirected into appropriate rather than self-destructive directions. Many personal evaluations were made at such events. The application of this mode of ministry is highly recommended for wives whose husbands are deployed on recognized high-risk assignments.*

In other words, he viewed the religious retreat as beneficial for military families experiencing *routine* military separations, as well as for families in the PW/MIA situation. Whether or not the perceived benefits persist over time for either wives or mothers is another question which cannot be answered by data from this study. However, the findings of this study appear to support our previously stated hypothesis that religion is a greater source of consolation for the MIA parent than for the MIA wife. When interpreting the statistics and the differences found to exist between the groups, however, we must realize that we have only looked at these families at one specific point in time when the wives and parents may have been asking two different questions. This does not mean that the wives may not have asked the same questions the parents asked at another point in time. In short, we should not interpret these statistics or these findings as static or permanent.

It may be that adjustment falls along a continuum, and that needs or concerns may shift along this line, even over a period as short as one week. For example, at the beginning of the retreat, one MIA mother in the group was emotionally torn about the loss of her son; it was only after having discussed and reconciled this loss through religious reference that she was then able to channel her emotions and efforts towards the pragmatics of coping with daily stresses. She came to terms with her grief and loss in the religious group; in a discussion group with the behavioral science personnel, she was then able to focus upon her guilt about neglecting the family because she had devoted so much time to thinking about her lost son. Assuming that the normal grieving process occurs in varying stages, any program put forth to assist families adjusting to the loss of a family member should be designed to benefit the bereaved in whatever stage the family member may be at any particular point in time. Observations made throughout the sessions also appear to point up the importance of cooperation between the disciplines of the behavioral science counselor and the religious counselor, with a view towards offering a wider range of services, tailored to individual needs which can answer both the philosophical "whys" and the pragmatic "how" questions of grieving wives and parents.

Summary of Findings

The purpose of this study was to examine the role of religion in helping the families of servicemen missing in action find answers to their questions and come to terms with their inner feelings and beliefs. The responses on pre- and post-retreat questionnaires of 83 MIA wives and 65 MIA mothers were compared to determine whether or not religion had a differential value for the wife than for the mother. Statistically significant between-group differences were found for reasons given by the wives and mothers for their attendance at the retreat, their expectations as to what benefits might be derived from the retreat, their preferences as to type of activity participated in during the retreat, and their overall feelings about their experiences at the retreat when it had ended.

Services To Families

15

Social And Mental Health Services To Families Of Servicemen Missing In Action Or Returned Prisoners Of War [1]

HAMILTON I. MCCUBBIN

BARBARA B. DAHL

Introduction

Experience in the provision of social and mental health services for families of servicemen missing in action (MIA) or returned prisoners of war (RPW) has led us to the growing conviction that an increased knowledge of families in these unique situations, together with a positive orientation to the extension of services can lead to viable and comprehensive community based programs designed specifically for these family populations. As the staff at the Center for Prisoner of War Studies examined past research and experiences, sought information from the French social workers regarding their contacts with families during and following the French-Indochina war, interviewed and worked intensively with the MIA and RPW families of the Vietnam War, we were afforded a view of the families' predicaments from a different perspective than that usually afforded a clinician. We came to appreciate the insecurities, difficulties and unhappy experiences of the wives, children and parents of these men and the importance of services to their families. It appeared quite obvious that family functioning was influenced profoundly by the stresses brought about by the months and, in most cases, years of waiting—so obvious perhaps, that it may have been taken for granted or forgotten and had not until recently received careful scrutiny.

1. Paper presented at the meeting of the American Psychiatric Association, Detroit, May 1974.

Family Adjustment. There are a number of reasons for predicting that the families of servicemen missing in action and families of returned prisoners of war will have a high incidence of "problems of readjustment" which are amenable to preventive mental health intervention. In addition to the fact that both populations have had to experience major adjustments due to the prolonged and indeterminate absence of a father/husband, the RPW family must cope with the reintegration of the returning father into the family after his prolonged absence, and the MIA family must face the fact that the husband/father may never return.

For the MIA family, father absence produces a modification and reorganization of the family unit (Benson, McCubbin, Dahl and Hunter, 1974; Hall and Malone, 1973; Hunter and Plag, 1973; McCubbin, Hunter and Metres, 1973) and has a profound impact upon the children (McCubbin, Hunter and Metres, 1974). Much of the social acceptance, stability and continuity of the family unit which is taken for granted in the intact family is lacking or severely taxed in the family of a serviceman missing in action. The military family without a father lives in a world of double isolation—as social deviants in the military system and as an enigma to the civilian community which has been struggling to reconcile the appropriateness of the Vietnam conflict.

The mental health, social adjustments and vocational problems of the returning Vietnam veteran have been documented (Lifton, 1973; Musser and Stenger, 1972; Polner, 1971). Although the emotional, social and family adjustments of the returned prisoner of war seem to be similar to those of the returning veteran, there is at least one basic exception. After a prolonged absence, in some instances eight or nine years, the returned prisoner of war must not only face an extremely changed society, but also a modified family whose patterns of adaptation to the stresses of father absence, social change and increased responsibilities have become a way of life.

The complexity of reintegration of the serviceman and his family following a long separation was the topic of a number of research studies during and following World War II (Duvall, 1945; Eliot, 1946; Hill, 1949; Waller, 1944). Reunion brought on major adjustments in family roles, responsibilities, and patterns of communication. More importantly, those studies pointed out the critical factors involved in reunions—the wives' development, their increased maturity and independence, role changes within the family, children's development and maturity, husbands' idealized expectations of the family and the marriage, changes in the wives' expectations of the marriage, and, most important, breakdowns in family communication.

The few personal reports of family experiences of returned prisoners of war (Chesley, 1973; Gaither, 1973; Plumb, 1973; Rutledge, 1973) and a recent study (Metres, McCubbin and Hunter, 1974) suggest that returning home after a long separation was indeed a trying experience. The associated stresses of reintegration into a family, demands by the public and press upon the returnee, changes in personalities and values, discrepancies in expectations of husband and wife, and changing lifestyles, all of which represent obstacles to a successful reunion, may be major contributing factors to the surprisingly high estimates of divorces among the recently returned prisoners of war. In view of the social and psychological complications so often accompanying the prolonged absence of a husband and the reunion after this period, it is perhaps surprising that the incidence of mental health casualties was not any higher than estimates have indicated.

Services to Families. Mental health services to MIA and RPW families have been the result of cooperation and coordination across all of the military departments: Army, Navy, Marine Corps, and Air Force. The scattering of families throughout the United States and Europe required that continuous communication be maintained across military branches to insure the provision of medical, psychological, legal and administrative services to all families regardless of their military affiliation. The concept of community mental health (Caplan, 1964; Hume, 1966; Visotsky, 1967), with its goals of prevention, reduction, and relief of psychiatric illness and social adjustment problems and its sequels, has been the guiding framework for the provision of mental health services. The emphasis has been upon the provision of comprehensive services to include remedial and rehabilitative services with a preventive aim. Because of the predicted incidence of readjustment problems among returnees and families of servicemen missing in action, we believe that prevention of major medical, social, emotional and behavioral problems is a primary facet in an effective program.

Within this community mental health framework, prevention is seen as occurring on three levels—primary, secondary, and tertiary. Simply stated, primary prevention entails the lessening and/or elimination of adverse psychological and environmental influences; secondary prevention refers to early and effective treatment to prevent the development of major social and psychological disturbances; and tertiary prevention refers to the rehabilitation of individuals or family systems diagnosed as having a definite problem or disorder of some duration and complexity. As part of the rehabilitative goals, work with these individuals or families is designed to reduce the extent of defective functioning within the family system and of inter-personal relationships outside of the family unit. Four important aspects of the program will be discussed: (1) "outreach" services; (2) collaboration with other agencies; (3) mental health consultation; and (4) research.

Outreach Services. In spite of the availability of mental health services in the military, there has remained a discrepancy between the numbers who could benefit from professional counseling and those who stepped forward to obtain help. A careful assessment of the families' comments, interview data, and follow-up contacts (Hall and Malone, 1973) revealed that unsatisfactory experiences with unin-formed civilian and military professionals, together with a natural reluctance to seek counseling, were critical factors mitigating the families' involvement in mental health services. In a few instances families experienced judgmental attitudes among health professionals, false reassurances and a reluctance among physicians to address the military family member's emotional problems. A bias against the Vietnam conflict or the military in general may, in a few cases, have interfered with the clinical evaluation and the establishment of a professional therapeutic relationship.

The challenge to link families who would benefit from services with available mental health programs has led us to look more closely at our present delivery system and to discover fresh approaches. Bridging this gap required us to suspend conventional notions of motivation, problems and treatment. We "needed to turn the usual clinical situation upside down". Specifically, we needed to move away from the tendency to characterize the hesitant but needy military family clientele as "not ready for treatment," "unmotivated," or "resistant". Such assumptions were inappropri-ate for a program which encouraged efforts toward early identifica-tion of problems or disorders and which emphasized early and effective treatment to prevent the development of major social and psychological disturbances.

Drawing from the experiences of the last fifteen years of experi-menting with a variety of approaches involving those individuals who seldom appear voluntarily within an agency (Overton, 1953; Sunley, 1968), the military has initiated an effort to extend services to MIA and RPW families. This provision of "outreach" services to families emphasizes the development of a continuous relationship between mental health agencies and families. Integrated as part of of the long-term care to returned prisoners of war, the family program emphasizes continuous contacts between the families and a mental health worker in order to examine the full range of family and individual adjustments. The emphasis of the contacts is not on family problems per se, but rather upon the overall social, and emotional health of the family system. It is assumed that through continuous family contacts an early detection of problem areas can be made, and, thus, a basis for the therapeutic relationship established. The military has developed a strong commitment to devote resources to providing this unprecedented service. In essence, through imaginative efforts on the part of mental health professionals, obstacles hindering the utilization of our mental health programs has been transcended in order to involve the military family and the community.

Through the establishment of a nation-wide program of family services involving mental health professionals and flight surgeons, the military has been able to respond to the needs for family services. The operationalization of "outreach" services, while still in its initial stages of development, has received strong support from the families. On the basis of data obtained from one branch of the armed services, we are encouraged with the progress. During an initial four-month period, social work consultants have extended assistance to 42.4 percent of the families of returned prisoners of war in that branch of service; this same team of consultants has involved 48 wives of servicemen missing in action and twenty-two children of MIA families in mental health services. These statistics do not necessarily reflect "psychopathology" within the family. The families may take advantage of the services for a variety of reasons, ranging from advice on legal matters to major family crises, and are referred to those professionals — lawyers, psychiatrists, etc., best able to evaluate and assist them. Thus, it is reasonable to assume that the families have seen the program in terms of its preventive value, since they have taken advantage of these services in order to assist them in coping with the "normal" problems of readjustment.

Collaborative Services with other Agencies. The adjustment of families of returned prisoners of war and families of servicemen missing in action is more than a psychological problem; it is a social phenomenon in which social, emotional, and legal issues are inextricably bound together. Thus, it is not surprising that these families require services from a multiplicity of disciplines. These include medicine, psychology, social work, educational counseling, and in some situations special education, as well as services from agencies which do not specialize in family counseling such as court and probation departments. It has not been unusual to find a few families in contact simultaneously with three or more agencies or professionals. Unfortunately, the multiplicity of necessary services to families has sometimes produced unintentional side effects. In a few cases different agencies gave opposing advice to wives and children, thus, precipitating additional conflict within the family unit. In addition, agencies not sensitive to or aware of the emotional and social problems faced by these particular families may have communicated a reluctance, if not a hesitancy, to respond to their total needs. An effective program of community organization and community psychiatry requires collaboration with other significant agencies in order to provide coordination of services, to reduce fragmentation and redundancy as well as to reduce conflict within the family and among community agencies.

Mental Health Consultation. An important component of a comprehensive program for MIA and RPW families is the provision for social work consultation and, in some cases, mental health education for civilian agencies as well as military agencies and professionals in private practice. Another emphasis of this program is to provide consultation to non-mental health agencies and professionals (lawyers, public welfare workers, etc.) who are involved in services to these families and, thus, may be in need of orientation or education. The actual consultation process with these families may vary from one social worker to another, but usually involves one or more of three major approaches: (1) evaluation of the family problem; (2) provision of advice to a consultee (a professional or an agency); or (3) provision of actual services in conjunction with the agency or professional.

The Role of Research. Research is considered to be an integral part of this comprehensive program of community psychiatry for MIA and RPW families. There is still relatively little available knowledge on a number of aspects of the social, psychological and emotional consequences of father absence. Very little is known about a number of aspects of family reunion following prolonged separations. In addition to the complications of child adjustment to a prolonged period of separation, more information on the effects of captivity on the returned prisoner and his future emotional, physical and social adjustment is needed.

It is also essential that we make an assessment of the relative impact of our "outreach" service to families. Presumably, an important test of a good military mental health program is how many preventable problems it removes from the shoulders of its citizens, the military families, and, after that, how rapidly and effectively it marshals its resources in order to remedy the damage done by non-preventable difficulties. It is expected that findings derived from examination of these basic questions supported by a continuous assessment of our services to RPW and MIA families, will lead to the development and application of comprehensive services for other families throughout the military system.

We at the Center for Prisoner of War Studies are in agreement with Russell (1974) who, in his review and study of psycho-social consequences in the families of survivors of the concentration camp experience, emphasized the importance of research and concluded: "Only further longitudinal follow-up studies of these survivor families ... will elucidate whether the outcome observed will last." " ... I would therefore like to associate myself strongly with those who stress the need for further and long-range studies of families of survivors living in various settings and environments; these studies obviously, might have to go on for several generations." It is also our position that only through these "long-range studies of families of survivors" can we truly understand the complex effects of such an experience on the families.

16

Consultants' Viewpoints

CHARLES A. STENGER
ROBERT E. STRANGE
FLOYD S. MESHAD
LEONARD M. ZUNIN

Outreach Services To The Vietnam Veteran: A Personal Perspective

FLOYD S. MESHAD

The purpose of this review is to briefly outline a program that was originally designed to deal with the Vietnam Era Veteran population, and, thus, has applicability for returned prisoners of war who have chosen to resume their civilian status. Strictly speaking, the program was established as a concept for the younger veterans, but it may also have implications as a model for outreach to returnees and their families.

The Problem

As recently as two years ago in the Los Angeles area there were no services per se for the younger veterans. By and large, the programs that were in effect were outdated, having changed little from World War II. Therapeutic type programs in existence in the veterans hospitals for in-patient care were available but a program which prepared the individual for leaving the hospital was virtually non-existent. What about discharge planning, the re-entry process, and the follow-up process? For, after all, successful treatment is not a measure of how well the patient functions in the hospital, but whether or not he can stick it out in the real world.

Procedures for Setting up the Program

In order to initiate a program of this type, which began in a Los Angeles veterans hospital, it was not only necessary to try to find out what resources were available in the outside community, but it was also essential to remember that the community must be kept up to date on the program as it progressed.

The Program

1. Residential Placement. In order to determine what residential placements were real for young men coming out of this situation—first out of the war, and then out of the Veterans Administration Hospital, the patients themselves were consulted as to what they would like to do so that they were given some choice and a chance to participate in in their own placement. After some discussion with the patients as to their preferences, it was discovered that most of them preferred living on the outside. Most were single and wanted their own place, and many wanted to get involved in educational programs, vocational programs and social activities. But none of them knew where to start. In the beginning, several days, and sometimes weeks, were spent with these individuals, placing them in residential sections and apartments where out-patient services would be available in a nearby facility.

2. Community Involvement. The problem of educating the community toward acceptance of the young veteran was helped through a volunteer program which was able to get a great deal of television coverage. It was felt that by exposing the whole situation faced by the Vietnam veteran as well as the total impact of his individual experience on him, several corporations, businesses, educational facilities, and people might volunteer time and money. One such project was with the Telephone Company, which conducted a "big brother" project. In most cases the volunteers were young, sometimes veteran managerial types, personnel that were interested in getting involved with these veterans. The "big brothers" spent their own time talking with the veteran about his interests and concerns, taking him to interviews, and setting up vocational connections.

A veterans "out-reach house", open 24 hours a day, was available to deal with anything and everything that may cause problems for the veteran. The "hotline" did not deal with the problems directly, but rather had the contacts refer the caller, who may be overdosing on drugs or contemplating suicide, to someone else, often arranging to pick him up and get him to some service as quickly as possible.

3. Educational Planning. Steps were also taken to locate people who were interested in veteran affairs on campuses to aid in educational planning or follow-up with individuals once they were involved in an educational environment. Volunteers took them to school, introducing them to other veterans and veterans organizations, helped them to get their G. I. benefits, helped them to find an acceptable residence, and assisted them in numerous other ways so that they might feel "settled".

4. Family Involvement. The program strongly supported the concept of family counseling. Since the population was young, it was felt that failure to get the family involved was a critical and serious omission. Whenever an individual was placed on the outside, if possible, family counseling was begun simultaneously in the home. Talking with the family and letting them participate aids in the re-entry process because the family, first of all, sees that some initiative has been taken, and, secondly, sees that someone has really taken an interest in helping their son.

Conclusion

A program such as the one that has been outlined here is only one attempt to update existing programs for facilitating veterans re-entry into their own communities. The specific techniques of extensive community involvement and participation on the part of the veteran himself in planning for his future may serve as a model for those personnel whose key role is to help the returned prisoner readjust to the community in which he has chosen to live and to facilitate his taking advantage of the available resources. Since many of the problems faced by the young veteran and the unmarried returning prisoner are identical, knowledge of established programs may be of benefit for those who are trained to counsel these men.

The Veterans Administration - Preparations For Returning Vietnam Era Prisoners Of War, Family Members And Families Of Servicemen Missing In Action

CHARLES A. STENGER

The Problem

Prior to the repatriation of American POWs from Southeast Asia in early 1973, the plight of the prisoners of war and their families was a matter of deep personal concern to millions of Americans. This concern rose to a phenomenal demonstration of public interest at their return and still continues to hold the attention of the public. Similarly, the institutions of our government with direct post-repatriation responsibilities were highly visible. How well they were doing their job was being carefully followed as well it should be. How responsive government agencies were to the PW/MIA situation was also a broader test of the capacity and willingness of public institutions to fulfill their responsibilities. If these men and their families were not given the full measure of compassionate responsive service, how can anyone else expect to receive it?

How serious a test this may be is suggested by a longitudinal study of public trust begun by the University of Michigan's Institute of Social Research in 1952 and continued at four-year intervals through 1972 (Miller, Brown, and Raine, 1973). This study revealed that public confidence in governmental institutions had deteriorated at an alarming rate since 1964 and by the close of 1972 was dropping precipitously. The study report concluded that the massive erosion of public confidence was creating not only a generation of Americans literally "turned-off" by their government but also conditions that could erupt in explosive social conflict. How well or how poorly we respond to the needs of the returned prisoners of war, their families, and MIA families will either help restore public confidence or further contribute to the dangerous rate of decline.

Charles A. Stenger

The Role of the Armed Services

Certain events in the PW/MIA situation do lend support to improved public confidence in our governmental institutions. In November 1972, the Department of Defense held a multi-agency conference that dealt with PW/MIAs and their families. The need to do an outstanding job in support of these families was strongly emphasized and aptly characterized as a "TOTAL FEDERAL CHALLENGE". "No one must be permitted to fall between the crack," was the phrase repeatedly used. Also, it was of concern that, after an initial massive effort, continued family support would dwindle down to an ordinary institutional approach. The importance of jointly developing a tight network embracing all branches of the Armed Services so that communication and cooperation between participating agencies would not be interrupted was strongly emphasized.

The central role of the military services in providing the assistance required was made clear and other federal agencies were properly tasked to provide back-up support. Consequently, the Veterans Administration (VA) was properly identified as the lead agency outside of the military establishment because its sole mission and resources were to serve those who served in the Armed Forces and their survivors.

Background Information on the Veterans Administration

Since the Veterans Administration is in the role of providing needed assistance to veterans, a few things of a background nature about this agency will help enable other military and civilian family services and agencies to best use its resources. The Veterans Administration is the largest health care system of its type in the world. There are more than 4,000 mental health professionals, psychiatrists, MA-level social workers, and Ph.D.-level psychologists, deployed in well over 200 VA hospitals and clinics dispersed throughout the country. Half of this staff has joined the Veterans Administration after 1964, the beginning of the Vietnam Era. In addition to these full-time mental health professionals, thousands of social worker and psychology students, and psychiatric residents are in training in the Veterans Administration at any one time.

Veterans of the Vietnam Era

There are currently 29 million veterans, including 6-1/2 million Vietnam Era veterans. The Veterans Administration, in fulfilling its responsibility to all the veterans and their families, actually touches the lives of half the population of the United States. There are also more than 70,000 living ex-PWs being served by the Veterans Administration.

In terms of the 6-1/2 million men involved, the Vietnam Era has the largest number in our nation's history next to World War II. These veterans, because they grew up as part of a generation that has lived its life during a period of rapid and unprecedented technological and social change, have had the greatest impact upon the programs administered by the Veterans Administration. In 1970, a survey of Veterans Administration mental health professionals in all its facilities was conducted to obtain pooled observations regarding the attitudes and behavior of Vietnam Era veterans. These veterans were found to be quite different than veterans of earlier wars in their willingness to challenge authority which they perceive as essentially indifferent to their right to be treated as individuals and to have a say in things that affect them (Stenger, 1971; Stenger, 1973).

Veterans Administration's Efforts on Behalf of the PW/MIAs

Veterans Administration planning for returned prisoners of war, MIAs, PWs, and the families of these servicemen, began in October 1971 with a meeting of health care professionals from the various military services and the National Research Council. The focus of the meetings was not upon plans for repatriation, since this was the responsibility of the Department of Defense, but upon the long-range health care to these men and their families and upon the overall implications for research.

In August 1972, it seemed evident the war was grinding to a halt and that the Veterans Administration would be called upon to supplement efforts of the military services and Department of Defense to meet the special needs of returned prisoners and their families as well as families of the MIAs. The Veterans Administration's Department of Medicine and Surgery established the function of a Vietnam POW/MIA Coordinator and the Department of Veterans Benefits did likewise. In the ensuing months liaison was established with Department of Defense echelons and was coordinated by the PW/MIA Task Force under the leadership of Dr. Roger Shields of the Office of the Assistant Secretary of Defense for International Security Affairs. The Veterans Administration was asked to plan for any eventuality, primarily in the role of a resource to the respective military services. Concomitantly, the National League of Families was intensely interested in the Veterans Administration's experiences with PWs from prior wars and related personal and family readjustment difficulties, and therefore sought the VA's consultation and participation in a number of their meetings. In this regard PW/MIA families had already sought counseling assistance from social workers, psychologists, and psychiatrists in VA hospitals near their homes. What emerged out of the meetings with the National League of Families was a reassurance that VA resources were available for emergency counseling assistance.

Over the next few months liaison was established between the Navy Center for Prisoner of War Studies and the Veteran's Administration in an effort to identify possible areas of cooperation and, also, to extract from their research efforts those findings which would help us to understand more fully the psychological dimensions of repatriation. Such information was essential to our planning. The Veterans Administration took the following steps: 1) On October 19, 1972, the VA Administrator alerted every VA facility by letter that VA resources would be provided to returned prisoners of war in a timely, compassionate and sensitive manner without any incidents of bureaucratic delay or failure; 2) In December 1972, all former prisoners of war on the staff of the VA facilities throughout the U.S. were identified and designated as local and agency-wide resource persons. Several hundred persons, including mental health professionals, were identified and their ideas and suggestions obtained. Together, these actions reflect the basic philosophy and operational principles of the Veterans Administration:

a. Appropriate VA resources would be made available upon request from the military or on an emergency basis to the man or his family, and particularly to the MIA families.
b. Specific, selected persons would be designated to be the point of contact for requests for assistance. These professionals would also monitor what had been done by others so that problems or delays would not occur.
c. Priority, personalized services would be provided.
d. The philosophy was to meet the demand quickly.

With regard to services to returned prisoners of war the following plans were developed and operationalized:

a. Within 24 hours after return to a Continental United States (CONUS) military hospital, a POW/MIA Survivor Card was to be prepared. This was to be used by the Division of Veterans Benefits for Central Office monitoring as well as by local offices that may be asked to provide direct services.
b. A Vetarans Benefit Counselor was to make initial contact at the military hospital with all returned PWs (with the medical staff's approval) to inform them of existing VA benefits

(educational, loans, etc.). This counselor was to give his home as well as office phone and could be called at any time.

c. When the PW leaves the military hospital for extended recuperation leave, he was to be given the telephone number and address of the nearest VA facility so that he could readily avail himself of any type of service or arrange emergency medical help as well as individual or family counseling.

d. Should a returned PW on leave call a VA hospital directly, he was to be put in touch with a mental health professional who would follow through as needed.

With regard to families of servicemen missing in action (MIA), killed in action (KIA), and returned prisoners of war, the following plans were established:

a. Within 24 hours after an MIA is reclassified KIA, the POW/MIA Survivor Card was to be completed and the name, address, and telephone number of the Casualty Assistance Officer (CACO) located nearest the survivor was to be included.

b. The CACO was to be contacted by the Veterans Benefits (VB) Counselor to arrange the timing and procedure for contacting the family. When feasible, the VA counselor was to accompany the CACO on his family visits.

c. For MIA families and those of returned PWs, VA medical facilities were to provide short-term personal or family counseling, or supportive psychiatric care.

Conclusion

The problems involved in enabling the returned PW to reestablish a meaningful identity and satisfying life-style, as well as the problems of enabling wives and family members of returned prisoners and those missing in action or killed in action to retain a meaningful identity and a satisfying life-style, are complex and urgently require attention on a preventative as well as treatment basis. It is my belief that the resources and experience of the Veterans Administration may be of assistance in such a complex and worthwhile endeavor.

Psychiatric Care For The Returned Prisoners Of War: The Navy And Marine Corps Experience

ROBERT E. STRANGE

Introduction

Expectation of severe physical and emotional pathology among the returnees figured significantly in the intensive planning and organization prior to their release. Although, when the release occurred, they were found to be in better physical and psychological condition than anyone had dared hope, there was considerable conscious and unconscious denial of symptoms and problems. Although their health and emotional states were better than expected, there were and will continue to be significant medical and psychiatric problems requiring identification and treatment.

Initial Examination. During their initial state-side hospitalization, all of the Navy and Marine returnees received extensive psychiatric examinations. They were interviewed for several hours by psychiatrists, after which they were given the opportunity for further psychiatric contact according to their conditions and desires. Their responses to this were generally positive. They were eager to talk and manifested a great need to ventilate and tell their stories. As a group they tended to be hyperactive, and they maintained for some days a state of post-return euphoria with general denial of emotional, physical, and situational problems. In most cases there was gradual return to a calm and realistic mood during the course of hospitalization. Some demonstrated reluctance to leave the sheltered medical environment, break off their group relationships, and return to a new world of freedom. These seemed to be the ones who had spent the longest time in captivity and therefore were required to make the most major changes in their lives and coping mechanisms. In contrast, some wanted immediate return to duty and flight status and were impatient even with the shortest medical hold. This group consisted of those returnees who had been imprisoned for the shortest times and who were in the best physical and emotional health.

Unique Clinical Situation for Examining Psychiatrists. The examining psychiatrists were all eager and enthusiastic, both because of great professional interest and the national significance of this unusual project. However, they faced some unique problems. Some felt concern about evaluating adequately the clinical significance of the returnees' emotional signs and symptoms. The examiners were sure that many of the returnees' responses were undoubtedly part of the natural and expected reactions to such prolonged stress, and the dilemma was that of clearly differentiating significant pathology from the stress reactions. Also, the VIP status of the returnees, with the social, military, political, and public affairs importance of their return, clearly complicated the psychiatrists' tasks of evaluation. It would have been easy to be awed by these patients and to over-identify with them. It would have been easy to hesitate in intervention when pathology was apparent, due to a variety of outside influences.

These dilemmas of the examining psychiatrist are well illustrated by the problems of evaluating the clinical significance of depressive symptoms among the returnees. From past experience and our understanding of psychodynamic principles, it was anticipated that depression would be endemic among the returned prisoners of war. The psychological losses and deprivation sustained during captivity and the need to suppress hostility for prolonged periods, along with many other factors, caused most psychiatrists to have a high index of suspicion regarding depression in these patients. It was assumed that the returnees would undoubtedly need to relearn mechanisms of expressing hostility and that the coping mechanisms they had learned to utilize effectively in confinement might appear as symptoms of depression on examination after release. The examining psychiatrists had to struggle with this puzzle of differentiating appropriate responses to captivity and release from the emotional illness of depression and/or hypomanic defenses against that illness.

The final determination regarding severity of depression and potential for self-destruction had to remain, as always, the responsibility of the attending psychiatrist. In an effort to give the clinician as much assistance as possible, however, the Center for Prisoner of

Psychiatric Care for the Returned Prisoners of War:
The Navy and Marine Corps Experience

War Studies collected data from the earliest psychiatric screening interviews, debriefing information about the confinement experiences, and family adjustment data. They extracted that information which is generally accepted as being related to depressive illness and suicide potential. This was then reviewed by clinicians who were not directly involved in the examination of the returnees. On the basis of this computerized data and without having examined the patients, the reviewers identified 34 of the 164 Navy/Marine returnees (21%) as likely to be either currently seriously depressed or with the potential for severe depressive illness. It was also their opinion that 53 others, another 32 percent, had or were likely to have depressive problems of a less severe nature. The actual examining psychiatrists, however, perceived this isolated data differently in the real-life situation of these most unusual patients. They established psychiatric diagnoses in very few of the returnees. Among the 138 Navy men, the following diagnoses were established: anxiety neurosis – 3; unspecified neurosis – 2; hysterical neurosis – 1; transient situational disturbance – 1. Among the 26 Marine returnees, only two diagnoses were established, both long-standing psychoses seemingly unrelated to the captivity experience.

Review of Findings – Initial and Follow-up. Following complete medical and psychiatric examinations of the returnees, recommendations were jointly prepared by all physicians, including the psychiatrists, who had been involved in the evaluations. The returnees' wishes, along with this medical opinion, determined his disposition from the hospital. All of the Navy men returned to some operational, staff, or training assignment, except for five remaining under prolonged medical treatment. During the year after return only seven left the Navy through retirement or release from active duty. The fact that 94 percent of the total group remain in service indicates the career orientation of these officers. Half of the Marine Corps group remain on active duty, this difference being due to a larger number of non-career personnel.

The low number of psychiatric diagnoses in initial examinations seems to have been supported by experience during the past year. There have been no readmissions for treatment of psychiatric problems. In our continuing psychiatric follow-up during this year, it appears that readjustment problems, when they have occurred, have manifested themselves primarily in family conflicts and behavioral symptoms. The Navy returnees continue to report few emotional symptoms, although there have been conflicts in marriage relationships and behavioral manifestations of tension. It is to be expected that these career officers will deemphasize intrapsychic problems and, therefore, the most successful means of giving psychiatric support frequently seems to be through the medium of family assistance.

Plans for the Future. For the Navy/Marine group, a follow-up program has been arranged for at the Naval Aerospace Medical Institute, Pensacola, Florida, where medical and psychiatric personnel have unusual and lengthy experience and expertise in the long-range physical and emotional problems of aviators. This group works with the Center for Prisoner of War Studies in San Diego to accumulate research data from the follow-up examinations. Each Navy/Marine returnee still on active duty is being sent to the Institute in Pensacola for approximately a week of medical and psychiatric evaluation. This is being done six months after the initial period of hospitalization and then every year thereafter. Those Navy/Marine returnees who are no longer in active service are invited to Pensacola for this examination at government expense. There may, of course, be situations in which the men may not participate; in these cases an attempt will be made to establish liaison with their civilian physician or clinic for exchange of information and records which will benefit the patient's medical care. It is important to point out that all the returnees who are no longer in active service have been designated by the Secretary of Defense as eligible for continuing medical care both for themselves and their families. As such, they are urged to take advantage of the military medical and psychiatric facilities near their homes, where care and follow-up examinations can be accomplished. Personnel from the Center for Prisoner of War Studies and the Naval Aerospace Medical Institute also work with the Veteran's Administration in providing liaison services and information exchange for those returnees in civilian life who choose to receive care at Veterans' Administration facilities. Throughout the planning of this program the philosophy has been to make psychiatric care easily and immediately available for the returnees and their families, yet to respect their individual privacy and avoid undesirable attention to and intervention in their lives.

This philosphy has been especially important in setting up the program of family services. Since almost all of the Navy returnees remain on active duty and all are aviation personnel, it was predictable where most of them would be assigned and would be living with their families. In these specific areas, a special out-reach program was initiated and built around a social worker in association with local psychiatric and medical facilities. This social worker contacted each returnee's family, offered assistance, and pointed out the availability of services. The Navy social workers maintain close collaboration with those of the Army and the Air Force, as well as the general civilian community. The program is a tri-service operation and provides assistance to returnees' families, both those who remain in the service and those who are civilian. Experience to date indicates increasing usage of the services provided by this program.

Obviously, these men who have undergone such lengthy emotional and physical trauma are a high-risk psychiatric population. The occurrence of one suicide in the Navy/Marine group shortly after repatriation underscores the critical need for comprehensive pyschiatric and medical follow-up. Such follow-up must be arranged to be as convenient and palatable, yet scientifically correct, as possible. Their individual privacy will be respected and undesirable and unnecessary attention and intervention in their lives will be avoided.

A Program For The Vietnam Widow:
Operation Second Life

LEONARD M. ZUNIN

When my husband was killed in Vietnam last year, it was the second time he had served there. We knew there was a chance of his being hurt or killed, and worried often, but he told us over and over that he knew how to take care of himself and would be back, and after so many times he had us almost convinced. The shock of being told of his sudden death by the Casualty Officer and Chaplain is too great to express with words. It has taken me a whole year to accept his death; even now sometimes I feel like he is still out there somewhere and will be back sometime. The children now mention him more often than in the previous months. They remember things he used to do or say, and there is less sadness in their voices when they talk about him. I know, though, they still hurt and—now and then— especially if they happen to see some news on TV about our servicemen in Vietnam, there is a grave look in their eyes and a twitch of their mouths which makes me think they are trying to hold back the tears. At times such as these, I suddenly put aside my own grief and turn into a clown. I say or do something silly, or tell them of something special we may do in the near future, and soon a trace of smile appears on their faces. To the world he was just one, to us he was the whole world.

These are the powerful, emotion-filled words of a woman whose husband was one of the many killed in action in the Vietnam War. She represents but one of thousands who share a common plight. The

217

purpose of this paper is to describe the experiences of one psycho-therapist in establishing and implementing a unique program in a military setting designed to assist these wives and families of service-men killed in action (KIA), a program which became known as "Operation Second Life."

Background

The idea of providing services to bereaved individuals in group dis-cussions was a new concept, and there was, thus, appropriate and considerable hesitation to the institution of an experimental program for widows—a program that had never been explored. One can easily imagine the potential repercussions of such a program if it should fall by the wayside, if there should be negative effects. No one wanted to use military widows as "subjects" for research, and this is what some people saw the project attempting to do. Nevertheless, there were many in favor of giving positive consideration to such a proposal.

Despite the number of individuals all the way up the military chain of command who supported the proposal, there were many unknowns and predictions of outcome were not clear. There were, indeed, no answers available for even simple questions that were posed. For example, what if a woman who was beginning to readjust, reorganize her life, and resolve her grief, was in a group just ready to leave in the next few weeks and another woman in acute grief entered the group. Would the woman in acute grief cause exacerbation and aggravation of this woman who was just getting on her feet or would the woman getting on her feet be able to help in a constructive way those who were in the phase of acute grief? The proposal eventually went as far as the Chief of Naval Operations who finally gave his endorsement and took the responsibility for instituting this program at Camp Pendleton, California.

In developing the program a number of individuals, including peo-ple like the late Dr. Fritz Perls, (Perls, 1969, 1973) the founder and developer of Gestalt psychotherapy, were consulted. Dr. Perls listened for a long time and then he looked up and said softly, "This is a group of women you will have to teach how to say goodbye." Only later was the full significance of the dynamics of "saying goodbye" under-stood by the psychotherapists involved. For indeed, one very interesting aspect for those who worked with women learning how to say "goodbye" was the realization that one of the most perplexing, if not the most difficult of all goodbyes that anyone has to make, is to a

218

loved one who is lost through death. Knowing when and how to say goodbye became important measures of an individual's mental health.

Establishing the Program

In order to establish the program, specifically a discussion group for widows, a number of guidelines needed to be established. Only women whose husbands had been killed in Vietnam were to be included in the group. The group met once a week for a period of two hours. Women came to the group as they wished; attendance was strictly on a voluntary basis and could be discontinued when the women saw fit. One of the most difficult tasks of instituting this program on a voluntary basis, was that if it was going to be voluntary for the women, it was believed to be important for the chaplains and any physicians or therapists that would assist in this program to offer their services on a voluntary basis; this program would be in addition to their usual duties and could only be done after hours. Also, it was necessary to insist on confidentiality, that is, that there would be no records kept, not even a note in the woman's service record that she was involved in "Operation Second Life". With these provisions, the program was started.

The Group

In general the women involved in the group ranged in age from about 25 to 35, had an average of one to three children, and most were officer's wives. While on the surface they appeared homogeneous, there were a few major subgroups which seemed to affect their participation in the group. One subgroup consisted of women who were younger, who had been married a short period of time, those who did not have children or perhaps had an infant, and who had been away from Mom and Dad for only a short period of time when they received word of their husband's death. These wives sought the comfort and refuge of their parent's home. However, officers' wives who had been married perhaps ten years, had two children, whose parents were much older; who had been a part of the military for all of their adult life; who had been a part of the military culture; who enjoyed the benefits of the military life; and whose friends were within the military framework; chose to stay, at least for the time being, within or adjacent to a military community. The latter group of women were involved in "Operation Second Life" for a long period. Many other women attended for only two or three sessions. Some, for example, were military widows passing through Camp Pendleton and, while perhaps visiting someone in the area, heard about the group and would come for one meeting.

The program was publicized in a variety of ways: in some of the newsletters at the base, through referrals at the Chaplain's office, by Navy hospital physicians' staff and by the participants directly involved. The main focus of the group was on the "here and now" and on understanding the strengths, the potentials, and the attributes of the women involved in the program. No attempt was ever made to suppress the normal and healthy grief reaction. Additional emphasis was given to the matter of beginning their lives anew and understanding that they had to begin. Understanding, also, that they may have had many beautiful memories and many overwhelming feelings of sadness but, whatever their memories and whatever their feelings, their life with that individual was over. To further emphasize the significance of a grief reaction as part of mental health and not as illness, the group did not meet in a psychiatric unit but at a separate location in the hospital, a neutral conference room. The program itself was referred to as "the group program" or "Operation Second Life" but never "group therapy"

Observations and Readjustment Issues

Generally, these women were very patriotic. Their bitterness was only in the conduct of the war; there was little question in their minds that we were justified being in Southeast Asia and that we were there for an important cause. Despite their powerful disagreements as to the way the war was being fought in Southeast Asia (often stimulated by some of the letters written by their husbands received periodically prior to their husbands' deaths), their strong patriotism remained.

Idealizations of marriage were common and descriptions of the husbands, during the wives' early phase of grief, differed little from descriptions of Greek heroes. In fact, although many of the widows are now remarried and some have children, it took a long time, sometimes two or three years, before they were able to really see their former marriages and their deceased husbands in a realistic framework.

One of the major recurring issues discussed was dating. In this regard we can note several very powerful differences between the military community and the civilian community and their attitudes toward dating for widows. The military community, generally encouraged early dating at about six, seven, or eight months after the death of a husband. The civilian community, on the other hand, seemed to encourage dating after about one to one and a half years. Thus, a woman who lived on a military base and had begun dating, eight months after her husband was declared KIA, might have been severely chastised by her in-laws or parents on a visit home. "Can't you even wait a year?" Whereas within the context of a military community, she is more likely to hear, "Come on, it's been nine months; it's time for you to get on your feet."

The military women appeared to be able to readjust earlier, not only because of the very powerful support of the military community, but because prior to their husbands' deaths, they had already been functioning autonomously, sometimes for a few weeks, sometimes for a few months.

They had been paying the bills, taking care of the children, taking care of the problems at home, the legal problems and the financial problems, and dealing with their friends on a "single" basis. Thus, they had already established a reasonable foundation for continuing to function autonomously and as independent single parents. This, then is to some degree very different from a civilian woman whose husband might have been killed in an automobile accident. Suddenly, the surviving wife is faced with taking over all of the functions she had continuously been sharing with her husband. Her repertoire of experiences probably did not include coping without her husband and assuming full responsibility for all family transactions.

The openness of communication between husband and wife appeared to be an important factor in the wife-adjustment after confirmation of his death. The women who were able to talk to their husbands about the possibility that he might not come home seemed to adjust better than those who were fearful or whose husbands were reluctant to bring up this subject. There were women who would say, "We ought to talk about the possibility of your not returning," and the husband would reply, "I'm coming back, don't be foolish." There were numerous discussions like this that the women related. Some husbands refused to have even the most superficial discussion. The ability to sit down and talk about the possibility that death might occur seemed to be an important reflection on many powerful aspects of the couple's entire relationship.

In addition to the usual criteria of adjustment, such as "planning for the future," following a grief reaction there appeared to be two special indices of adjustment which reflected when these women had reorganized their lives and were ready to begin anew. First, was a primary identification readjustment associated with the feeling that "I am a single women." For, when someone is divorced or widowed, and they are asked, "who are you?", they think of themselves first as a divorced person or as a widow, which becomes one of their two or three primary initial identities. As life goes on, as readjustment occurs, being divorced or widowed always remains part of their identities, but when this label shifts in priority and becomes significantly lower on the list of "who they are", then the person is ready to comfortably see herself in a whole different framework in relation to the world around her. The second index of readjustment was the time they chose to remove their wedding rings. There were many feelings and concerns related to this behavior and these were discussed by the group. There were no attempts to push them; they were simply told, "when you're ready to take it off, you will." For many, taking it off meant putting it on the other hand because, if they had children, they wanted to wear a ring; but then there was the fear that "men might ask you out," or they might be ostracized by their family and civilian friends. For each of the women, the decision to take off the ring and either put it away or put it on the other hand was a very meaningful event and was indicative of an important phase of readjustment to life.

Another facet of adjustment was the area of receiving medals. Many of the women did receive posthumously medals for their husbands. At first they went through a myriad of frustrations because the receipt of the medals sometimes was delayed many months. Some wanted "to get it over with". The event for most was traumatic and precipitated a recurrence of a grief reaction. Many of them in retrospect mentioned that "if I would have been given the medals a month after I had learned that my husband had been killed, I would have refused them." There was an antipathy which they had not worked through. However, when the medals came much later, the wives were able to accept them with pride. For example, what do you feel if you are a woman whose husband is a helicopter pilot on MEDEVAC and is asked to go in where there are two men wounded and surrounded. He is told that it is a suicidal mission. Would anyone go in? "My husband volunteered to go in and not only did he go in, he picked up one guy. He couldn't see the other Marine. He got in the air and everyone's firing at him and he goes back down to pick up the second guy and as he's rising above the ground the second time, he gets shot out of the air." It takes time to work through the feelings of anger, frustration and resentment. Is she proud of him or is she angry and full of suppressed rage? She questions, "did he love me or did he love a guy that he had never met before more?"

Until these feelings are worked through she couldn't really accept the medals in the spirit in which they were intended. They would only trigger the release of suppressed emotions. It takes many months. There were many situations that resemble this one.

Religion and religious attitudes invariably shifted following the death of a husband. The shift was however unpredictable and

222

occurred either in a direction away from religious interests or toward increased involvement in religion. The feelings varied from a sense of understanding of God and his ultimate purpose to extreme anger and resentment toward God and religion for what "He" had done. The philosophies of life that the women formulated in the months following their husbands' deaths were thought-provoking, deeply personal, sensitive, perceptive and often beautifully philosophical:

I think when you're married you tend to forget that other people are of any importance in your life and so when you've lost the person closest to you, you've sort of lost everything, and it came immediately to me that I hadn't lost everything because a great number of people cared and told me that they did, and I shared the burden with some of them who loved my husband also, and then I think I have a rather strong faith and I have always recognized that we all will die, you know, and I suppose my philosophy helped a great deal. Another wife added: "I feel that life is great and that it will always be great—the world is a lousy place if we make it a lousy place, and to be happy we have to work at it."

Another interesting aspect brought out by these group discussions was in the area of antipathy, anger, and resentment directed towards the children; these feelings evoked guilt. With respect to children, two points of view emerged in the group discussion. Those women who did not have children felt that those who had children in the group were lucky since they had part of their husband. On the other hand, the women who had children jokingly expressed their frustration with the children. For them, having no children to worry about was enviable. "I've got two children; what am I going to do?" Sometimes the women deeply appreciated the fact that they had children, and other times, were quite resentful of them. Again, the importance of a group situation was demonstrated when the wife feeling guilty about her "resentments" would hear from four or five other women that they, too, felt this way at times. As one wife said, "My gosh, I thought I was going crazy, I thought I was sick. You mean it's o.k. if I resent them?"

Four Difficult Periods. There appeared to be four exacerbations of their grief. The first occurred for those that did not have R & R (the military term for Rest & Relaxation, a period of time when the wife meets her husband in Hawaii for a seven-day vacation). When the time came that they would have been scheduled to have R & R, they repeated the grief reaction. The second exacerbation occurred when the husband's remains arrived, since there were many days, often weeks, and sometimes many months' delay. Not the funeral itself, but just the arrival of the remains produced a renewed exacerbation of grief. The third was the date the husband was scheduled to return to CONUS (Continental United States) from Vietnam. The fourth reaction which caused a severe exacerbation of grief was the return of American PWs. Telephone calls came in from military widows all over the United States who were confused about their feelings. Many of the widows living in the Camp Pendleton area wanted to have a discussion. A number of these women were remarried and found themselves experiencing grief again as a result of witnessing the return of the American prisoners of war. Fortunately, the women in the group were able to help each other understand, prepare for, and perceive the "normalcy" in having these recurring reactions. Thus, instead of a woman being confused by the sadness of depression, and asking, "Why am I going through it again?", they could recall the feelings of others who shared a similar experience—"I did the same thing, and it's a perfectly healthly and normal thing."

Conclusion

The Vietnam war has created thousands of personal crises for parents, wives and children. This is only part of the story, the story of some of the wives who have chosen to continue their relationship with the military and take steps towards building a "second life" where they are. Almost without exception they have benefited from the group experience, resolved their crises, and met their problems head-on. These widows are a very special group of people, who have jumped high over hurdles. They do not exude bitterness about the war that cost the lives of their husbands. They deeply believe their men died for an important cause, in defense of their country and in defense of their own convictions and values of right and wrong, good and bad. They want their children to believe that too. Like most widows, they are lonely, they find adjustment difficult and at times slow, but they have not retreated, they have not withdrawn, nor have they glued their eyes to the ground or pulled down their window shades. They have not run away and given up; but rather they have decided to begin a new life, each in her own way, and proudly, with the help of the military, maintaining in some measure the kind of life they knew. They do not pity themselves, loathe pity from others, and do not ask sympathy from anyone. They are standing on their own and living with, they believe, the same courage, and the same convictions for which their husbands died.

References

References

Allen, A.M., Taplin, D., Lowy, J.A. and Twigg, L. Skin infections in Vietnam. *Military Medicine,* 1972, *137,* 295-301.

Allen, H.E. Shilling Manor: a survey of a military community of father absent families. Unpublished doctoral dissertation, Catholic University of America, 1972.

Anderson, C.L., Boysen, A.M., Esenten, S., Lam, G.N. and Shadish, W.R. Medical experiences in communist POW camps in Korea. *Journal of the American Medical Association,* 1954, *156,* 120-122.

Archibald, C.H., Long, D.M., Miller, C. and Tuddenham, R.D. Gross stress reaction in combat — a 15 year follow-up. *The American Journal of Psychiatry,* 1962, *119,* 317.

Asch, S.E. Effects of group pressure upon the modification and distortion of judgments. In H. Guetzkow (Ed.) *Groups, leadership and men.* Pittsburgh, Pa.: Carnegie Press, 1951.

Baker, S.L. Fagen, S.A., Fischer, E.G., Janda, E.J. & Cove, L.A. Impact of father absence on personality factors of boys: I. an evaluation of the military family's adjustment. *American Journal of Orthopsychiatry,* 1967, *37,* 269. (Abstract)

Baker, S.L., Cove, L.A., Fagen, S.A., Fischer, E.G. & Janda, E.J. Impact of father absence: III. problems of family reintegration following prolonged father absence. *American Journal of Orthopsychiatry,* 1968, *38,* 347. (Abstract)

Ballard, P.A. Psychological aspects of captivity and repatriation. In C. Peck (Ed.), *Medical care for repatriated prisoners of war: a manual for physicians.* San Diego, Ca.: Navy Medical Neuropsychiatric Research Unit, 1973.

225

Barry, M.J. The prolonged grief reaction. May. Clinic Proceedings, 1973, *48*, 329–335.

Beebe, G.W. Follow-up studies of World War II and Korean War prisoners: II. morbidity, disability, and maladjustments. Washington, D.C.: National Research Council, in preparation.

Benchimol, A.B. and Schlesinger, P. Beriberi heart disease. *American Heart Journal*, 1953, *46*, 245-263.

Benson, D., McCubbin, H.I., Dahl, B. and Hunter, E.J. *Waiting: the dilemma of the MIA wife.* (NPRU Report No. 74-32) San Diego: Navy Medical Neuropsychiatric Research Unit, 1974.

Berger, J.W. A pastoral concern for POW/MIA families. Paper presented at a symposium for social workers given by the Center for POW Studies, San Diego, September 1973.

Berle, A.A. Legal background of communist methods of interrogation and indoctrination. *Bulletin of the New York Academy of Medicine*, 1957, *33*, 616.

Bettleheim, B. Individual and mass behavior in extreme situations. *Journal of Abnormal and Social Psychology*, 1953, *38*, 417-452.

Biderman, A.D. Communist attempts to elicit false confessions from Air Force prisoners of war. *Bulletin of the New York Academy of Medicine*, 1957, *33*, 616.

Biderman, A.D. Socio-psychological needs and "involuntary" behavior as illustrated by compliance in interrogation. *Sociometry*, 1960, *23*, 120.

Biderman, A.D. *March to Calumny.* New York: The MacMillan Company, 1963.

Biderman, A.D. Life and death in extreme captivity situations. In M.H. Apply and R. Trumbull (Eds.), *Psychological stress.* New York: Appleton Century Crofts, 1967.

Boulding, E. Family adjustment to war separation and reunion. *The Annals of the American Academy.* 1950, *272*, 59-67.

Bowlby, J. Grief and mourning in infancy and early childhood. In *The psychoanalytic study of the child.* New York: International Universities Press, 1960.

Bowlby, J. Childhood mourning and its implications for psychiatry. *American Journal of Psychiatry*, 1961, *118*, 481-498.

Brown, D.E. Dark and lonely is the silent night. *U.S. Navy Medicine*, 1972, *58*, 4-7.

Caplan, G. *Principles of preventive psychiatry.* New York: Basic Books, 1964.

Chesley, L. *Seven years in Hanoi.* Salt Lake City: Bookcraft, Inc., 1973.

Chodoff, P. C. Late effects of the concentration camp syndrome. *Archives of General Psychiatry*, 1963, *8*, 323-342.

Chodoff, P. C. Effects of extreme coercive and oppressive forces. In S. Arieti (Ed.), *American Handbook of Psychiatry.* New York: Basic Books, 1966.

Cohen B. and Cooper, M. A follow-up study of World War II prisoners of war. *V.A. Medical Monograph,* Washington, D.C.: U.S. Government Printing Office, 1954.

Cruickshank, E. K. Painful feet in prisoners of war in the Far East: review of 500 cases. *Lancet,* 1946, *2,* 369-372.

Deutsch, H. Absence of grief. *Psychoanalytic Quarterly,* 1937, *6,* 12-22.

Dickerson, W.J. and Arthur, R.J. Navy families in distress. *Military Medicine,* 1965, *130,* 894-898.

DiGirolamo, M. and Schlant, R.C. Etiology of coronary atherosclerosis. In J.W. Hurst (Ed.), *The heart, arteries and veins.* New York: McGraw-Hill, 1974.

Duvall, E.M. Loneliness and the serviceman's wife. *Marriage and Family Living,* 1945, *7,* 77-82.

Eitinger, L. *Concentration camp survivors in Norway and Israel.* London: Allen and Unwin, 1964.

Eitinger, L. and Strom A. (Eds.) *Mortality and morbidity after excessive stress.* New York: Humanities Press, 1972.

Eliot, T.D. War bereavements and their recovery. *Marriage and Family Living,* 1946, *8,* 1-6.

Engel, C.L. Is grief a disease? A challenge for medical research. *Psychosomatic Medicine,* 1961, *23,* 18-22.

Engel, W. Reflections on the psychiatric consequences of persecution. *American Journal of Psychotherapy,* 1962, *26,* 191.

Ewing, C.L. Vertebral fracture in jet aircraft accidents: a statistical analysis for the period 1959 through 1963, U.S. Navy. *Aerospace Medicine,* 1966, 505-508.

Fagen, S.A., Janda, E.J., Baker, S.L., Fischer, E.G. and Cove, L.A. Impact of father absence in military families: II. factors relating to success of coping with crises. *Proceedings of the Annual Meeting of the American Psychological Association,* 1967, 2.

Farber, I.E., Harlow, H.F. and West, L.J. Brainwashing, conditioning and DDD (debility, dependency and dread). *Sociometry,* 1957, *20,* 271.

Frankl, V.E. *Man's search for meaning.* New York: Washington Square Press, 1968.

Freud, A. and Burlingham, D. *War and children.* New York: International Universities Press, 1943.

Freud, S. Mourning and melancholia. In *Complete Works.* Vol. 14, London: Hogarth Press, 1957.

Friedman, P. Some aspects of concentration camp psychology. *The American Journal of Psychiatry,* 1949, *105,* 601.

Fulton, R. and Fulton, J. A psychological aspect of terminal care: anticipatory grief. *Omega,* 1971, *2,* 91-100.

Furman, R.A. Death and the young child. In *The psychoanalytic study of the child.* New York: International Universities Press, 1964.

Futterman, E.H. and Hoffman, I. Crisis and adaptation in the families of fatally ill children. In E.J. Anthony and C. Koupernik (Eds.) *The child in his family: the impact of disease and death.* New York: Wiley, 1973.

Gabower, G. Behavior problems of children in Navy officers' families. *Social Casework,* 1960, *41,* 177-184.

Gaither, R. *With God in a POW Camp.* Nashville: Broadman Press, 1973.

Glickman, I. Periodontal disease. *New England Journal of Medicine,* 1971, *284,* 1071-1077.

Glusman, M. The syndrome of "burning feet" (nutritional melalgia) as a manifestation of nutritional deficiency. *American Journal of Medicine,* 1947, *3,* 211-223.

Grinker, R.R. and Spiegel, J.P. *Men under stress.* New York: Blackeston, 1945.

Group for the Advancement of Psychiatry. GAP Symposium #3: Factors used to increase the susceptibility of individuals to forceful indoctrination: observations and experiments. New York: Group for the Advancement of Psychiatry, December, 1956.

Halberstam, M.J. North Vietnam's medical care: sparse, equitable, and efficient. *Internal Medicine News,* 1973, *6,* 12 and 22.

Hall, R. and Malone, P.T. Psychiatric residuals of prolonged concentration camp experience. Paper presented at a symposium for social workers given by the Center for POW Studies, San Diego, September, 1973.

Hall, R. and Simmons, W.C. The POW wife – a psychiatric appraisal. *Archives of General Psychiatry,* 1973, *29,* 690-694.

Hartog, A. Group therapy with psychotic and borderline military wives. *American Journal of Psychiatry,* 1966, *122,* 1125-1131.

References

Hilgard, J., Newman, M. and Fisk, F. Strength of adult ego following childhood bereavement. *American Journal of Orthopsychiatry,* 1960, *30,* 788-798.

Hill, R. *Families under stress.* New York: Harper and Brothers, 1949.

Hinkle, L.E. and Wolfe, H.G. Communist interrogation and indoctrination of "Enemies of the State." *Archives of Neurology and Psychiatry,* 1956, *76,* 115.

Hirsch, C. and Nachemson, A. Clinical observations on the spine in ejected pilots. *Acta Orthopaedica Scandinavica,* 1961, *31,* 135-145.

Hocking, F. Psychiatric aspects of extreme environmental stress. *Diseases of the Nervous System,* 1970, *31,* 542-545.

Horowitz, M.J. & Becker, J.S. The compulsion to repeat trauma: experimental study of intrusive thinking after stress. *Journal of Nervous & Mental Disorders,* 1971, *153,* 32.

Horowitz, M.J. Cognitive response to stressful stimuli. *Archives of General Psychiatry,* 1971, *25,* 419.

Horowitz, M.J. & Moskowitz, M. Intrusive thinking in psychiatric patients after stress. *Psychological Reports,* 1972, *31,* 235.

Hume, P.B. General principles of community psychiatry. In S. Arieti (Ed.), *American handbook of psychiatry,* Vol. 3. New York: Basic Books, 1966.

Hunter, E.J., McCubbin, H.I. & Metres, P.J., Jr. *Religion and the PW/MIA family.* (NPRU Report No. 74-30) San Diego: Navy Medical Neuropsychiatric Research Unit, 1974.

Hunter, E.J. & Plag, J.A. *An assessment of the needs of POW/MIA wives residing in the San Diego metropolitan area: a proposal for the establishment of family services.* (NPRU Report No. 73-39) San Diego: Navy Medical Neuropsychiatric Research Unit, 1973.

Isay, R.A. The submariner's wives syndrome. *Psychiatric Quarterly,* 1968, *42,* 647-652.

Jackson, E.N. *Understanding grief.* New York: Abingdon Press, 1957.

Jacobs, E.C. Memoirs of a medical P.O.W. *Military Medicine,* 1970, *135,* 991-997.

Jones, W.L., Madden, W.F. & Luedman, G.W. Ejection seat accelerations and injuries. *Aerospace Medicine,* 1964, 559-562.

Kantor, M. *Andersonville.* Cleveland: World Publishing Co., 1955.

Kardiner, A. Traumatic neuroses of war. In S. Arieti (Ed.), *American Handbook of Psychiatry.* New York: Basic Books, 1959.

Kinkead, E. *In every war but one.* New York: W.W. Norton, 1959.

Klein, H., Zellermayer, J. & Shanan, J. Former concentration camp inmates on a psychiatric ward. *Archives of General Psychiatry,* 1963, *8,* 334.

Kral, V.A. Psychiatric observations under severe chronic stress. *The American Journal of Psychiatry*, 1951, *108*, 3.

Kubler-Ross, E. *On death and dying.* New York: MacMillan Co., 1968.

Lewis, R.B. Painful feet in American prisoners of war. *U.S. Armed Forces Medical Journal*, 1960, *1*, 146-157.

Lifton, R.J. Thought reform of Western civilians in Chinese communist prisons. *Psychiatry*, 1956, *19*, 173.

Lifton, R.J. *Home from the war.* New York: Simon and Schuster, 1973.

Lindemann, E. Symptomatology and management of acute grief. *American Journal of Psychiatry*, 1944, *101*, 141-148.

Lindequist, R. Marriage and family life of officers and airmen in a Strategic Air Command Wing. (Technical Report No. 5) Chapel Hill: Institute for Research on Social Science, 1952.

MacIntosh, H. Separation problems in military wives. *American Journal of Psychiatry*, 1968, *125*, 260-265.

McCubbin, H.I., Hunter, E.J., & Dahl, B.B. *Residuals of war: families of prisoners of war and servicemen missing in action.* (NPRU Report No. 74-49) San Diego: Navy Medical Neuropsychiatric Research Unit, 1974.

McCubbin, H.I., Hunter, E.J. & Metres, P.J., Jr. *Adaptation of the family to the prisoner of war and missing in action experience: an overview.* (NPRU Report No. 73-62) San Diego: Navy Medical Neuropsychiatric Research Unit, 1973.

McCubbin, H.I., Hunter, E.J. & Metres, P.J., Jr. *Children in limbo.* (NPRU Report No. 74-24) San Diego: Navy Medical Neuropsychiatric Research Unit, 1974.

McKain, J.L. Needs of the military family. *Medical Bulletin U.S. Army Europe*, 1965, *22*, 294-297.

Meerloo, J. *The rape of the mind; the psychology of thought control, menticide and brainwashing.* Cleveland: World Publishing Co., 1956.

Metres, P.J., Jr., McCubbin, H.I., & Hunter, E.J. *Families of returned prisoners of war: some impressions on their initial reintegration.* Navy Medical Neuropsychiatric Research Unit, 1974.

Miller, A., Brown, T. and Raine, A. Social conflict and political estrangement, 1958-1972. [Summarized in *Institute for Social Research Newsletter*, 1973, 1 (18)].

Miller, J.G. *Discussion of methods of forceful indoctrination: observations and interviews* (GAP Technical Report No. 4) New York: Group for the Advancement of Psychiatry, 1957.

References

Montalvo, F.F. Family separation in the Army: a study of the problems encountered and the caretaking resources used by career Army families undergoing military separation. Unpublished doctoral dissertation, University of Southern California, 1968.

Musser, M. & Stenger, C.A. A medical and social perception of the Vietnam veteran. *Bulletin of New York Academy of Medicine,* 1972, *48,* 859-869.

Nagera, H. Children's reactions to the death of important objects: a developmental approach. In *The psychoanalytic study of the child.* New York: International Universities Press, 1970.

Nardini, J.E. Psychiatric concepts of prisoners of war confinement. *Military Medicine,* 1962, *127,* 299-307.

Nefzger, M. Follow-up studies of World War II and Korean War prisoners: I. Mortality and morbidity. *American Journal of Epidemiology,* 1970, *91* (2), 123-128.

Niederland, W. Clinical observations on the "Survivor Syndrome". *International Journal of Psychoanalysis,* 1968, *49,* 313.

Overton, A. Serving families who don't want help. *Social Casework,* 1953, *34,* 304-309.

Pearlman, C.A., Jr. Separation reactions of married women. *American Journal of Psychiatry,* 1970, *126,* 946-950.

Perls, F.S. *Ego hunger and aggression, the beginning of gestalt therapy.* New York: Random House, 1969.

Perls, F.S. *The gestalt approach and eye witness to therapy.* Calif: Science and Behavior Books, 1973.

Plumb, C. *I'm no hero.* Missouri: Independence, 1973.

Polner, M. *No victory parades: the return of the Vietnam veteran.* New York: Holt, Rinehart and Winston, 1971.

Reed, E.P. Experiences of a medical officer in a Japanese prison camp. *Texas State Journal of Medicine,* 1947, *42,* 543-547.

Reeves, G. The new family in the post-war world. *Marriage and Family Living,* 1947, 7 (4), 73-76.

Russell, A. Late psycho-social consequences in concentration camps survivor families. *American Journal of Orthopsychiatry,* 1974, *44,* 611-619.

Rutledge, H. & Rutledge, P. *In the presence of mine enemies.* New Jersey: Fleming H. Revell Co., 1973.

Santucci, P.S. & Winokur, G. Brainwashing as a factor in psychiatric illness. *Archives of Neurology and Psychiatry,* 1955, *74,* 11.

Schein, E.H. The Chinese indoctrination program for prisoners of war. *Psychiatry,* 1956, *19,* 149.

Schein, E.H. Reaction patterns to severe, chronic stress in American Army prisoners of war of the Chinese. *Journal of Social Issues,* 1957, *13,* 21-30.

Schein, E.H., Cooley, W.E. & Singer, M.T. A psychological follow-up of former prisoners of war of the Chinese communists. (Contract No. DA-49-007-MD-754) Cambridge: Massachusetts Institute of Technology, 1960.

Schein, E.H., Schneir, I. & Barker, C.H. *Coercive persuasion: a socio-psychological analysis of the "brainwashing" of American civilian prisoners by the Chinese communists.* New York: Norton, 1961.

Scrimshaw, N.S. Report from Hanoi. *Nutrition Today,* 1973, *8,* 16.

Segal, H.A. Initial psychiatric findings of recently repatriated prisoners of war. *The American Journal of Psychiatry,* 1954, *111,* 358.

Segal, J. Therapeutic considerations in planning the return of American POWs to continental United States. *Military Medicine,* 1973, *128,* 73-77.

Shambaugh, B. A study of loss reactions in a seven year old. In *The psychoanalytic study of the child.* New York: International Universities Press, 1961.

Shannon, R.H. & Munson, H.G. Spinal injuries in nonfatal USAF aircraft accidents: 1 January 1968 – 31 December 1972. Paper presented at the Aerospace Medical Association Convention, Las Vegas, 1973.

Smith, J.J. & Furth, J. Fibrosis of the endocardium and the myocardium with mural thrombosis. *Archives of Internal Medicine,* 1943, *71,* 602-619.

Solomon, R.L. and Wynne, L.C. Traumatic avoidance learning, the principles of anxiety, conservation and partial irreversibility. *Psychological Review,* 1954, *61,* 353.

Spellman, W., Jr. Orientations toward problem solving among career military families. Unpublished doctoral dissertation, Columbia University, 1965.

Spolyar, L. The dynamics of grief of wives and families of military personnel missing in action. *Medical Service Digest,* 1973, *24,* 20-24.

Stenger, C.A. Profile of Vietnam era veteran. *Counseling Psychologist,* 1971, *2* (3), 77.

Stenger, C.A. Vietnam: a different war, a different veteran. *The Jewish Veteran,* 1973, *28* (9), 16.

Strom, A. *Norwegian concentration camp survivors.* New York: Humanities Press, 1968.

Sunley, R. New dimensions in reaching-out casework. *Social Work,* 1968, *13,* 64-74.

Szasz, T.S. The communication of distress between child and parent. *British Journal of Medical Psychology,* 1959, *32,* 161-170.

Tas, J. Psychical disorders among inmates of concentration camps and repatriates. *Psychiatric Quarterly,* 1951, *25,* 679.

Todd, K.W. European into coolie: P.O.W.s adapt themselves to the tropical villagers' diseases. *Journal of the Royal Army Medical Corps,* 1946, *86,* 179-185.

Toffler, A. *Future shock.* New York: Bantam Books, 1969.

Toffler, A. On future shock and the freed POWs. *Los Angeles Times,* March 1973.

Tyhurst, J.J. Individual reactions to community disasters. *American Journal of Psychiatry,* 1951, *107,* 764.

Visotsky, H.M. Primary prevention. In A. Freedman & H. Kaplan (Eds.), *Comprehensive textbook of psychiatry.* Baltimore: Williams-Wilkens, 1967.

Walker, E.R.C. Impressions of a repatriated medical officer. *Lancet,* 1944, *1,* 514-515.

Waller, W. *The veteran comes back.* New York: Dryden, 1944.

Weiss, R.J. & Payson, M.E. Gross stress reaction. In A.E. Freedman & H.I. Kaplan (Eds.), *Comprehensive textbook of psychiatry.* Baltimore: Williams-Wilkens, 1967.

Wenger, N.K. Myocardial involvement in systemic disease. In J.W. Hurst, (Ed.), *The Heart, arteries and veins.* New York: McGraw-Hill, 1974.

West, L.J. *U.S. Air Force prisoners of the Chinese communists.* (GAP Report No. 4) New York: Group for the Advancement of Psychiatry, 1957.

West, L.J. Psychiatry, "brainwashing" and the American character. *The American Journal of Psychiatry,* 1964, *120,* 842.

Westling, L.L., Jr. Ministry to prisoner of war returnees and their families in the long-term readjustment period: a manual for Navy chaplains. Unpublished doctoral dissertation, Navy Post-Graduate School, 1973.

Whelan, T.J., Jr. Testimony before the Subcommittee on Veterans' Affairs of the Committee on Labor & Public Welfare. United States Senate, Ninety-first Congress, first and second sessions on Examination of the Problems of the Veterans Wounded in Vietnam. November, 1969.

Wolfenstein, M. How is mourning possible? In *The psychoanalytic study of the child*. New York: International Universities Press, 1966.

Young, M.D. Malaria. In G.W. Hunt, W.W. Frye, J.C. Swartzwelder (Eds.), *A manual of tropical medicine*. Philadelphia: W.B. Saunders, 1966.

Zunin, L. Why did our husbands have to die? *Coronet*, 1969, 7, 28-38.